Modern Fresh
& Salt Water
Fly Fishing

Modern Fresh & Salt Water Fly Fishing

Charles F. Waterman

Winchester Press

Book & Jacket Design by George H. Buehler

Library of Congress Catalog Card Number: 70-188598
ISBN 0-87691-063-0

First printing April 1972
Second printing April 1974

Published by Winchester Press
460 Park Avenue, New York 10022

Printed in the United States of America

To my wife Debie,
who continues to cast while I eat lunch.

Contents

Introduction

AT FIRST, all flies were wet flies. Then, when the dry fly came along, the wets were considered unsportsmanlike. Then came the nymph, a refinement that was conceded to require great skill—more than dry-fly fishing in some instances—and more books were written, some rather hurriedly. I believe the consensus was that an upstream nymph is ethical, a cross-stream nymph is questionable, and downstream nymph is almost as bad as wet-fly fishing. With all this, it was hard to answer the fisherman I knew who caught a big brown trout on a streamer when everybody else was fishing dry flies. His defense was that he put the fish back anyway.

Now there are thousands of trout-fly patterns, perhaps five hundred of which are fairly well known in one part of the world or another. Some of them are direct imitations of specific insects, some are rather impressionistic vagaries, and some are tried-and-true patterns with no attempt at resemblance to any natural insect. Some fishermen say that the latter are "lures," and as such are unethical in true fly fishing. But nearly all Atlantic salmon flies are technically "lures," as well as nearly all freshwater bass and pike bugs, and streamers, and almost all saltwater flies. Not many American fly fishermen are bothered by these distinctions anymore.

Only in recent years has the sinking line been accepted by American traditionalists, and until recently it wasn't considered fly fishing by many. But there has been special interest in big trout lately, and the sinking line and bottom-bouncing streamer are an excellent way of getting them in many big rivers.

Saltwater fly fishing is relatively new and has been widely

Using a boulder for protection while fishing water too swift to stand in. Fly fishermen are eager enough to overcome most obstacles.

practiced for only about fifteen years. With it came tackle so different from light trout and bass equipment that fish of more than a hundred pounds are not unusual—and are especially impressive to those who have not examined the gear closely and are thinking in terms of trout or bluegill equipment. One veteran saltwater guide said he was most confident with fly tackle on a very heavy fish because the long and pliable rod absorbed a great deal of fisherman error without sacrificing much in the way of tackle strength. The standard 12-pound-test leader with a much stronger shock tippet is enough for heavy fish, and the new big-game fly reels are precise, capacious, and very rugged.

Only a few of the traditionalists are now using silk worm gut or silk lines; the modern synthetics are better in most situations. At one time, split bamboo seemed about to be replaced completely by fiber-glass rods but, whether better or not, bamboo can give a different feel, and there are new buyers for high-quality wood, especially from the well-known old makers. Glass is still the acknowledged leader for heavy fishing.

When spinning boomed in America in the late forties it took over one chore of the fly rod, that of casting very light spinners, spoons, and plugs—a job at which the fly rod was inefficient anyway—but it never completely supplanted fly fishing as many of its proponents promised. It was spinning that made casting simple for the occasional fisherman, but some who learned the easy method first, later accepted the challenges of fly fishing for some forms of angling that spinning did not fit.

Fly fishing owes the long cast of today to the tournament competitors who perfected the method of throwing a heavy "shooting head" with monofilament backing and developed line-handling techniques readily adapted to practical fishing. It was the West Coast steelhead anglers who needed the extra distance, got it with the new methods, and taught them to others. Many were tournament casters themselves.

Most of the bass fishermen could do without distance casting but they happily adapted it to special situations. The new methods of distance casting had a great effect upon trout fishing, for they enabled casters to cover big, fast runs formerly fished by other methods. They went to big streamers, fished deep, and found that they could catch much larger fish than had been coming to their dry flies and nymphs. In fact, the long cast and the big streamer subtracted considerably from the number of dry-fly experts, for a time at least. This is now the dominant method on big trout rivers where late-fall fishing is permitted.

The long cast is a boon to saltwater fishermen, who now

throw 70 feet with little difficulty, even with a "whole line" (no monofilament backing for the shooting part). The distance methods added power and made much larger streamers and bugs completely practical. There was an immediate jump in saltwater records as bigger fish took bigger lures, and the manufacturers built new rods and new reels epecially for the new heavy loads and the big fish.

An exploding population of fishermen is posing new conservation problems on many trout streams. Many fly fishermen want to have waters set aside for fly fishing only, a plan that has worked in many instances. The fact that trout suffer little from the single hook of a fly makes the release of fish practical, whereas bait methods are apt to be fatal, even if the fish is returned to the water.

Most serious fly fishermen recognize that habitat retention and improvement is a better tool than hatchery production in most trout waters, as the survival and reproduction of hatchery fish are nominal. Therefore, fly fishermen have strongly advocated "wild trout," which seems like simple logic at first glance but gives trouble to fisheries management people. This question is discussed at greater length in Chapter 7, but basically the problem is that the public must be served—the "public" in this case being the occasional or tourist fisherman. He can catch naive hatchery fish but faces certain disappointment when pitted against the cagy "wild trout." Thus, the very expensive hatchery fish cannot be given up completely, even though they present only temporary fishing with no benefit for the future.

Although the fly rod is still a leader in creek and river bass fishing for both large and smallmouth bass, and more than holds its own on shallow lakes, it has been overshadowed by new developments on deep lakes, especially the large impoundments. It is simply a matter of bass spending most of their time at depths beyond practical applications of the fly. Although shoreline fishing may be as good as ever, the new bottom-bumping techniques of spinning and baitcasting tackle have proved more consistent than edge casting. Thus the fly rod has taken a back seat for most

Not all trout streams are swift and rocky. This meadow brook runs slowly through pasture land.

deep-lake black-bass fishing. The electronic fishfinders are of little use to a fly angler if his quarry shows up at great depth.

Few anglers use the fly for pike and pickerel but they have proved surprisingly gullible for large streamers and popping bugs. In many cases they have chosen feathers and hair over the hardware formerly recommended and almost universally used. This kind of fly fishing is likely to grow.

While fly rods take 100-pound fish, and some of the tackle is quite appropriate for that, one of the strong points of fly fishing is its ability to afford pleasure from the smaller fish; many a master angler can enjoy six-inch trout or small sunfish when nothing larger is to be had. The adaptation of the light fly rod to very small fish is one of its greatest attractions.

Fly fishermen are studious, a characteristic of someone who adopts a sport that is not entirely mechanical. Strangely, fly-fishing schools are attended by experts as well as beginners. Books and articles on techniques continue to attract readers who have cast flies for decades, and there is always something new. The product of more leisure time, better equipment, and the experience of those who have gone before, today's fly angler is better than his predecessors.

The fly-fishing hobby can take many directions. There are the casters who glory in distance and/or accuracy and prefer fishing where the rivers are deep and wide or where the bonefish will tolerate no mistakes. There are trout fishermen who have become students of entomology. There are flytiers who cannot tolerate use of a purchased fly and who devote time and money to acquiring exotic materials for special patterns. They invent and name their own creations, and if the world little notes their inventions they do not care, for their satisfaction is in the production. Some of them discard patterns that work too well, and even go so far as to seek some outwardly presentable fly that will be refused by eager fish. They then endeavor to learn what there is about the failure that so effectively provokes the fish's disapproval.

Some are challenged by the most difficult fish, which require the most delicate of presentations, and will fish for days to catch a certain brown trout that seems especially selective, ignoring larger and more willing specimens. Others are obsessed with catching the heaviest possible fish on the lightest possible leader. At the other end of the fly shop is the big-fish angler who will go to the very limits of the rules to land a saltwater monster on flies, continually asks himself if he is really using fly tackle, and argues incessantly with others of his cult about the ethics of their marginal game. But if he were convinced he had violated some fly-fishing rule, any triumph would be irreparably tarnished, so that he is a strict purist in his way.

All of these are fly fishermen.

Modern Fresh
& Salt Water
Fly Fishing

ONE

Who Fishes with Flies?

BECAUSE IT requires skill and, in many cases, even a little study, fly fishing has long been the most respected form of angling. In this age in which much fishing has become increasingly mechanical, it is not surprising that fly fishermen have become addicted to considerable pleasant snobbery, most of it inoffensive.

The field has widened so greatly and can be entered from so many directions that fly anglers have different heroes; a bass bugger from Kansas may never have heard of the British pundits so faithfully studied by trout fishermen of the Pennsylvania limestone streams. A steelhead fisherman, up to his belt in a cold Washington freshet and throwing a sinking line with a weighted streamer, may not know a male Adams dry fly from a female Adams and possibly isn't too concerned about the distinction. He might even wonder a little at the saltwater fly fisherman who uses an 80-pound-test shock tippet. But remember that flies are tied on hooks from number 28 to 6/0.

The method started out, of course, with imitations of flies, which probably followed the use of natural flies as delicately

Fishing Firehole River in Yellowstone National Park, a spot where the fish can choose the temperature they like, as snow-fed water is warmed by hot springs.

hooked bait. The name isn't strictly correct these days, for the "flies" may now represent baitfish, spiders, crabs, shrimp, crayfish, fish eggs, frogs, or squid.

Fly fishing has many purists, some of them addicted to the dry fly only, others who will fish only to rising fish, and some who would not use a shock tippet for saltwater fish or freshwater pike. There are fly-tackle purists who would use no other kind of tackle, but will use fly rods to troll or baitfish.

Some of these "fly-rod-only" purists can be very happy fishermen, in the sense that an archer can be a happy big-game hunter, but many of them spoil their sport by making one fishing technique compete with all other methods. For the fact must be faced: fly fishing is the most productive method for many kinds of fish in many times and places, but there are also conditions under which the method is a handicap. A bass bug will not always outdo a deep-fished shiner, and worms will often defeat a dry fly on a muddy spring trout stream.

Of course, the purist may not get the most fun from using the most productive method in every instance, and may recognize the futility of trying to sell his concept of sport to more logical operators. The curse of appearing a little strange to other fishermen in some localities is then a cross he must learn to bear.

2

Fly fishermen for trout and salmon are the scholars of the fishing business, buying innumerable books, some of which delve into entomology far beyond the needs of merely fooling a fish with feathers, and some of which are incredibly pretentious. This latter characteristic is accepted and even desired by some anglers, for the language of fly fishing for trout becomes high-flown in many circles. It is startling to find that a man who is down to earth about politics, automobiles, or his own profession will burst into pompous phrases when fly fishing is mentioned, quoting learnedly from fishermen from both past and present. A few beginners are scared off by this phenomenon.

Some of the most informed and literary of the authorities have drawn their conclusions from only a few hundred yards of water, and although concentrating on small areas is undoubtedly the way to learn thoroughly, their pronouncements have often been accepted as applicable to completely different surroundings. Some fly-fishing masters have become totally engrossed with their own short streams, ignoring the vast fishing world that exists outside their own beloved areas. Their information must be accepted for what it is, but readers should still be thankful for it. After all, fly fishing is a hobby, and few practitioners would have the time to cover it on a worldwide basis. Thinking students can acquire broad knowledge from an assortment of local reports.

Some trout streams have been so hallowed by rhetoric that the common man is afraid to fish them, feeling certain his crudities of fly choice or casting would offend both the fish and the masters

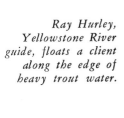

Ray Hurley, Yellowstone River guide, floats a client along the edge of heavy trout water.

who have waded before him. He is so afraid he will do something wrong he may even stand on the bank and watch worse fishermen sloshing about and speaking in the unknown tongue of the far-out fly-flinger.

Fly fishermen are likely to take themselves pretty seriously, and fly-fishing ethics, although important, vary with the individual. For more than a hundred years the British chalk-stream trout fishermen have been writing argumentative and even caustic books about what is and isn't fair on their favorite waters. As you run back through the various volumes it is rather obvious

Flies go far from land. A defeated dolphin comes alongside after striking a streamer in the Gulf Stream off North Carolina.

that no conclusions have been reached, that no conclusions are likely to be reached, and that each writer has collected his own coterie of loyal quoters and name-droppers. It has finally reached the point where it is quite possible to write books about the other books without ever going fishing.

"Fishing the water" is listed as one of the worst sins on an English chalk stream, and simply means fishing without sighting a fish before your cast. However, one author concedes it might be all right to cast to a particular spot if you were reasonably sure a fish were there, even though you hadn't seen him.

TWO

Fly Casting

THERE ARE many ways of casting a fly, and any method that works well for someone can't be completely wrong. Real experts, consciously or unconsciously, combine a variety of casting gimmicks, often can't tell you exactly what they're doing, and are dismayed when the beginner can't learn all these things in a few minutes. Individually, these little tricks are introduced from time to time as revolutionary fly-casting breakthroughs. Helpful though they may be, there hasn't been much completely new in flycasting methods in recent years, although equipment has improved tremendously. Most veterans ignore the basic principles, making the essential moves automatically, and this is a handicap, for nearly every expert wants to teach somebody how to cast and you can't teach him an automatic response.

Of course, in fly casting, you throw the weight of the line instead of the weight of the lure, and it is thrown in the form of a loop, first formed in a backcast, then pushed forward and allowed to straighten out. What goes up is what comes down, and if you make the backcast good, the fishing cast should be automatic. The backcast loop is the key to the whole performance, and when you learn what a good loop looks and feels like, the rest gets pretty simple. Good casters picking up strange equipment generally look over their shoulders to watch the loop form. It is even more important for beginning casters to look back, too, catching their mistakes early in the game. A beginner should watch someone else throw a good loop, and then imitate it. If the backcast loop is right, the timing is right. That's basic and one of the few things that are undebatable. The feel of the line in the air comes quickly to many casters; others do it more mechanically and are likely to have bad days, not quite sure of what they're feeling for.

I was disgusted about Hugh Peltz. Hugh is a tall, tough, and athletic rancher who didn't begin fly fishing until he was around fifty. Most of the true experts have started much earlier. Anyway, Hugh got basic instruction from a good caster and a short while later mentioned to me that he was having no trouble throwing off the entire fly line—and a little more. I believed him, but it seemed cruel injustice that he could easily learn in a few days what often takes years of experience. He was too casual about it anyway, and as I watched him and his big hat leave the coffee shop I tried to be analytical. Granted that he had the coordination—he's a top-notch horseman, from polo to rodeo—I'd seen a lot of good athletes who took considerable time to whip the fly-casting game. It was the following day when I finally recalled that Hugh Peltz was a master calf-roper and that throw-

Enrollees of the Orvis fly-fishing school, in Manchester, Vermont, string up their rods for their first instruction at the Orvis casting pools.

ing a rope and throwing a fly line are very much the same thing. A man who gets the feel of a swinging rope has a head start with a swinging fly line. He would have made a topflight tournament caster. I emphasize the business of *feel* which comes sooner or later.

A beginner can learn with any well-matched rod and line, but I'd recommend what approaches an all-around outfit. This adds up to something like an 8 or 8½-foot rod, taking an 8 line, and it will get by on everything from meadow streams to the ocean. It is powerful enough for its action to be easily felt but not so potent as to cripple the beginner who swings it with poor timing. For the very basic moves, a level line is satisfactory, but I'd recommend the more expensive forward taper for learning. That's a line with a short, heavy section next to the leader and lighter line back of it.

The "weight-forward" line pulls or "shoots" the lighter line through the guides easily and is the right type for distance casting. We're not after distance to begin with, but the heavy weight-forward is easily felt by the caster, and the feel of a line curling in the air does more than anything else to establish timing. The double-taper line, which is smaller at each end, is primarily for a delicate delivery and not quite so good for distance. Nevertheless, the procedure is the same, regardless of line and rod combination.

The simple cast begins with line on the ground or water, laid out fairly straight ahead of the caster. He picks it up with gradually increasing speed of his rod tip, ending the pickup with a quick flick of wrist or forearm, and throws the line back over his shoulder. This is called the backcast and, done perfectly, the line goes with a fluid motion, the rod tip changing smoothly from its forward bend into a backward bend as it follows the building loop, then increasing its backward bend as the line is driven forward into the fishing cast.

If the line does not go high over the shoulder, the pickup probably has been too slow or too weak, but too quick a jerk can fold it, too. If the line strikes ground or water behind the caster, the backcast recovery has been too slow. If the fly snaps like a whiplash, the backcast and fishing-cast motions have been too fast. If the leader tangles in the line, the backcast loop has been too narrow.

It is common for the beginner to use so short a line that he fails to bring out the rod's action. It's actually easier to cast with 30 or 40 feet of line than with 15 or 20. In getting started, he should stick to the same length of line on every cast. Changing line length will change the timing, but after a little practice the adjustment will be automatic.

For many years it was preached that the caster should toss the backcast over his shoulder and then wait until he felt a little tug as the line straightened out behind him. Such a system will work, but it lacks the smoothness of fluid motion, and although you can get by with it, you'll find it limits your efficiency.

There is no necessity for stopping the rod at "one o'clock" on the backcast, although such a classic move is good on many kinds of fishing. "Three o'clock" would be pointed straight back and parallel to the ground. If a beginner sticks to about one-thirty or even two o'clock on his backcast, he can avoid the common fault of getting the backcast too low. Most of us throw a lower backcast than we think, and I've seen beginning casters actually hit the ground behind them with their rod tips. I'm frequently

The one o'clock position, the classic point at which the backcasting motion is stopped. Such casting employs a great deal of wrist action and some forearm work. For longer casts, most anglers allow the arm to drift back and the rod tip to go much lower.

embarrassed when I wade deeply and start flailing the water be-hind me after a long period of boat fishing. The backcast always ends up lower than I thought it was. Later on, the experienced fisherman can use different tactics for special purposes, but he should make a special effort to begin with a high backcast. It'll be low enough at best.

Whatever other casting gestures he makes, most of the power is applied to the pickup after the caster has started the line moving toward him on the water and before it passes one o'clock. As he picks up the line, his wrist is bent downward. As the rod tip comes up, the wrist straightens in what can be de-scribed as a "quick flick," adding to the acceleration of the line, which is also being moved by the forearm coming upward.

As he brings the line off the water and steers it into a back-cast, the caster generally lifts his elbow; just how much he lifts it is an individual matter, but the zone of applied power is still between the pickup and one o'clock. That's also the zone where most of the power is applied in the forward, or fishing cast.

Once the pickup power has been applied and the one o'clock point reached, many casters prefer to bend the wrist backward and "drift through" with the rod tip going lower behind on the backcast. This won't prevent a high backcast unless carried to the extreme, for the backcast has already begun going up at that point. Still, I predict trouble if you let the tip ride back past two o'clock, unless you're very cute with a left-hand line-haul. One valid reason for lowering the tip a little is that the line can be fed backward through the guides with less friction. That happens in advanced casting.

It is important to cast well, but you must learn to do it without great effort. Poorly timed casting will beat you down, and older people or slightly built anglers simply can't cast all day unless they have their timing well adjusted. Great strength can actually be a handicap at first, for the athlete sometimes learns to force the line out and never bothers to do it right. Someone with less strength *has* to do it correctly in order to do it at all. No matter how good a line you cast, if you tire quickly, something

The true backhand cast is helpful in avoiding obstacles, but few fishermen can throw for great distances while using it. The action is mainly wrist and forearm.

can be improved. Often it's a subtle thing. When I first started fly fishing, I'd blister my hand and end every day with a sore arm. Finally, the blisters quit showing up and the arm quit hurting, but for twenty-five years I had a casting callous on the heel of my right hand. Then, although I made no conscious change in tackle or casting method, the callous simply disappeared and never came back. Somewhere along the line I had started doing things an easier and better way without noticing it. We can safely say that if it's hard work, it's wrong.

Most of the fly-fishing dropouts occur at about the same point. The candidate has learned to get out a fairly long line without hooking his ear or splashing water in back. He decides he's learned all there is to know about casting but finds it's a lot of work—so he drops the whole project. If he'd stick with it just a little longer, things would get easy. When you wade a stream or stand in a rolling boat to fly cast, your legs should get tired before your arm. It's that simple.

In the days when fly fishing was considered a classic and somewhat stylized performance, there was a great to-do about casting a fly with a book held between your elbow and your side. The "educated wrist" did it all, and anyone who waved a fly rod with his arm was a crude fellow indeed. Then, along came distance casting and the realization that there was no need to

10

handicap yourself by holding your arm stiff. So we all laughed scornfully at the old way and waved our arms joyously. Last summer I was wading gingerly in a small stream of spooky trout, using a very light rod, making short casts, and furtively drying my fly with quick flicks of the tip. It suddenly occurred to me that I was using the old picture-book method of casting, stiff elbow and all. In that particular situation, it worked better than anything else.

It is restful to alternate during a day's fishing. Use a lot of wrist for a while, then move your forearm for a few casts, then try waving your whole arm. It provides enough variety to prevent fatigue for hours. Fatigue is more important than most of us will admit, and almost anyone's casting suffers after three or four hours. The fatigued veteran drops his backcast occasionally, finds that his fishing casts are inconsistent, and loses just a bit of accuracy no one else would notice. The beginner comes apart completely, hooks his waders, and snaps off his flies.

My wife and I used to give casting demonstrations in those innocent days when 70 feet of fly line in the air was enough to bring admiring gasps from the gallery. I cockily accepted the job of instructing in a casting seminar for people who had never held a fly rod. The sponsors furnished bundles of matched outfits.

I knew that the simple throwing of a proper loop was the quickest way of becoming a caster, so I set the class up with a row of pupils holding rods. Then I got out in front of them, facing just as they were, pulled in my stomach, and began to false-cast, calling out about loops that were too loose, loops that were too tight, and loops that were just right. My poor wife panted about among the victims trying to tell them what they were doing wrong. My idea was that if they'd imitate my motions for ten minutes straight, they'd have the basics. I was too thick to realize that a beginner, doing everything wrong, would almost faint from exhaustion after ten minutes of steady false casting. I heard later that my students decided fly casting was on a par with marathon running and they wanted no more of it—all sixty of them.

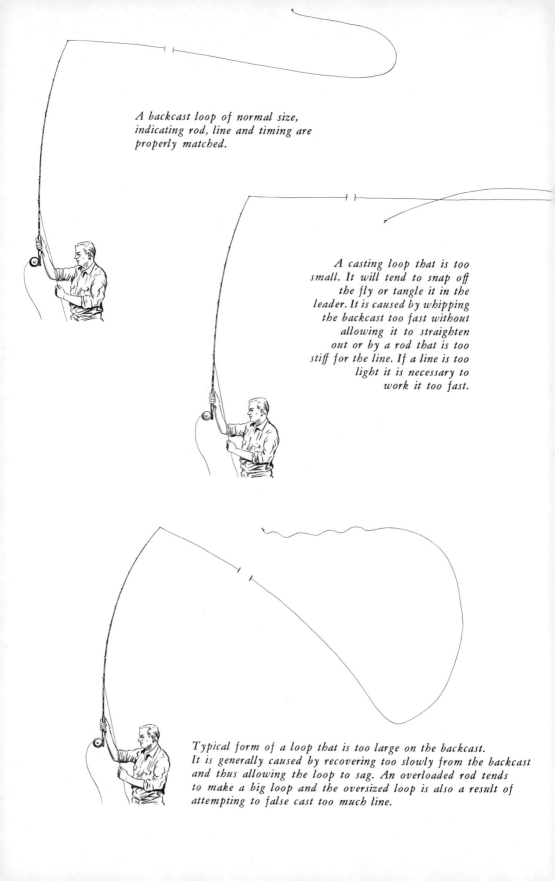

A backcast loop of normal size, indicating rod, line and timing are properly matched.

A casting loop that is too small. It will tend to snap off the fly or tangle it in the leader. It is caused by whipping the backcast too fast without allowing it to straighten out or by a rod that is too stiff for the line. If a line is too light it is necessary to work it too fast.

Typical form of a loop that is too large on the backcast. It is generally caused by recovering too slowly from the backcast and thus allowing the loop to sag. An overloaded rod tends to make a big loop and the oversized loop is also a result of attempting to false cast too much line.

The bare basics of fly casting can be taught in a few minutes, but it takes more practice than that to fish efficiently. I once promised to teach anyone to fly-cast in half an hour but found some of my pupils amazingly uncoordinated and stupid. Then, to demonstrate that a normal person could learn in thirty minutes, starting from scratch, I endeavored to learn to cast left-handed, something I'd never done. With all my professed knowledge of timing and technique, I found that nothing seemed to work for me. I'm still a terrible caster with my left hand.

Most casts are aimed too low. The perfect cast travels as a loop, unrolls parallel to the water, and drops straight to the surface. The caster should aim some distance above the water, except in a high wind when he may have to slap his fly down. A fly that is thrown too hard for the distance it must go will slap down and then snap back. If it is thrown too gently, the loop will not turn over and the leader won't straighten out.

As the cast is finished, the rod tip should be pointed in the direction the line is traveling, a simple matter of reducing guide friction as much as possible. Once the line has nearly straightened out on the fishing cast, it may help to lift the rod tip to prevent line from striking the water too near the caster. If the fisherman feels it's important to have the fly strike first, he can pull back rather sharply just as the loop straightens, but most of us are satisfied to have the line, leader, and fly alight at about the same time.

The distance caster goes with lots of line speed and shoots a great deal of running line. The commonest fault of beginners in distance casting is to attempt to false-cast too much line, believing the farther they must cast, the more line they'll need to carry in the air. When using a weight-forward line, it's best to get all the head out, then extend enough more to make things feel right and get distance from line speed. When a shooting head backed by small running line is used, the false-casting length is pretty well set up even before starting.

"Shooting" line is simply a matter of feeding line through the guides as your cast pulls it out. Most fishermen feed it through the fingers of their line hand. The shooting line is held in coils in the fingers, or dropped on the deck of a boat or on the water, or hooked over clothespins or bobby pins fastened to wader tops, or held in the mouth, or carried in a line-stripping basket. When casting from a boat on windy days, I like to use a big plastic trash can for my shooting line. These storage plans are necessary only when you're throwing for long distances.

Added distance is gained by aiming the cast quite high and by a single haul on the line as the rod drives forward on the fishing cast. The line hand simply gives a pull as the cast starts forward, thus speeding the line considerably. The line speed comes from the forward motion of the rod hand, from the straightening of the rod as it pulls the line forward, and from the tug given by the line hand (left hand in the case of a right-hander). That's a single haul. The double haul is more complicated, takes practice, and is a little like patting your head and rubbing your stomach at the same time. You do it this way:

First, you must work out the amount of line you want to false-cast. If you are using a powerful rod and heavy line, you'll probably want to use about 35 feet, or whatever feels right. Now you throw a backcast and as it goes back you feed some line back through the guides. Your rod hand will be somewhere near your ear as you make the backcast, and the line hand, without releasing its grip on the line, will move up beside it and "push" two or three feet of line back through the rod. Then, as you come forward with the rod you haul down with the line hand, bringing that two or three feet of extra line back through the guides. In doing this you speed up your line travel and gain distance. This is not simply a method of false casting more line. It is a system of adding line speed.

Then, as the line comes forward with the added impetus of your hauling, you let your shooting line go, and complete the cast. The line hand makes a sawing motion. You are using the same section of line, both as you feed back and as you haul forward. A tournament distance caster will double haul all the way from his left knee to his right ear and back again. When extreme

In casting for distance the fisherman feeds
line back over his shoulder with his left hand as part
of the double haul. Many casters lower the rod
tip as shown here to allow the line to slide
through the guides easily on the backcast although
the "follow through" does not add to power of
the cast. Such a long reach with the left hand
is needed only to increase the length of
pull as the cast comes forward.

As rod comes forward on fishing cast, angler
sweeps downward with his left hand to increase
line speed and to load rod for maximum
power thrust forward.

In casting for extreme distance the left hand is
swung clear to the left hip on the forward application of power. This angler has now completed the
haul and as his line straightens out in the forward
cast he will release the line with his left hand
and shoot his running line forward. These illustra-
tions show the extreme moves used in long-distance
casting. For most fishing the hauling motions are
much shorter although the timing is similar.

distance is your object, you are more likely to make several false casts before firing. In competition, a tournament caster will watch his loop very closely and let it go when he thinks it is as nearly perfect as possible. That much false casting is a nuisance when fishing, however, and it is not necessary to make false casts just because you are double-hauling. You can use the double haul without false casting at all in many instances—just pick up, feed back, and haul forward.

When casting for extreme distance, there is a tendency to overdo things at the last split second. You have false-casted a loop several times and it looks just right, so you decide to let it go on the next forward motion. Then, in anticipation of the distance you're going to throw, you drive at a different speed, fold up your cast, and fail dismally. I suppose everyone adds just a little steam to the final gesture, but if the line is working properly, the cast should be a simple continuation of the false casting—except that you let the line go.

Most fishermen false-cast more than is necessary, especially those fishing large streamers and bugs, and it's the false casting that makes work out of fishing. If you false-cast twice for every fishing cast, you're doing three times the amount of work necessary in many instances. When casting distance must be changed constantly, extra false casting is excusable; when every cast is just like the last, there's no need for all that waving.

For example, when drifting in a boat and casting blind with a floating line, I see no need for false casting at all. This situation occurs when drifting through weed or grass flats for black bass or pike, when covering grass flats for saltwater trout, and when working shallow bays for tarpon. Of course if you see, and cast to, individual fish it's a different proposition, but if it's just a matter of covering the water, you can establish the amount of line you want to pick up—say 40 feet—and then make your casts for 70 feet. After retrieving 30 feet, you just pick up and cast again, with no false casting at all. I confess very few fishermen do this, but can you think of any reason why they don't? Is there any purpose in a false cast if you already have the exact amount of line out, neatly stretched on the water? As the years took the starch out of my casting arm, I began a personal crusade against false casting and I really believe I put forth as little effort per hundred casts as any of my fishing friends, no matter how well they cast. I put out much less effort than the young and athletic types who, at this stage of the game, see no point in conserving the little extra energy demanded by a few false casts. My only argument to them is that they're not fishing when the line's in the air.

When fishing a sinking line, it's necessary to retrieve farther than with a floating line, simply because the water holds the line so hard that you can't pick up until it's pretty well in. False casting then becomes necessary unless you can manage a good pickup with a roll cast. Unlike the old silk lines with their prima donna ways, the new floating lines float without dressing, and even when they're pretty dirty. But there are all stages of floating, from the line that rides high like a cork and picks up slick as grease, to the logy and dirty line that appears to float but is more than half below the surface. Regular cleaning and doping will keep a floating line high on top and make it pick up much easier.

It may sound a little wild, but there are certain conditions when a low-floating line may actually help in some kinds of fishing. When you pick up the soggy number it pulls harder than the high-floater, and this means you can retrieve closer to the rod tip and still get enough resistance to bend the rod well and make a throw without false casting. A big, bulky fly or bug accomplishes a similar purpose. But generally, the higher things float, the better.

The stripping basket is used by some big-river fishermen, especially steelheaders. It's simply a canvas basket that's fastened at your waist, and the idea is to store your running line in it so that it doesn't tangle or get carried downstream. The chief difficulty with the stripping basket is something few fishermen note until they try it: when you use a basket you must put *all* of your line into it as you retrieve. Otherwise, a little loose line hanging outside will pull out the stored line and it will end up on the

Above: Stripping basket provides excellent storage for surplus running line, but must be filled carefully to avoid large loops outside basket which pull out coiled line before caster is ready. *Right:* Plastic trash can provides perfect line storage in boat. In windy weather, two can be nested, with a weight in the bottom can.

ground or in the water, an eerie performance that makes it appear spitefully alive. You see, the coils inside the basket are not very large and just a couple of feet of line hanging out will spill the whole business.

However, the stripping basket is ideal for a fisherman who works a stream with a dead drift and does not retrieve until his bottom-hugging fly has swung completely below him. Then a steelheader like Johnny Walker of the Kispiox will put his rod under his arm and retrieve his line hand over hand, tucking it into his basket. The system works with either a "whole" line or a shooting head and lightweight backing. If you want to manipulate the fly as it swings down, you must be careful in the way you stuff it into the basket, but it will work. Nevertheless, this is a little technique some casters don't like to bother with. It's good, but it isn't perfect.

The big plastic trash can, used in a boat, grates on the esthetic senses of many anglers but is a marvelous help when the wind blows or when you must change casting directions frequently, as when casting to breaking fish. Use a can that is

18

quite tall so that you won't have any trouble feeding your retrieved line into it in a high wind. If it blows very hard, you may
have to weight the can. I have seen days when more than a third
of a fisherman's casts went awry, blowing around an outboard
motor or somebody's large feet. Since the angler is throwing a
pretty long line, he feels he can't coil it satisfactorily in his line
hand and he is forced to drop it on the deck where the wind
playfully takes over. I note that such fishermen rip off their old-
school ties and smile happily when I produce my plastic can
under such circumstances.

Once the basic timing comes naturally, the matter of getting
the extra line through the guides on the shoot is the main problem. The cast can be killed by that line slapping the rod, or
kinking as it goes through the guides, or sticking to your line
hand. Some fine fishermen have earned their reputations as exceptional casters largely through their ability to coil extra line in
their hands and feed it smoothly. Work out your own method.
Most of us can carry about three coils of line in the line hand
without getting it tangled. Some fishermen who use only short
casts have systems of wrapping the retrieved line around their
fingers, and while this keeps the line off the ground, boat, or
water, the coils come off so small that distance is hindered.

When I am wading I can carry about three coils in my line
hand and about three coils in my mouth, but this mouth business
is questionable, especially with the pollution problems in many
rivers. I can't say that I've ever contracted anything from that
continual transfer of river water to my mouth, but I'm pretty
careful to use the method only where I think the stream is fairly
clean. If you're standing in strong current, the line-tending work
is complicated by the downstream pull, and even a floating line
comes off jerkily if the current is breaking over it downstream.
If it's whirled down in an eddy, your casts come to aggravating
halts. If the water's deep, the lower parts of the coils are generally in it, even those held in your mouth. I've had pretty good
luck looping line over clothespins hooked to the tops of my
waders after I worked out the right angle at which to clip them

Caster holds coils of line in mouth while throwing for distance on large river. Note that rod rides back past two o'clock to wait for loop to form properly.

on. Bobby pins are all right, too. Some casters will stick an extra loop into a shirt or pants pocket.

I confess to the occasional use of a "doily," a cheap trick that has caught me quite a few fish. Some years back I found some bass striking small bait on the far side of a highway canal. Not only was the gusty wind from exactly the wrong direction, but the short grass underfoot was of some type that imprisoned any fly line dropped into it. No matter how valiantly I double-hauled, two-thirds of my casts aborted because of grass tangles. Beside me stood two other fly fishermen, grunting mightily and volunteering remarks about the wind, the grass, and the smug bass smacking the minnows on the distant shore, just out of reach of our best efforts. It was so long a cast that the running line *had* to be dropped into the grass because none of us could hold that many loops without getting tangles. After half an hour of frustration, I went back to the car and pulled out a small piece of tarpaulin, spread it over the grass, coiled my line on it, and started catching bass. After all, the tournament casters do it all the time and I've used the thing several times since with only minor embarrassment, but if I'd had my trash can it would have worked just as well.

It was the tournament competitors who invented long-distance casting, and it was the steelhead fishermen who made it practical for fishing. The big thing in distance is the shooting

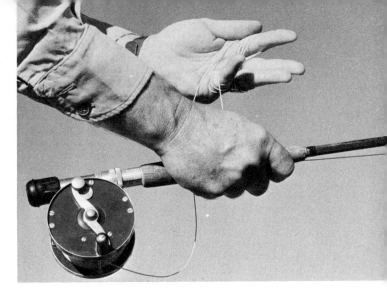

head or shooting taper, a heavy section of fly line spliced to monofilament or very light floating material. Most fishermen use the shooting head only as a sinking line, but others go all the way and use nothing but heads, floating or sinking, fastening them to whatever running line they prefer. When you start weighing the heavier shooting heads, as used for steelhead, Pacific salmon, and saltwater fishing, you begin to understand what makes a fly rod work. A common fishing weight for a fast-sinking head is 330 grains. That's heavier than the 5/8-ounce plugs used with bait-casting outfits. No wonder it goes.

In tournament distance casting, the monofilament running line is carefully coiled and tended by a gillie. It's no wonder the tournament lads can use very small stuff that goes very lightly through the guides. For fishing, somewhat heavier "mono" is used to avoid tangles. A more recent product is a floating material, made like a fly line but very small in diameter. Before that was introduced, some casters had been buying the smallest fly line they could get and splicing their shooting heads to it. The idea was that the wading fisherman wouldn't have to cast his monofilament up from a sunken position in the stream, but simply peel the floating stuff off the top. You can get more distance with monofilament, providing it is not sunk too deep, as it goes through the guides more smoothly, but the other running line is easier to handle without snarling it.

The fishing head is generally 30 feet or less in length, but the tournament casters use longer ones. The casting procedure for most fishermen is to retrieve the head until one end of it enters the rod guides, then pick up and make a false cast before letting go. They leave just enough running line out through the guides to allow them to double-haul without working their splice through the tip guide. It is easy to ruin a cast by false-casting too much of the running line, for it has no appreciable weight and can cause your shooting head to sag as it runs out of speed.

Any cast longer than 70 feet can be termed a long one. That would be almost the extreme with an ultralight trout rod and double-tapered line. Using a fairly powerful rod and forward-tapered line, most veteran casters can get very close to 100 feet and may do a little better if winds are favorable. There are very few casters who can do more than throw off the line and leader, which may extend slightly beyond a hundred feet. When it comes to the shooting head used with monofilament or light braided material as running line, the 100-foot cast becomes routine. A tournament caster will throw more than 140 feet with a one-hand rod. Fishermen will consistently get slightly more than a hundred feet with steelhead tackle.

Extreme distance with fly tackle requires very delicate timing, even though the distance caster may appear to be engaged in a rather crude display of muscle. Most of the best distance-casters who compete in tournaments are fairly athletic, big men, but one of the consistent winners has been Bob Budd of Jeffersonville, Indiana. He was still winning national distance events past sixty years of age and weighing no more than 145 pounds. Muscular though he is, Bob Budd obviously gets his results through superior timing as he gives away reach, height, and weight to his competition.

Having never done any tournament casting, I felt that long distance was primarily a matter of equipment. To prove my point, I once coaxed Bob Budd to coach me a little some twenty years ago. He rigged up a "distance trout rod" for me—a stiff nine-footer with heavy tournament head and light monofilament. It

*The moment of power application for a long cast. Left hand
is hauling to gain line speed.*

turned out that I could throw pretty far with the outfit—occasionally. The difference was that he could do it consistently, a
matter of judging the timing and the backcasts almost to perfec-
tion. After several days of practice, I became more consistent but
I had learned just enough about the distance game and its special
tackle to know that there was more to it than first met the eye.

Probably the best grip for a flyrod is with the thumb on top
of the handle. This position slightly inhibits wrist motion as the
rod tip goes back in the backcast, but this may even be desirable
in keeping the backcast from sagging. I am convinced that keeping the thumb on top, or nearly on top, of the handle helps guide
the cast and adds power on the delivery, especially if you use
considerable wrist in your cast. Some rod handles are specially
shaped for this grip. When the thumb is bent *around* the handle,
the grip will rock back and forth in the hand, is under less control and, with powerful rods, can cause blisters. Some good casters
cant the rod somewhat, thus turning the reel out, away from their

bodies. They say this makes power casting easier. This doesn't help me, but I think they probably use more wrist movement than I do; the wrist will bend more with the thumb extended along the side of the grip. At this point we come to the business of wrist casting, forearm casting, and full-arm casting. Emphasize the forearm to begin with, but learn to use everything you have.

With very light rods some fishermen extend the forefinger along the upper side of the handle. The idea is that this finger position will positively prevent the rod tip going too far back. Also, it helps the fisherman conform to classic style, as well as giving him his forefinger to aim with. I use this system only when I think someone is watching, as it hurts my finger.

There's nearly always a wind from somewhere, and the more faint-hearted fly fishermen give up even when it's only a breeze. The diehards can actually do a fairly good job with winds as high as 35 miles an hour. Up to 15 or 20 miles per hour it should be no great hardship if you can adjust your casting direction a little. There are ways of cheating the wind, however, no matter what direction it comes from.

To cast straight into the wind you may have to sacrifice delicacy to some extent; it's difficult to put a dry fly down gently. And if the wind is strong enough to blow *your* fly around, it may be blowing natural flies around too, possibly adding tricky riffles to the surface and befuddling the trout as much as it befuddles you. The way to cast into a head-on wind is to throw it hard in a tight loop and keep it low. Nearly all of us sideswipe slightly in normal casting, rather than swing the rod through a completely

Heavy rods may be supported by the forearm for casting and for playing fish, but the wrist snap is lost.

With wind coming from his right, fisherman tips rod to his left and allows the entire cast to work on left side of his body, thus avoiding tangles and hook dangers.

vertical arc. Some good casters sideswipe even more when facing a bad wind, but, however it is delivered, the loop should be tight—simply a matter of offering less wind resistance. Throw the backcast high and loosely and the wind will pull it back effortlessly as it catches your open loop. So it is best to keep the fishing cast low because there's usually less wind close to the ground, where it's broken up by vegetation, folds in the land, or wave action. Then, in driving forward, aim very close to the surface or right at it.

When the wind is behind you, throw your backcast low to keep it "under the wind" and then cast high into the air on your fishing cast, keeping the loop large enough to catch the breeze, and the line and leader will straighten out smoothly and drop gently.

The worst wind for the right-handed caster comes from his right side, for that's the one that blows his fly into his ear or around his neck. When you feel your line being blown into your face, there's a tendency to sideswipe and try to hold the whole thing off to your right. It will work in a light wind, but in a heavy blow you'll still get the fly where it hurts. The most satisfactory remedy is to do your casting with your arm a little high and with the rod tip slanted toward your left, over the top of your head. This carries your cast to the left of your body. For most of us, it's a simpler method than a true backhand, which would put the entire rod on the left side of the body with the casting arm across in front of the chest.

The ideal wind direction, and one that can often be arranged, especially in boat fishing, is from behind the left shoulder—a thrust that helps push the fly out and at the same time carries it well to the right of the caster. None of these wind-beating tricks is difficult, but many otherwise proficient fishermen don't stop to reason them out. Incidentally, when choosing a rod for a windy day, most anglers prefer a stiff one that works happily with tight loops. Heavier and stiffer leader material goes better in the wind.

Fly construction is important too. Dry flies in trout sizes have little effect on casting, but when we come to big streamers and bass bugs, the lure must be reckoned with and it isn't always the size or the weight that makes casting difficult or easy. There's a thing we'll call "planing quality" that simplifies or complicates casting.

For example, there are some large steelhead flies tied rather skimpily on No. 1 hooks and slightly weighted with lead wire so they'll probe the bottom in fast water. Such a fly will weigh about 17 grains and I consider it very difficult to cast. Even with heavy steelhead tackle, big sinking head and all, it always takes me a few minutes to get the rather tricky rhythm of throwing one of the things, and misjudgment can whack it into your back or neck sharply enough to keep you gun-shy for an hour or two.

On the other hand, I do considerable fishing with some giant saltwater streamers that are six inches long and carry 2/0 hooks. When one of those is wet, it weighs a full 38 grains, much larger and heavier than the inch-long steelhead pattern, yet I consider it much easier to cast. The answer is that although it's bigger and heavier, it planes smoothly through the air and demands less exact timing than the weighted fly. When wet, it's streamlined, but there is enough body to the six-inch silhouette to make it soar. Of course, either of these flies requires husky equipment for efficient casting. Usually it's the lure, rather than the fish, that demands big powerful rods and heavy lines.

Any fly-making material that flutters in the air will be hard to cast. In early experiments with Mylar streamers, everyone tried the coarser strips—the things sounded like low-level strafing runs as they went past your head—that didn't even go very far. It was not until the strip size was reduced to 1/64-inch wide that the Mylar streamers became pleasant to cast. In dressing "breather" streamers, some tiers spread the feather tips so far apart at the tail end that they stay apart in the air, even when wet, and casting suffers. They twist the leader too.

Some fly-rod bugs, especially those intended for salt water, are made with very heavy, rust-resistant hooks. I weighed one commercial number that came to 64 grains, much heavier than ultralight spinning lures. It requires a very heavy rod and something like a No. 11 line to turn over satisfactorily. I have another bug in my box with an even longer silhouette, but a lighter hook and body, that weighs only 24 grains. Not only that, but it is more streamlined, offering less resistance in the air.

The large saltwater flies are frightening to many freshwater fishermen trying them for the first time. After the first two or three casts, the average trout fisherman will announce that it's impossible, but a good caster will adapt to any timing and in half an hour he'll be casting smoothly. Before such things were taken over by spinning tackle, many fly fishermen were casting tandem spinners on their bass rods. It wasn't much for distance but it caught a lot of fish.

Most of the fancy casts required in specialized fishing can be worked out easily once the basics are mastered. There are many excellent fishermen who claim to do it without these trick casts, but when fancy moves will catch more fish, they tend to learn.

Overhanging bushes or trees and undercut banks require some special techniques if the fish are in close. It happens with black bass, panfish, some saltwater fish, and freshwater trout, and a very tight loop is the solution. Some fishermen working toward overhung banks throw their casts so low that the belly of the line strikes the water well out from shore, long before the leader and fly begin to turn over. Then the cast actually rolls out on the surface, rather than in the air. Others make the delivery with a sort of modified whip-cracking motion, and the final turnover is short and fast, the fly usually striking the water pretty hard. That's a difficult situation with small drys, and timing must be just right if the fly is to escape drowning.

You can lower the final stage of the cast by dropping the casting elbow just as the leader starts to turn over. Part of this is a simple matter of getting the whole operation closer to the water; part of it is a psychological gesture that makes you throw lower—just knowing the overhang is there cramps your casting style.

The other way of casting under an overhang is the wide sideswipe in which the cast is made with the rod almost parallel to the water. It works well, keeping the entire cast low, but it is good only at shorter ranges. Extralong casts require that the rod tip be fairly high.

It's in dry-fly stream fishing that the casting tricks come on strong in solving all sorts of current and wind problems, and although no two problems are ever quite the same, three or four techniques can usually handle them. The basic idea is to give the dry fly a dragless float over the fish's lie, preferably without first showing him the line or leader. Between the caster and the fish there may be several current speeds, and the first rule is to "use your waders more and your arms less." Careful wading and fish-stalking can enable you to avoid adverse currents more effectively than any amount of trick casting, and extremely long casts should be avoided if trout are spooky, and especially if the casts are being made to an individual rising fish.

Assuming that the fish is upstream from the caster, and that the currents, as usual, have cooperated to make things as difficult as possible, you may want to throw a curve cast, to the right or to the left, so that the fly can float over the fish before he sees the line or leader, and before drag sets in. (Drag, of course, is any motion of the dry fly, other than a dead drift with the current, and it's caused by the leader holding back upstream or pulling downstream. The resultant wake causes thoughtful trout to stop feeding and hide under rocks.)

For a slow retrieve, the fisherman uses a "hand-twist" with his rod hand, and gathers line with his left hand by grasping it alternately with thumb and forefinger, with little finger against heel of hand.

A curve cast to the right is one in which the fly, leader, and line form a hook bending to the right of the fisherman. Imagine an ordinary fishhook formed by the line. The fisherman would be standing at the eye of the hook and the fly would be at the barb, well off to the angler's right—curve to the right. Turn the hook over and the barb would face to the left—curve to the left. This may be oversimplification to many, but I have heard experienced fly fishermen fussing among themselves about curve casting, obviously not talking about the same things at all.

A curve to the right can be thrown by a sidearm cast that is slightly weak for the amount of line out. Instead of the leader and fly swinging out into a straight line as they come around from the right, they simply settle to the water with the fly still lagging behind the front of the loop. Then, as the fly starts downstream with the current, it should be seen by the fish before he sees the line or leader. A downstream wind can make this cast easier.

A curve to the left is accomplished by using a cast that is thrown a little harder than necessary for the distance to be reached. It is made sidearm, and some fishermen pull the cast up short with the line hand. In any event, the fly and leader not only straighten out at the end of the throw, they continue on around and hook to the left before dropping on the water. The right-hand curve is underpowered; the left-hand curve is overpowered.

Plenty of fishermen can throw these curves well, but none can always do it perfectly on the first trial in a new situation. I know that I need a couple of practice casts before things work right and I like to make those practice throws where there are no fish rising. Some excellent dry-fly men never attempt curve casts since a sloppy performance over a touchy fish can end your chances.

Chester Marion, a hard-fishing western trout man, is one of the best dry-fly anglers I know and says he never uses the curve cast. At first I thought he might be throwing the curves subconsciously to reach difficult lies, but after a little spying I concluded he really does not use them. He throws his dry flies harder than most fishermen do and seems to bear down on accuracy rather than long floats. When he locates a regularly rising fish in tricky currents, he throws his fly very close above it, hoping for just a few inches of dragless float in exactly the right place. Few catch more fish than Chester Marion, but I don't consider this to be ultimate proof of anything. Perhaps he could catch even more fish if he employed the curve casts, but he certainly gets along very well without them.

The slack-line casts are very helpful in dry-fly fishing, sometimes with nymphs as well, and are much simpler than the curves. A slack-line cast is simply one in which the line falls on the surface crookedly so that the fly will not drag until the currents have straightened out all of the bends in line and leader. You can throw the slack cast by making a normal effort and then waggling the rod tip to left and right as the line settles to the water. You get a similar effect by simply lobbing the line weakly, so that it never quite straightens. You can cast hard and yank back at the last instant, causing the line to kick back into a series of curves as it drops.

The rod-tip waggle that works with the slack-line cast can be used "in reverse" for a gentle pickup of the leader and fly, providing the cast is not too long. The waving motion is executed as the rod tip comes up, and the wave of line movement is transmitted to the leader and fly, which leave the surface with a minimum of

Louis Nordmann, casting for spotted weak-fish, demonstrates why line handling is important. Loose running line offers great resistance to any cast.

commotion and are in the air before the dragging motion of the pickup begins.

The slack casts are also used in fishing a dry fly or nymph downstream, not exactly classic style but very effective at times. The cast is made from above the feeding fish, stopped a few feet short of his feeding station, and then allowed to slide down with the stream, the curves in the line and leader designed to overcome dragging tendencies of intervening currents. It's likly to be a clean drift, possibly a perfect presentation, but if the fish doesn't take on the first cast, the fisherman is confronted with the problem of having to pick up fly and leader against the current and above the fish, likely to be a sloppy operation. Then too, setting the hook may be difficult when the fish takes from directly below the fisherman, since the hook tends to pull straight forward out of the fish's mouth instead of pulling into a corner of the jaw. But again, no two situations are exactly alike, and many fish are taken with the downstream slack cast. One effective variation is done with a floating shooting head and monofilament backing, the shooting head floating freely at the proper speed, and the light running line being paid out so that it does not interfere with the drift. Such a float can be continued almost endlessly under the proper conditions; one proponent said he "could stand in one place and fish the whole crick." It isn't quite that simple, but specialists can do very well with it.

The "change-direction" cast comes in here somewhere, a simple matter of picking up from one cast and laying the new cast in a different direction, as much as 90 degrees from the route of the first. If the direction of the cast is changed only slightly, the change can be made with no extra thought to the backcast. But if the change approaches 90 degrees, the caster should deliberately throw his backcast a little higher and a little harder. Then, while the backcast is in the air, he should turn his body to face the direction of his new cast and push the rod in that direction. The backcast will swing around in a curve and go the way he is facing. If all goes well, the caster will never completely lose the feel of weight in his backcast. This won't go for long distances but is very simple out to 40 or 50 feet.

Obstacles bring out the unusual casting forms. The roll cast has its place when there's no room for a backcast; it's a matter of lifting the rod tip to about one o'clock (slightly past the shoulder) so that some line sags beneath it, and then throwing it forward, rolling up line from the water and throwing it into a fishing cast. This maneuver reaches its highest form of development with fishermen who spend much of their time in brushy streams, and some of them can get remarkable distance by shooting line as the cast goes out. Those who fish in more open waters use a roll cast primarily to get their line into the air where they can false-cast it satisfactorily. It becomes a standard procedure with many anglers using the sinking head, when the heavy line is so far down it is hard to recover with a routine pickup. By rolling it forward and then backcasting it, you can get back into business promptly, and with practice you may be able to eliminate the false cast—just roll forward, throw back over your shoulder, and make a fishing cast.

The practice of watching your backcast becomes a necessity when you're backcasting between trees, bushes, or other obstacles, and there are some fishermen who simply turn their backs on the fishing water, make careful false casts into openings in the cover, and actually change their backcasts into fishing casts. The reason for facing away from the fish is to cast as accurately as possible between the obstacles. However, most of us can get by in most cases by simply watching over our shoulders.

I have had some excellent practice at backcasting while fishing roadside ditches alongside main highways. The idea is to get the backcast over or between passing cars and trucks, and the penalty for a mistake can be the loss of a fly, leader, and line—or worse. One of my less auspicious efforts left me a temporary cripple when I misjudged and allowed swirling air currents to suck my fly line down and around an outboard motorboat being

Many casters look backward occasionally, in order to watch their loop form on the backcast. In fishing on this roadside canal, the backcast is especially important—and high!

towed at 60 miles an hour. Letting go of my outfit proved a little difficult, and by the time I had sense enough to throw the rod on the ground and jump on it, my hands were badly cut and burned and the innards of my fly reel had melted down and frozen. I lost fly, leader, line, and backing, but saved rod and reel. The line and backing were strong enough to have whipped the rod and reel into the traffic stream if they had gotten away from me. Since there were several delighted fishermen watching, it was not exactly a highlight of my angling career.

Many of the world's best fly fishermen have no names for the fancy casts they make subconsciously. Many of them are amused at any effort to classify casts, or to write detailed instructions. No one can describe to anyone just how a good cast feels, but by setting down the mechanical factors, I may have helped someone.

THREE

Rod and Line

ONE FLY ROD could do it all. It would be made of fiber glass or split bamboo, around 8 or 8½ feet long, and it would take an 8 line. Admittedly, it would be awkward for small trout in placid brooks, and it would be a little over matched against an offshore cobia, but it would work. With just this one rod, you could be happy with a variety of lines, or even with only one line if you were handy at choosing leaders.

It's a pretty good place to start, and when you decided to get a trout rod you'd certainly appreciate the delicacy of a 7-foot dry-fly wand. Then, when you got your big 9-foot saltwater stick, you'd really feel the horsepower. Still, the rod I described first could do it all; if you never tried the others you wouldn't know any better and you'd learn to do a good job with it. But that's the hard way to go, and few serious fly fishers have only one rod. In fact, some of them have too many and spend more time fooling than they do fishing. A rod collector is sometimes in the same fix as a firearms collector who is continually outshot by the fellow wedded to one well-worn gun.

Three fly rods can make up a pretty efficient battery. In

recent years there has been a trend to somewhat lighter and shorter rods through the entire field of fishing; some of the current heavy-duty numbers are shorter and lighter than "light" trout rods of some years back. This is partly the result of improved rod construction, but I think line developments and casting techniques have contributed as much or more. For fifty years the real experts have been using ultralight equipment for some of their fishing. More recently, the less accomplished casters began to realize that such fishing does not require supernatural powers, and since then everybody's gear has been getting handier.

If the latest line-weight designations would only be accepted in tackle talk, the whole thing would be simplified. Line manufacturers have made a valiant effort to standardize by designating the weights of their lines with numbers instead of letters. The larger the number of the line, the heavier it is. Thus, if you say such and such a rod is a "number nine," you mean that it takes a 9 line, and anyone who knows about line weights will understand what you're talking about. A "10" rod would take a heavier line,

Rough treatment like this shows the way a fly rod is built. This one, being used on a jack crevalle, shows a fairly slow action. Note that it is even bending slightly all the way into the butt.

and so on. Fishermen have been slow to accept this system, and some veteran fly people still don't know what you mean. Therefore, many rod discussions are prefaced by a conference on definitions.

There are complaints that a 7 line made by one manufacturer is lighter than another's, but this is really a minor beef and you can come pretty close by talking in numbers. I'm first to admit there are some differences, but a real effort has been made by the AFTMA (American Fishing Tackle Manufacturers Association), Best of all, the manufacturers have begun to mark the line number for each rod on the rod itself, so you can have a pretty good idea of what you're getting, even if the clerk who waits on you has just walked over from the candy counter. Line number does not cover all the finer points of rod action, but a few years ago you had to start from scratch, and judging rods in a tackle store is hard enough at best.

There is less of it these days, but I have seen many frustrated souls waving expensive rods with lines that bore no relation to them. Usually, the fault is with a line that is too light. The beginning fly fisherman is a little awed when he sees the large diameter of a fly line for the first time, often not quite understanding the principle of the thing. He thought he was going to light tackle, and here is a character trying to sell him a line that looks like anchor rope!

SOME BASICS

Let's try to simplify our language before we get into the nuts and bolts of rod and line combinations. By using line numbers we can say a great deal about rods in a few words.

As fly lines progressed through the stages of braided horsehair, combinations of horsehair and silk, and then to silk, their sizes became standardized and were indicated by letters. The letters used were "A" to "I" and referred to the diameter of the line. This was satisfactory, since all of the silk lines of a given size had about the same weight, regardless of the manufacturer. If your rod took a "C" line, you could confidently order one from

LIGHT TAPER   HEAVY TAPER

|—————————————— 75' ——————————————|

The "Variweight" fly line is constructed to provide proper weight for two different fly rods. Its purpose is to facilitate matching line to rod action in cases where it is inconvenient to try several lines. In casting, it has the same qualities as the conventional double taper.
DIAGRAM COURTESY SCIENTIFIC ANGLERS, INC.

any catalogue and it would be a pretty good fit for your rod. Incidentally, a "C" would be nearly right for many trout rods, being close to what is called a number 6 by the current system. In the early fifties, when new fly-line materials began to take the place of silk for most uses, the old size designations weren't valid because the new materials varied in weight. Since the weight of the line, rather than its diameter, is what makes it fit a given rod, it was necessary to come up with a different set of designations. The AFTMA number system refers to weight rather than size. Roughly, an 8 line is about the same as the old "B" designation. An "A" line was bigger, and some of the ultraheavy lines were marked "AA" or even "AAA."

The four basic types of fly lines. The measurements of the tapered lines are typical, though they vary greatly in lines built for specific purposes.

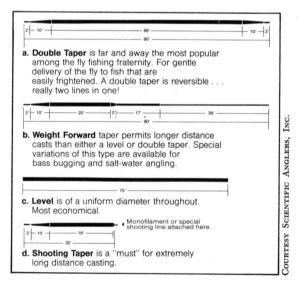

2'|— 10' —|——————— 66' ———————|— 10' —|2'
|————————————— 90' —————————————|

a. Double Taper is far and away the most popular among the fly fishing fraternity. For gentle delivery of the fly to fish that are easily frightened. A double taper is reversible . . . really two lines in one!

2'|— 10' —|——— 20' ———|2'|— 17' —|——— 39' ———
|————————————— 90' —————————————|

b. Weight Forward taper permits longer distance casts than either a level or double taper. Special variations of this type are available for bass bugging and salt-water angling.

|———————— 75' ————————|

c. Level is of a uniform diameter throughout. Most economical.

Monofilament or special shooting line attached here.

2'|— 10' —|——— 18' ———|
|————— 30' —————|

d. Shooting Taper is a "must" for extremely long distance casting.

COURTESY SCIENTIFIC ANGLERS, INC.

Fly lines come in four basic designs:

The *level line* is the same diameter over its entire length, is inexpensive, and is used mainly for short casts.

The *double-taper* has a heavy section in the middle and tapers down to a small tip at each end. It is best for delicate presentations of small flies. When one end shows wear, it can be reversed on the reel for longer life.

The *forward-taper* has a heavy section near the front and is designed for distance, or for turning over heavy and bulky flies. The rear section of this line is small enough to feed easily through the guides and offer little air resistance.

The *shooting taper* has a short section, resembling the front part of the forward-taper, and it is attached to a shooting line of another material, quite small in diameter. It is used when distance is needed. The shooting taper is not usually listed as a basic line form, but I have done so for the purpose of simplification.

In setting up line specifications, the first 30 feet of tapered lines are weighed to establish the number designations. The weights and numbers go like this:

Line Number	Weight in Grains
1	60
2	80
3	100
4	120
5	140
6	160
7	185
8	210
9	240
10	280
11	330
12	380

There's quite a bit of leeway, but these weights give us a mighty good start.

Now we can talk about a No. 5 rod and understand that this means a fairly light-actioned trout stick. We don't need to worry about the rod's weight, only the line that it works best with, and although I may like a heavier line than you do for the same rod, we can at least discuss it.

By the old designations, a fairly heavy weight-forward line would be a "GAF," meaning that the heavy section was "A" size, the running line was "F" size, and the front taper went down to "G." The newer designations don't bother with the smallest parts of the tapers but use these letters:

L—Level
DT—Double-taper
WF—Weight-forward
ST—Single-taper
F—Floating
S—Sinking
I—Intermediate (requires
dressing to float)

Thus, a floating line that is weight-forward, with the fishing section weighing 210 grains, would be a WF-8-F, the description of the taper coming first. This cuts through a great deal of explanation.

A BATTERY OF RODS

Three rods cover most of the needs for all fly fishing, and most of us wouldn't catch any more fish if we had a hundred. (A few of us have.) I can describe a pretty good choice of three rods. Beyond that my advice would be neither needed nor heeded, although I have a few further suggestions.

The trout rod is best for small dries, wets, nymphs, medium-sized streamers, and small panfish bugs. It usually takes about a 6 line. At one time the rods used for this fishing tended to be much longer, but casting techniques, rod structure, and line design have improved, making 7½ feet a favorite for general trout

Streamer fisherman makes a long pickup of floating line. Note coils of running line hanging downstream in water.

fishing these days. In this class, I think bamboo usually has an edge, although it actually has more weight than glass.

For many years there was a great to-do about wet-fly action versus dry-fly action. Most of our present trout rods are something of a compromise. Wet-fly action is slow, with the rod bending into a pretty even curve all the way. Dry-fly action is described as faster and crisper, with more tip-work. The wet-fly action helps somewhat to pick up a sunken attraction, while dry-fly action helps in flicking a floater dry in false casting and in laying it daintily on the surface. At the risk of outraging some perfectionists, I'd say to forget this distinction and simply get a rod that casts well with something like a 6 line and a small fly. Most late-model rods of good manufacture are fairly good compromises. In split bamboo, such a rod would weigh around 4 ounces. In glass, it would probably weigh $3\frac{1}{4}$ to $3\frac{1}{2}$. But these weights are not too important—simply a rough indication.

To get back to the question of length—don't be disturbed about a few inches here or there. Many top-quality rods are sold, to everybody's satisfaction, in the lengths they just happened to come out in. The $7\frac{1}{2}$-foot specification is a general one. With a rod this size you can also cast fairly large hair bass bugs if you keep them well doped and floating high. This is not a rod for heavy bass bugging; it doesn't do well with big streamers in heavy rivers, and a big 2/0 bass bug will ruin your day and disposition, if not your arm.

Now to the rod for bigger bass bugs, for big trout streamers and bulky dry flies, and for light saltwater use. This rod should be more than eight feet long and less than nine. It would take an 8 line in most cases, although I have a tendency to overload it by one weight and come up with a 9 outfit. A 7 outfit will work too, although slightly on the light side. Most of the time, this rod would be used with weight-forward lines, even when casting big dry flies on big water. It would handle sinking lines, either as single-piece units or as shooting heads with light backing. Its action would be medium to slow, with power on down to the butt. This is your workhorse rod and it will take some abuse. It will be good for big trout, steelhead, salmon, bass, and light saltwater fishing. Some of us prefer something in this range for bonefish.

I am not going to enter into any bamboo-versus-glass brawls (I'll discuss that business later), but this middleweight rod can be of either material. I use bamboo and glass interchangeably here. In lighter rods (by action) I prefer bamboo by a small margin. In this No. 8 I don't care. In rods taking lines heavier than 8 I have come to prefer glass, largely because of its lighter overall weight. A lot of good fishermen agree with me.

The third rod in your lineup would be about nine feet long, take something like a 10 line, and would throw the biggest bugs and streamers in the strongest winds you'd attempt. I choose fiber glass in this model, and, since you're likely to lay a bit of muscle to this one, it will need to stiffen up as you load it down. This could be your salmon rod, although the No. 8 would be more pleasant most of the time.

That is a basic three-rod battery for most men who are going to do a lot of fishing. The heaviest of the rods will be too much for most ladies and youngsters. With skill, they'll manage to cast with it, but it would be too much effort over the long haul, so most of them should make do with the No. 8 rod. However, it would be a mistake to try to do the heavy stuff with the little trout outfit. Remember that it's less work in many cases to choose the heavier stick, even though there is an understandable impulse to cling to what feels feathery.

Expanding this basic three-rod battery, a fourth rod would probably be a lighter-actioned trout specialist of around six feet. A fifth rod would be a fish-fighter, preferably made with heavy glass walls, for extraheavy saltwater fish. It might not be particularly pleasant for anyone's casting, because it's constructed primarily for the heavy strain of hauling tired giants to a gaff. But by the time you get to a fourth or fifth rod, you'll probably have your own ideas.

ROD MATERIALS

The earliest fly rods were made of solid pieces of wood, often with a stiff butt section of one kind and a whippy tip of another. Then came carefully shaped rods of one piece of solid wood. The big development came with the split cane or split bamboo rod, made from strips glued together. The six-strip bamboo has been on the American market since about 1870 and is

Fly fishing is the oldest form of light-tackle gamefishing, and before split bamboo became popular, fly fishermen used solid wood.

the most popular combination. For extra power with moderate weight, some of the bamboos have been built hollow at the butt.

Quality metal fly rods are almost a thing of the past, although many were sold in the thirties. After World War II, fiber glass took over most of the rod business in both solid and hollow models. The best glass fly rods are hollow and afford a wide variety of actions. They can be made at moderate cost, are remarkably uniform in mass production, and are owned by thousands of fishermen who have never handled bamboo.

It is hard to find serious fault with high-grade glass rods. Until about 1965, the glass-rod business was hurt by a series of sales gimmicks in the form of trick actions. For that reason, older rods should be examined carefully. One of the rod-making kicks included a very whippy tip and a very stiff center section. The idea was that the very light tip would work with light lines and flies, and, the main section of the rod would handle the heavier lines and bulky lures. It was not as bad as some of its disgusted critics claimed, but it was not as good as a more conventional bend.

The special qualities of beloved rods are vague and hard to describe. Perhaps the most concrete criterion of bamboo quality is that a good bamboo rod does the casting and then quits flapping around. Perhaps "resilience" is the best term to use. It is a compliment to bamboo that the more astute glass-rod makers have tried to get the bamboo feel and have compared their finished product to "the finest of bamboo." They've come very close to it in many cases. I believe they're ahead of bamboo in the heavy-duty rods, breaking even in the middle range, and still a little behind in light trout rods.

Bamboo rods are expensive, many of them costing up to two hundred dollars and more. I will not say the extra cost is justified by performance. That's up to you. I will say that good bamboo rods are built with much handwork. Their cost is justified by the effort of manufacture, and their tolerances are often as fine as those of precise metalwork.

Although many of the largest rod manufacturers deal in nothing but glass, there is a current revival of interest in some of the fine old rod names of yesteryear. Some of these rods are being made now with the old names but with new manufacturing techniques. It would be risky to name them, as the picture changes constantly, but some of them come from England, which was the cradle of fly fishing as it is known in America, and there are several American firms building high-grade rods. There are also some rods from continental Europe.

There is some snobbery connected with bamboo, especially that sold under old and revered names, but some of the fishermen who would have nothing else would cast almost as well with willow branches. Nevertheless, possession of a fine bamboo carries prestige, even if you don't know how to use it.

Some of the basic actions in light bamboos have not been changed in fifty years and are still being manufactured. Since no one can suggest improvement, there's no complaint there. Since most of the cane suitable for rod-building comes from China, there have been importing difficulties, the cane stocks of the seventies being acquired in America by somewhat devious, although completely legal, means.

Although the actions haven't been changed much in recent

High-grade bamboo fly rods still require considerable hand-work, but the handles are shaped on lathes. This work is being done at the Orvis plant, in Manchester, Vermont.

years, bamboo rods have been improved. Glues are much better and fittings reflect the latest in metallurgy. At one time, many rods were wrapped almost from butt to tip with various colors of thread, an expedient for reinforcing the glue that held the segments. Modern glues will hold with no assistance, and the only thread wrappings needed are those that secure the fittings.

Impregnated bamboo has been provided for many years by the Orvis Company, in Manchester, Vermont, and that material is very tough indeed since the impregnation goes all the way through. Varnish is unnecessary, so the exterior is simply polished in most cases. The stuff is actually tougher than glass, but few fishermen try to find out about that, as impregnated rods are fairly expensive. Now, impregnated bamboo is being listed by other builders.

Ferrules on high-grade bamboo rods are usually of nickel silver. Of late, many of the glass rods have joints that simply employ the glass itself. In some models, the large end of the tip section simply slides down over the small end of the butt section. Various means are used for reinforcing the female part of the ferrule, using wrappings and metal rings. Other rods have a solid male plug attached to the butt section, which simply slides into the female fitting of the tip. The glass ferrule is welcome to anyone who has suffered the agonies of ferrule corrosion, sticking, and loosening with glass rods. Although continually improved, glass connections have given some trouble. I have had the tip section split at the connection and, although it never gave way, I can see potential trouble through prolonged use. I have also had the male plug come loose on another type of rod and slide back down into the butt section, putting the rod completely out of service. But I am told the later models won't do that, and I haven't had recent trouble.

Both bamboo and glass rods can be worn out through long and heavy use. It is usually a gradual process that sneaks up on the proud owner, who finally decides there's something wrong with his casting or that his new line isn't the right weight. Once or twice it seemed to me that it happened rather suddenly with glass rods, but I had not measured the change in stiffness on those occasions and it may be it was a sudden realization, rather than a quick change in the rod.

I have a friend who fishes very hard all season and who uses a great many large dry flies on fast water. Through a rather energetic casting style, and violent false casting in drying the big flies, he takes the starch out of two glass rods each year. The rods simply soften up, to the point where they require lines at least one size lighter than originally called for. This has been going on for several years and I have checked these sticks as new rods, and then as used-up ones. You can wear out bamboo, too.

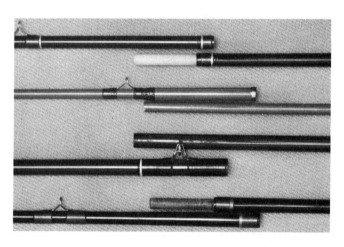

Many glass fly rods are jointed without metal ferrules. Here are the glass ferrules of four different manufacturers. Glass connections have advantages in resisting sticking and eliminating corrosion.

Most fishermen do not cast enough to wear out their rods, but it is a very important matter. I am sure many rods have worn out so gradually that their owners didn't know it, and many fishermen are still trying to cast with badly softened rods.

If you want to keep track of the wearing qualities of a rod, put a weight on the handle so that the rest of the rod projects out horizontally from a table or bench. The tip will sag slightly. Tie a small weight to it and measure the exact distance that the tip bends away from a straight line. After using the rod for a season, or for the greater part of a season, repeat the measurement, using the same weight, and compare the amount of bend. It's easy to see whether it's softened appreciably.

A bamboo rod is beginning to lose its starch when it's slow in straightening after a sharp bend. A little "set" doesn't hurt a rod, but if it becomes excessive you're probably losing casting power. Sets can be removed in many cases by hanging the rod by the tip, although that won't affect casting qualities. Some sets are permanent. Some are temporary. Glass rods can set, too, but it isn't common.

Most rods are now built in two pieces instead of the three sections that were standard until recent years. This eliminates a set of ferrules and improves casting qualities, in theory at least. Ferrules interrupt the smooth bend of the rod and increase stiffness. The new all-glass connections minimize the stiffening effect. Fishermen who must pack equipment in very restricted areas can get rods in four sections from several firms. At the other extreme from these suitcase rods are the one-piecers demanded by a few perfectionists. Most one-piecers are short, ultralight trout rods, but there are some big-game, ferrule-doubting fishermen who manage to get about with custom-built nine-footers.

ROD LENGTH

Rods have become shorter, but it appears now that we've reached the right lengths. The more powerful rods have settled between eight and nine feet, and the lighter trout rods between seven and eight. There have always been much shorter rods for very small streams, but anything shorter than six feet is a highly specialized tool and requires special casting techniques. Timing becomes more precise.

For some years I have been using a 6½-foot rod for most of my light trout fishing. It is very light and handy to carry and will cast as far as needed on small streams, but I have no proof that it's better than a 7½-footer, and I confess it has some deficiencies. Perhaps I am using it simply to show what a hotshot fisherman I am.

The short rod has one advantage: it does not stick up into

the air so far and is thus less visible to the fish. It also takes up less room when working tight, brushy streams, but it does require more effort in long casts and doesn't hold as much line off the water as a fly is being fished. Keeping line off the water as the dry fly comes downstream is an instant method of simplifying drag problems. There are some stream situations which call for throwing the backcast over shoreline brush, and the longer rod is helpful there.

Casting with a very short rod requires good timing and generally a little more effort than with average lengths. You may have seen an exhibition caster throw line with his arm only, using no rod at all, but nobody thinks this is the easiest way, and some who preach the convenience and ease of ultrashort rods put out a lot of muscle when the fishing starts. The commonest system, when distance is needed, is to extend the casting arm to full length, thus, in effect, adding to the rod measurement. Arm-waving may be a demonstration of dexterity, but it's out of step with the delicate approach that's supposed to go with ultralight stuff.

Very long two-handed salmon rods were standard in England and Canada for years and are still seen there. In some very swift rivers the extra length is necessary to keep the fly line above the water and get a proper drift. Some of those very long rods, perhaps 14 feet or so, were tried in heavy saltwater fishing but simply didn't work out there. They are rarely seen now except on a few salmon rivers. Most casters would rather have a line-hand free and use a lighter weapon.

ROD ACTION

The terms commonly used to describe rod action do not tell the whole story. Modern action can best be compared to a circle for descriptive purposes. If a rod bends so evenly, from tip to butt, that its silhouette would fit smoothly into the outline of a circle, you'd have the extreme in "using the whole stick." Rods approaching that description are usually described as "slow and powerful," but that isn't necessarily so.

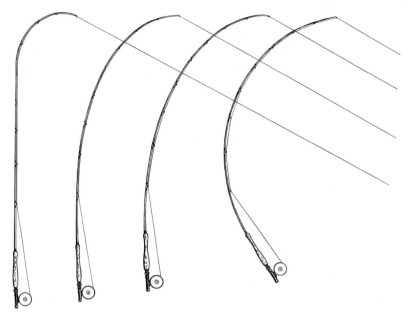

Some degrees of rod action. From left, a tippy rod with stiff butt and midsection; a typical all-purpose action with moderate midsection stiffness; a "slow-action" rod that works clear down into the butt in casting; the extreme in "slow" action in which the rod forms a segment of a circle.

The average rod, if there is such a thing, would have a tip that bent much more sharply than the center section, and the center section would bend more than the butt section. Thus, as the rod "loaded up," the action would move progressively down to the handle.

The "tippy" rod bends readily at the small end and is extremely stiff farther down. The term "fast tip" is often used to describe it, but that's not quite correct because the soft tip can be quite slow.

All these rod types cast somewhat differently. The caster of long experience can usually get the feel of a rod quickly and do a creditable job with it, whether it's his favorite action or not. Still, there are some very good casters who are lost when handling a strange type of rod, and not all adequate casters are expert analysts of casting form or rod action. Those who do not adapt readily stick to the rods that work best for them and are better off without too many.

In seeking the ideal of a moderately slow, powerful rod, the individual and his casting style must be considered. There are real extremes. For example, I tend to use a line that is one number heavier than recommended by manufacturers, but I am a conservative compared to some. I used to fish with a saltwater expert who insisted on a short, stiff rod, and he worked it with very fast arm action, which meant he could use a lighter line than most of us. He persuaded me that his was the right way to fish the salt, and I finally got one of those rods, just like his. He was using a No. 8 line; to get satisfactory use of the rod I went to a No. 11. This is a ridiculous extreme but shows why it's hard to please all of the fishermen all of the time.

A rod that is loaded too lightly must be worked rapidly, and the line usually moves in a tight, or shallow, loop. An overloaded rod is worked slowly to give it a chance to recover from the severe bends and get the extra weight moving. Thus, with a heavy line a rod feels slower, and just where its slowness stops and your slowness begins is anybody's guess. For most of us, it is lost in the mathematics of rod construction.

With practice, you can cast with miserably mismatched outfits—not so surprising when you remember that it's possible to cast a fly line with no rod at all. In trying to work up a casting demonstration with matched and unmatched tackle, I used some wildly mismatched rods and lines. I was surprised that it was possible to cast 80 feet with a No. 5 rod and No. 11 line, and approximately the same distance with a No. 11 rod and a 5 line. I'm no casting wizard but, as I practiced, I was able to compensate for the exaggerated disparities in tackle.

There are fishermen associated with the tackle industry who pick up a rod and assess its power and qualities without attaching a line. They do this by various mysterious wiggles and wavings. I cannot. Several times, I have come home with rods that were not what I thought they were at all, and my wife has shown equally sorry judgment in tackle shops. My assessment is especially poor when I have been fishing recently with a very different type of rod. Without the line and leader, most of us don't learn

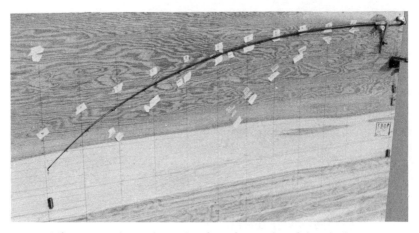

The action of a rod can be charted on a board by placing a weight on the tip and measuring its bend at various points.

too much, regardless of the sage wavings and critical facial expressions we produce at the store.

Some of the things the fisherman hardly notices about a rod are actually scientifically worked out—the number and placement of guides for example. If he wants to build his own rods he should study that. For another thing, rod action can be tragically oversimplified. I once declared a new rod too soft and arbitrarily whacked six inches off the tip to "give it backbone." I gave it backbone all right, and I assume it is now in use somewhere as a frog-gig handle. Two inches would have been enough. Lest you lose all faith in me, I hasten to add that experiment occurred many years ago.

Shapes of the cork handles are a matter of personal preference, pure and simple, and my only recommendation is that the handle be large enough for a firm grip if the rod is powerful. I once had a big saltwater rod that blistered my hand, but when I taped up the grip it was comfortable. In making a graceful grip, the builder had simply turned it down too small. That fault appears more often with ultralight rods, in which the cork grip is made very tiny to add to petite appearance and cut down the actual weight. Very light rods sometimes have inefficient reel

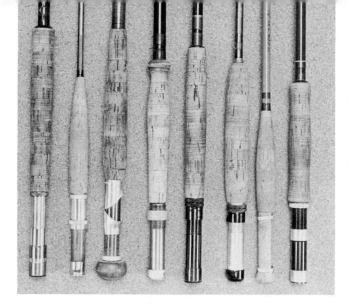

Shapes of rod handles are a matter of individual preference, but the more powerful actions require considerable gripping surface. Ultralight rod handle is shown second from right.

seats for the same reasons. Much of the esthetic value is lost when you have to apply rubber tape to keep from losing your reel.

I don't own one, but I have been impressed by "hammer handle" rod grips, on which the cork is shaped into an oval with flattened planes to give what is a nearly perfect hand-hold. Since these handles cannot be turned quickly in a lathe, they show up only on custom rods, as far as I know. If there's a minor fault it's that your handle works well in only one position. The same criticism applies to handles with thumb and palm depressions. They're wonderful as long as you don't turn the rod or your hand.

Except for the first, or stripping, guide, most fly rods have common snake guides of hard wire. A few that are used for long-distance casting have lightweight ring guides. For very heavy fishing, the stripping guide should be a ring with a wide bearing surface to minimize wear on backing line under heavy tension. This guide is sometimes too light on otherwise high-grade big-game rods.

THE LINES

Silk lines have almost given way before nylon and Dacron. New fly lines do not require the care that silk did, and they are made in many specialized forms for specific purposes. Most of the newest floating lines have a center, or core, of uniform-diameter material, and the taper, or shape of the line is created by the coating. Some of them are made of the same material all the way through. There are fast-sinking lines, slow-sinking lines, lines that can't seem to make up their minds, and floating lines with sinking tips. There are level lines, double-tapered lines, a variety of forward-tapered lines, and shooting tapers, all of which have their uses. The fly fisherman never had it so good.

A level line is not built for distance casting, but you can increase the delicacy of its delivery by using long leaders tapered up to very heavy butt sections. In effect, you're putting a taper to the front of your line and it performs something like the double taper used by most careful trout fishermen. When you put on the monofilament leader butt, simply choose material that is only slightly smaller than the line diameter and taper down from that. Is isn't the easiest way but it will work. Your only problem will be that the heavy leader butt won't want to float, but you can keep it afloat fairly well, if necessary, by treating it heavily with dry-fly dope or line dressing.

The *double taper* consists of a long belly with duplicate tapers at each end and is the favorite of the small-stream trout fisherman. When one end is worn, it can be reversed. There is no danger of the double taper being abandoned, but I see trout fishermen using more and more forward tapers, especially for the larger flies. They're much better for distance bcause the line back of the taper is quite small.

The *forward taper* is the distance line and the one that turns over the big bugs and streamers. Recently there have been forward tapers that are very short for their weights, thus bringing out the action of the rod on short casts. The other important feature of the short taper is the ability to get into action with a minimum of false casting. One of these short tapers is called a saltwater taper and was developed with flats fishing in mind, a situation where the fish is sighted before the cast, and the fisherman can carry the forward section of line in his hand, toss it into the air, make a single back cast, and then lay his fly on the water. This saves time and avoids false casting over spooky fish.

The *shooting taper* is a short section of tapered line that is used ahead of very light shooting material—monofilament or specially braided, fine-diameter line that floats. This is the best of all combinations for extreme distance, with either floating or sinking heads, and was developed by tournament casters. It is especially popular for steelhead fishing, where heavy sinking lines must be thrown a long way. Those who employ monofilament running line generally use about 20-pound test. Recently there has

There are appropriate fly lines for many specific kinds of fishing, whether the objective is floating, sinking, slow-sinking, or distance casting.

been a move to a running line that floats. Some fishermen were already splicing their heavy shooting heads to very light fly line, but manufacturers now make a light level line especially for the purpose described above. The advantages are that it does not tangle as much as monofilament, and that it can be picked up off the surface of the water as the cast is made, whereas monofilament will sink and cause a drag on the cast. This, of course, refers to a wading situation. However, the light fly line will not go quite as far as the monofilament.

Most of the shooting heads are of sinking material, but some good fishermen use shooting heads for everything, floating or sinking. There is no doubt of their efficiency, providing the fisherman is adept at handling the small shooting line without tangles and is not too disturbed by the splice. You can now buy shooting heads with carefully spliced running line that eliminates most of the lumpy-connection problems.

The old silk lines sank slowly when fished without line dressing and floated when doped. Some modern lines are made to do just this but are used by only a few fishermen. There are floating lines with sinking tips, excellent for use with nymphs under some conditions. The floating line acts as a strike indicator for the deep nymph, and it can be easily picked off the surface for the next cast. Some lines are built with all of the forward head sinking and all of the running line floating (very nearly the same combination as a shooting head spliced to floating running line). There are slow-sinking lines for use at moderate depth. There are very fast-sinking, or "high-density," lines for very deep fishing or for use in fast water that tends to carry a slow sinker too fast. We'll mention these special lines again as we come to fishing conditions that require them.

BALANCE

In fly fishing, "tackle balance" is concerned mainly with rod, line, and fly, although some anglers make a big thing of the proper reel for a rod and line. A tiny reel looks good on a tiny rod and rather strange on a heavy one, but as long as it will handle the line and the fish, the "balance" is not overly important in casting efficiency. The ideal combination would be a reel that balances the weight of the rod tip as the rod is held in casting position. A heavy reel will greatly reduce the effort with heavy rods, but there are some fishermen who say they do not feel the rod's action unless the tip overbalances the reel. If this attitude is valid, it is most important with very light rods. Reels are a separate subject.

FOUR

Some Things that Help

THE IMPORTANCE of some basic equipment is too often minimized, so that some essentials are examined hurriedly and bought carelessly. The fly reel has been called "simply a spool to store the line" so many times that it ranks as one of the neglected items, often bought solely for appearance. Its value increases with the size of the fish to be caught, and a poor one can be an abomination, even with ultralight tackle. The less you notice the fly reel while fishing, the better it's doing its job. If it freezes up, falls apart, or drops off the rod, it suddenly becomes a closely scrutinized and loudly maligned item. Rod and line may be the basic necessities of fly fishing, but don't overlook the other essentials, which should be collected with care. There are countless gadgets of varying importance that crowd many a vest, bag, or box, and one man's necessities may be another's junk.

FLY REELS

Because they took up line fast, held lots of backing, were hard to smash, and didn't make corkscrews of my line, I used to equip my lightest rods with big lightweight reels. My wife finally

Left: *A moderately priced, heavy-duty fly reel, produced by Shakespeare. Such reels emphasize adjustable drags of more power than is required on reels to be used for lighter fishing. Right*: *English reel built with multiplying feature, for use with light- or medium-weight fly tackle. Fast take-up is an aid in keeping excess line out of the way, but too much multiplication makes handle hard to turn.*

pointed out that such a windlass detracted from the esthetic appearance of a miniature rod, made me look like a fish hog, and caused my fish to appear smaller in photographs. I scoffed at the other criticisms, but having your fish look small in photographs is serious business. So I got some little reels.

The smallest fly reel I have has an overall diameter of less than two inches. By contrast, the diameter of most medium-capacity reels is around 3¾ inches, and the high-capacity big-game reels measure about four inches. My little reel makes me look like a sure-enough expert when it's fastened to a midge rod, but it's not very practical. I can get a piece of small-caliber fly line on it all right, but there's no room for backing, and the arbor is so small that my line comes off in kinks. The takeup is slow and laborious. A better size is a little over three inches in diameter, holds some backing in addition to the fly line, and is big enough to wind easily. I use that size nearly all the time on little trout rods. It balances pretty well and weighs 6½ ounces with line. Big-game fly reels will weigh around a pound. Some of the large but light reels have a storage chamber for lead shot, so weight can be adjusted.

Most good-sized fish should be played with the fly reel rather than with the line hand, although there are times when that's inconvenient. For most trout, panfish, and bass fishing, drag setting isn't critical, and some light reels use only a click. There's nothing wrong with that if the click is durable, but those on the very cheapest reels may not be.

It's traditional that a fly reel should have a click which squalls when the fish runs, and the louder the better for some fishermen who want the world to know when they have one on. I won't object to that part but would like my reel to use a little moderation when I'm simply stripping line to cast, so I vote for a modest click. Some of the finest big-game reels do not use clicks, and their manufacturers say no drag can be as smooth with a click as without. Smoothness to that degree is important only when the fish are long and fast runners, if then.

The drag is unimportant on light-duty reels, as long as it holds a little when needed. But some of them cannot be set tightly enough to keep the reel from overrunning as you strip line fast, something that happens when you are casting to moving fish. Once using a brand-new reel with a minimum of click and drag, I tried to yank line off quickly with my stripping hand when I saw a fish strike nearby. The reel overran into a bird's nest, and the spool had to be removed to get it back into commission. I've seen this happen several times to other fishermen when bass and salt-water fishing from a boat. It would be less likely on a trout stream.

Some lightweight reels can be easily bent if dropped, and the damage is nearly always worse than it looks. Once the frame is out of line and the spool tied up, it takes a mechanical genius with luck to make it turn again. When in doubt, I'd pick up one with a heavier frame; it won't hurt your casting. Interchangeable spools are worthwhile on light- and medium-duty reels, making it possible to carry several kinds of lines in your vest ready for

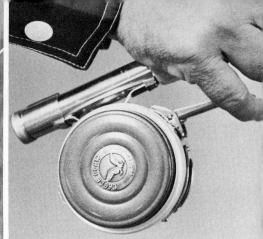

Left: The Bogdan salmon and saltwater reel is a heavy-duty, lightweight, multiplying model, with a 2-to-1 take-up. Frame and spool are machined from solid aluminum. *Right*: Automatic fly reels like this one are not used for fish that make extremely long runs, but are very convenient when loose line must be handled quickly. Automatic reels have limited capacity but leave a hand free while line is being retrieved, and are especially convenient when the fisherman is working from brush

use, but get at least one spare reel before collecting a vestful of spools. Otherwise, one breakdown can put you out of business. Standardization of reels and spools is a happy thought, but most anglers aren't satisfied with only one make.

Since they don't have level-winds, fly reels come with rather narrow spools to reduce tangles and cut-ins by line that is wound on under pressure. At best, you'll probably need to spread the line on a little if you have a large reel, but if the spool is fairly narrow the level-winding is a minor thing and can be forgotten unless you have a lot of line out. Spools up to an inch in width give very little trouble with level-winding. Wider spools, as on some large-capacity salmon and saltwater reels, demand more attention. The widest spool I have is on an excellent salmon reel and is 1½ inches.

The *single-action* reel is the basic fly design, but there have been some excellent *multipliers,* usually in the large sizes. I have used one that multiplies 1½ to 1 and appreciate the advantage, especially when I have a fish on and a lot of loose line in water or boat. There can be problems with a reel that multiplies too fast as you're turning a big spool, and it can become very hard to crank.

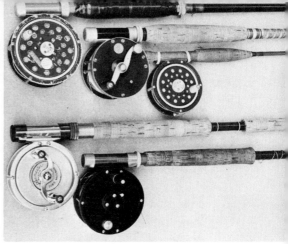

Left: Some of the best big-game fly reels are built from bar-stock aluminum and have large capacity and sturdy drags. From left to right are the Seamaster and the Fin Nor, both of which have landed many record saltwater fish. Right: Large-capacity reels compared in size to the typical reel used for trout fishing on small streams (third from top). From top: Pflueger Medalist, Zwarg (no longer available), small Medalist, Seamaster, and Rogue.

The *automatic* is rather heavy for ultralight rods and lacks line capacity and drag efficiency for long-running big fish, but it is excellent for boat use on bass and most trout as it keeps line from underfoot. It is satisfactory for most wade-fishing for medium-sized fish and it is a line and time saver when you're fishing from a bank. It's a specialty reel, not an all-around one.

Most fly reels are made for right-hand operation, although left-hand models are available in many makes. I can crank faster with my right although it requires changing hands on the rod. I consider changing hands a convenient way of resting my casting fist, but it's a minor thing. One fisherman I know uses a right-handed reel but winds it backward on the left side so he doesn't have to buy left-handed models. That's all right if you're used to it.

There are some reels constructed so that the rim of the spool turns outside the frame, and the fisherman can add drag by simply playing his hand along the turning edge. Some free-spooling big-game reels have handles that remain stationary as a fish runs, so you can play the spool with your finger or thumb. The other method of providing a manual brake is to put pressure on the line as it rides on the spool. These systems are unimportant unless you expect long-running or large fish. For lighter fishing, all you need is enough drag or click to prevent overrun.

Any medium-duty reel should have some backing, in addition to the entire fly line. A heavy-duty reel needs 150 yards of backing, plus the fly line. Backing is discussed on pages 311, 331.

Until recent years there were so few high-quality reels available that they could be listed and discussed in a few pages, but now there are a great number of both domestic and imported models. Some of the most expensive lightweights are not intended for rough use, even though their workmanship merits the high price. It is not a question of quality, simply ruggedness, and you must judge your own needs.

THE LEADER

Leaders are basic fly-fishing equipment but receive less attention than they deserve while other things are frequently blamed for their shortcomings. It is so easy to make this leader business complicated that it might help to list some simple facts about them:

The leader is a less visible extension of the line, and the *tapered leader,* far from being needed only for highly delicate fishing, is almost invariably an aid in any sort of casting. It serves as an extension of the fly line's taper and can produce delicacy or can aid in turning over huge streamers and bugs.

The knots used in many tapered leaders add a little weight where it is needed in rolling out the cast. Knots are visible to fish but do not seem to frighten them if the cast is properly delivered. Small fish often strike at the knots, pretty good proof that the little lump isn't a bad influence. Still, knotless tapered leaders have a place with fishermen who don't want to build their own from scratch. For most fishing you will need a piece of heavier butt section and in much trout fishing you will need a length of lighter tip material. Most fishermen seldom change the butt section, leaving it permanently attached to the line. Tippets are changed frequently, receive much wear, and are often broken off.

Beginning fly fishermen are notoriously afraid of long leaders, feeling they will be hard to cast. Except in very heavy fishing or very deep fishing, there is little need for any leader shorter than the rod. At the other extreme, there is seldom use for a leader longer than 15 feet, simply because very long leaders require heavy butts which tend to defeat the purpose of delicacy. Except for its translucency, an extremely heavy butt is no less visible than the line tip—and some lines are translucent.

Although there is disagreement as to how much is needed, some stiffness in leader material is a help in casting. When leaders are made up of several brands of monofilament, they perform erratically and turn over in uneven curves. Leader materials of the same strength may vary greatly in diameter, and casting quality depends on diameter and stiffness, rather than strength. It is easy for the careless leader builder to come up with a piece of 20-pound stuff that is "stepped down" to a 15-pound material which is actually larger in diameter than the 20-pound mono, and he accidentally makes a reverse-tapered leader.

In trout fishing, very small flies with little wind resistance require very light tippets for delicate casting, completely aside from their appearance in the water. Heavy, stiff leaders will slap down very small flies. Bushy flies are hard to cast with very light tippets as their wind resistance holds them back so that the slender monofilament loses its momentum and crumples as the cast dies. Bugs and large streamers demand fairly husky leaders for casting purposes.

Roughly speaking, the leader butt should be about two-thirds to three-fourths the diameter of the line to which it is attached. If you're using a double-tapered line for trout fishing, the point or tip of the line will be around .030, so the butt end of the leader would be about .020, usually being around 30-pound test. With heavy lines for other types of fly fishing, the line tip may be as large as .050, meaning a leader butt as large as 45 or 50-pound test. However, in this coarser fishing the diameter becomes much less critical.

A rough rule for leader construction is 60 percent butt, about 20 percent short sections for stepping down, and 20 percent tippet. For a nine-foot leader tapering down to a 6X tippet for delicate casting of small flies, there would be around 40 inches of about .018, 30 inches of .016, six inches of .014, six inches of .012, six inches of .010, and 20 inches of .008 or 6X. This is a nearly ideal profile. Frankly, few fishermen measure these things out exactly.

Those are some basics on leaders.

The gut leaders of bygone years have almost disappeared, being largely replaced by nylon monofilament. Gut requires soaking before use, is more expensive, and varies widely in quality. Some of those who swore ten years ago that they'd never use monofilament have quietly adopted it because it's stronger, cheaper, and easily available.

The "X" rating of leader material is confusing to new fly fishermen and refers to leader size rather than strength. It's the size that affects the casting and either fools or scares the fish. The X ratings are as follows:

0X	—	.011
1X	—	.010
2X	—	.009
3X	—	.008
4X	—	.007
5X	—	.006
6X	—	.005
7X	—	.004

A 5X tippet will test about 2½ pounds and is a good choice for light trout fishing with fairly small dry flies, 14 to 16 hooks. For very small dries and nymphs, fished in slow-moving and very clear waters, a 6X tippet, testing less than two pounds, is about as small as most anglers go. A 7X tippet, testing about a pound, is used only in delicate situations by delicate fishermen with delicate flies, and those who use 7X extensively aren't looking for advice from me. Incidentally, by the time the tippet has been knotted and dragged across a rock or two, the test is considerably reduced. I can get by pretty well with 6X, but I have numerous breaks when I go to 7X, even on small fish.

The really persnickety angler should change most of his leader for each tippet size. In practice, he generally adds or subtracts here and there to fit the situation. If his 5X tippet is too coarse, he'll shorten it a little and simply tie on some 6X or substitute the entire tippet. Not one in a dozen anglers could tell you within a foot how long his leader actually is. Most fishermen simply go by the designation the manufacturer puts on the leader spool, but some carry their own micrometers. It's a good thing to have but cheap micrometers are awkward to work with and you'll get inconsistent measurements with them. I wouldn't spend my rod money for a forty-dollar instrument unless I intended to use it a great deal.

In the stronger tests there is a great deal of variation in diameter. There is some monofilament labeled 12-pound test that mikes more than .020, and some that shows less than .013. The large-diameter monofilament is actually desired for some kinds of heavy fishing in which stiffness is desirable for casting, and a relatively light test is needed for fishing contest requirements. Visibility of the material is unimportant in such operations.

A corkscrew leader is the curse of small fly users, but a small piece of innertube material can help straighten the leader that retains the curlicues it acquired on the reel. Draw the leader through the folded piece of rubber, and do it slowly, getting a little of the stretch out of the material as you go. Although this does a good job on light monofilament, a really stiff and wiry butt section will defy your efforts. It's best to use limp nylon for that part, even when you desire a little stiffness in the light end.

In casting against a high wind, long, light tippets will fold up and tangle, so the common practice is to shorten up the leader, especially the tippet. Nobody wants his leader to fall in a bird's nest, but I have caught many choosy trout that took when the leader hadn't straightened out, the fly falling back into a coil of tippet and floating beautifully in a brisk breeze. I do not keep fish caught that way, and after an especially good day of sloppy casts against a high wind, I make a small contribution to my local Trout Unlimited chapter. The same wind that crumples your cast will add to surface disturbance and impair the trout's vision. .

Evidently, a trout can see any size tippet you use if the water is calm and clear. The small tippet is simply less noticeable and is ignored, or confused with surface movements when dry flies are used. Sinking the leader is a ritual with many dry fly casters and they invariably apply a sinking solution to the tippet, in the belief that it shows less under the water than when floating. There is no doubt that a floating leader creates a reflective streak on the surface, but the sunken leader can be examined more carefully by the fish. Perhaps the ideal solution is a tippet that sinks very slowly, without altering the fly's stance or interfering with the pickup.

There are no two situations exactly alike. I have fished where considerable debris floated on the surface of otherwise clear water. Even selective trout can thus become used to floating things and often pay little attention to a leader. Then, too, some of the clearest and most gently flowing streams have a rolling motion that produces undulating lines of surface movement. Since I have often mistaken one of those little reflective lines for my leader, it's likely that trout can be equally confused. It is an exaggeration to term such a vagary of the current "broken water," but any unevenness in the flow helps to hide a leader.

Long leaders traditionally go with delicate fishing, but there are some tough situations where length is of little help. If water is quite shallow, the fish simply can't see much of the leader. If it is very deep and still, it would be difficult to find a leader that was long enough. Of course, the limiting factor in an extra long leader is that the thing must have a lot of butt section to cast well, and a heavy butt will create almost as much disturbance as a fly line.

The colors of leader material vary considerably, so careful trout and salmon fishermen sometimes dye them to fit specific situations. It's a matter of what kind of background the fish sees the leader against. A few minutes with a diver's face mask shows that a leader alters in appearance as the light changes. Most of the monofilament material is translucent and, in theory, it takes on the color of its surroundings. Some monofilament has a more reflective finish than other makes, but some fishermen think the reflections are actually helpful. Only a fish can decide, and fish may disagree.

There has been much talk about the effect of cold on leader material, but my crude tests show no great difference in nylon strength down to freezing temperatures. I confess to some puzzling breakoffs in chilly water, and it is harder to make knots hold when the material is cold, but these observations are inconclusive.

A simple overhand knot in leader material reduces its strength greatly, the exact amount depending on how long the knot stays and the type of monofilament used. Whether it's caused by wind or simply sloppy casting, fishermen commonly call it a "wind" knot since they must blame something. Frequent inspection is the only antidote. Leader splices and connections will be covered in the section on knots. (pages 358-364).

FISHING VESTS

I used to say that no fishing vest ever contained enough pockets, but some new models have compartments I haven't even found. I am partial to vests instead of long-sleeved fishing jackets since they're cooler in hot weather and can be worn over all sorts of coats or sweaters when it's cold. Get a large size and be sure there's a large pocket for rainwear, sandwich, and insect spray. Leader storage has been a problem, most of us carrying a double handful of little spools. You can string the spools on a cord or chain, in the proper order of their measurements, and easily tell when one size is running out, storing the whole works in a large pocket of the vest. I generally keep a couple of spools of small tippet material in a separate pocket since that's what's most often needed. One manufacturer sells a vest with a row of small pockets, each designed to hold one spool of leader material.

Most of the vests are short enough for small-stream wading,

but they'll get wet if you go in near the tops of armpit waders. So, when you anticipate such situations, wear them inside the waders. When you wade wet in very deep, warm water, a sheepskin hatband will hold quite a few flies dry and ready for use. If you expect to travel in a boat or walk through brush, small safety pins stuck into an old hat will work for bugs, streamers, and large flies.

CONTAINERS

Storage of wet flies is pretty simple. In sizes larger than 14 they can be kept in boxes with clips, or with spring or plastic grippers. You get a good look at the entire contents when you open the lid. Bugs and very large streamers are best carried in boxes with compartments.

It is the very small stuff that causes problems. When you get down to 14s and smaller you need very small containers. For some years I have been using little boxes with compartments having individual transparent lids. The spring-loaded lids come up at a touch to expose the flies, and you can get the little ones out with your fingers or with tweezers. But the springs and hinges are delicate and won't take much banging around. When a lid comes up accidentally as the big main cover is lifted, a little wind can whip ten dollars worth of flies into the wilds before you can swear. The little springs should be checked often, and the box should be shielded from wind each time it's opened. Extra boxes are good investments, as you shouldn't have too many flies in each one. In searching through a crowded compartment, I have often let one or two flies get away in the breeze—a very expensive business and often unnoticed in excited fumbling on the stream.

For that matter, a collection of flies is usually more valuable than the owner realizes, one little box often holding the price of a good rod, reel, and line. Because you add to them gradually, you're often unaware of the total cost. A friend of mine lost a little box of his salmon flies and considered it a minor mishap until he figured up its total worth—over two hundred and fifty dollars. For this reason, I'd rather not carry everything in one

Extremely durable rod tube is made from plumbers' conduit in a variety of sizes. Cap is held by friction, but can be taped for long, rough trips.

box. Regular checkups will keep you from toting things you have no intention of using on a given trip.

Sheepskin-lined books are good for storage of large streamers and wets, as long as you don't put flies away without drying. I don't like to use them around salt water. Felt-padded leader boxes have pretty well disappeared, along with the silkworm gut they were made for.

The best fly boxes are good investments. Magnifiers and tweezers are a help if you use lots of little stuff. Small pliers, scissors, and forceps are a help, too, and some fishing tools are efficiently held on retractable chains that pull out of small spring-loaded containers.

Aluminum rod case is used as a walking stick during this trip in the North Carolina mountains. Stream is Hazel Creek, noted for rainbows.

Canvas shoulder bags will carry much tackle for their size, but I wouldn't check them on an airline. A tackle box should be roped or strapped shut if it's sent as luggage by any common carrier. All contents should be wrapped in individual packages, as the airlines seem to consider such boxes personal challenges. If rods are shipped, they should be in aluminum tubes and taped shut. Collapsible tubes should have something to hold them rigid —I use a stiff aluminum tube inside the bigger one. It is slightly longer than the longest rod to prevent collapse of the whole works when the Paul Bunyan of the baggage room goes to work.

If you carry insect dope in box, bag, or vest, be sure it doesn't leak. Some of it will destroy fly lines and even eat up some plastic boxes.

If you carry a camera in your vest, it can be wrapped in a plastic bag to escape rain and sudden duckings, but it should be taken out and inspected at each day's end. I say this bitterly as I recall the condition of a Leica that had gotten wet and was left to soak for a week in a cozy plastic wrap. The perfect camera for a fisherman is one of the small, underwater 35-millimeter units that can be washed under a faucet if necessary.

WADERS AND WADING

My friend bought an expensive pair of felt-soled waders and left for an unsettled section of western Canada where the steel-head didn't know their own strength. A long auto, plane, and boat trip later, he put on his new waders—to find that the cold water came up inside almost as fast as it came up outside. Many brand-new waders leak copiously, and this is no place for blind faith. I test new waders by getting into them and then sitting down in a bathtub nearly full of water. I look pretty silly doing that, but not as silly as I'd feel fifty miles from nowhere, with wet underwear. High price is no warranty, and anyway, guaranteeing waders is a little like guaranteeing parachutes.

Some very good fishermen use inexpensive, plastic, stocking-foot models and get felt-soled wading shoes, aluminum-studded shoes, or simply tennis shoes to wear over them. The advantages are that the light waders are easy to patch, easy to dry, easy to store, and light to walk in. The *dis*advantges are that they are generally easily torn, require socks between wader and shoe to reduce chafing, and are little protection against cold. They also take longer to get into, and I never know what to do afterward with the wet socks, generally full of mud or sand. Stockingfoot cloth waders are usually more durable than the plastic ones.

Boot-foot waders are easy to put on but hard to dry out unless you hang them up where the air circulates. Good, waterproof cloth uppers with rubber boot feet are the most durable waders of all, but tend to be a bit heavy. The all-rubber boot-foot waders used by surf fishermen are frequently employed by fly casters, often with the addition of special soles to suit the situation. They last well but are heavy for hiking.

Nearly all waders are damp from condensation after use, thus convincing many fishermen that their waders leak when they really don't. Such citizens are highly offended when a dealer insists his merchandise is good, even though his customer has wet feet. I know some dealers who never buy waders for themselves, using only those that have been returned for "leaking."

"We fill 'em with water, and if none comes out, we figure it's just condensation," said one merchant. "We've learned not to

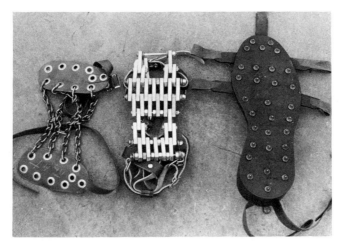

Types of sandals used in slippery streams. Left to right: Steel chains, hinged aluminum plates, hobs set in flexible sole.

argue with a good customer, so we just give him a new pair, even if we know there's no leak."

Such footwear gets wet inside but the boots don't fill up. There is no way of beating condensation when you have warm feet in cold water. Some anglers I know wear an extra pair of pants or insulated underwear between their regular clothing and the waders, so their inside clothing stays dry. But such combinations are bad for long walks on dry land.

Some waders are more comfortable than others, but all of them are something of a burden, so you may as well get used to it.

The crotch is the most likely spot for wader wear and that's the part you snag going over a fence. It is also one of the most difficult places to patch, so make sure that new waders are well reinforced there. Carry the patching kit in your vest on every trip.

Because of cold water and condensation, you will want to wear two pairs of socks and you may prefer three, so wader feet should be a little oversize. Neat, sleek-looking waders are likely to be a little short in the leg. Check your ability to bend over and to lift one knee while standing on one foot. There is some variation in the height of waders, but I have never owned any that came too high. Use husky suspenders—some of those that come with waders are pretty flimsy.

Since before I fell on my first slick rock, stream fishermen have been trying to develop something to keep their soles from slipping. I consider the shallow, slippery stream about the most dangerous thing associated with trout, salmon, and smallmouth fishing. If you fall in two feet of water you may get wet and cold, but if you fall in two inches of water you can get broken bones. I know several trout fishermen who have been badly hurt in shallow-water falls and one who was permanently disabled. He was an all-American quarterback and considered something of an iron man. So if you want to wade in waist-deep water that's too fast, go ahead if you're a good swimmer, but go easy in the shallow stretches. I have ignominiously crawled from such places on hands and knees when I found the rocks were impossibly slick. It can be that bad.

Felt soles are the most popular protection on slippery bottoms and they hold well unless the rocks are too heavily coated with slimy growth. In those cases, aluminum studs or hinged aluminum sandals are better. Aluminum acts the same as soft iron hobs in clutching rock surfaces, and iron hobs are seldom seen any more. Golf spikes are preferred by some of my fishing friends but have a decidedly adverse effect on living-room floors and tend to pick up all sorts of trash as you walk. They may trip you in the woods, however efficient they are in the stream.

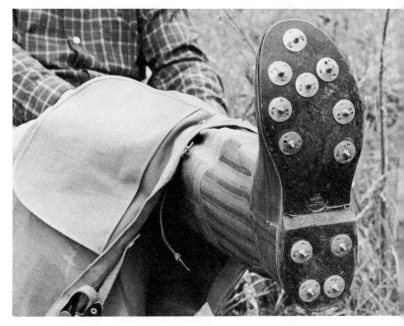

Golf spikes used on waders for slippery stream. Soft metals give excellent footing on slippery rocks, but most fly fishermen use felt soles.

Felt soles can be replaced, although it's expensive. In getting new waders, check the depth of the felt and ask about its quality, for there are many kinds. No rubber sole, however cleated, can compete with felt or aluminum when things get slippery. Nylon carpeting, however, has proved efficient if you stick it on properly.

There have been some nonskid combinations involving carborundum shavings that you fasten with stickum to an ordinary boot sole. It really takes the slide out of the rocks and it is quite possible that some of the newer stickum will stay with you. But the first time I tried the system things didn't work out too well. It was years ago, on the Madison River just north of Yellowstone National Park, during salmon fly season, and the river was as slick as I've ever seen it. In my motel room, I applied the rubbery base and the metal particles according to directions, and after the drying period I found I could walk the slippery Madison like a mountain goat on a sidewalk. Exhilarated by my new-found proficiency, I waded right across the river and fished along the other shore for nearly two hours. But when I decided to go back to the car, I found my stickum had worn off. There was only one way to get back, and I took it. I swam.

Most fly fishermen have frequent use for hip boots. Some of the lighter models come with felt soles and cloth tops, excellent for small streams, and a comfort in warm weather if the water's shallow, but when there's any doubt at all, use chest waders. Water is often deeper than it looks, and there is something to the old saying that the only advantage of hip boots over knee boots is that they hold more water.

Eventually, I guess, every wader gets knocked over in heavy current, falls in through awkwardness, or simply gets in too deep. Waders are certainly no help in swimming, but they are not the deathtraps commonly believed. After numerous accidental duckings, usually through my own carelessness, I did some experimen-

Waders handicap a swimmer but do not plunge him head downward except in very unusual circumstances. This is the typical attitude of a fisherman who simply relaxes in the water after going into a deep hole. He can swim from this position.

tal diving while wearing boot-foot waders. They add little to your weight in the water, but they do hamper your movements. In most cases, the air is pushed out of the wader as the water gets deep, and the material is held close to your body. When you fall in, the legs do not fill tightly and balloon out. Your body remains on a pretty even keel and there is no tendency for the feet to float upward. It is possible that the waders could fill with air and float you head down for a few seconds if you went in head first, but it wouldn't last long.

A belt fastened about the waist will keep much water out during a brief ducking and will keep the waders from bellying out when you're right-side up in the current. Oversized wader legs are a problem for persons of slight build, giving the current that much more shove. It takes no physicist to conclude that greater body weight is a help in wading, but there are some excellent waders among smaller people, folks who have just enough nerve at the right time, refuse to panic, and can actually keep dancing upright when they lose solid footing.

For example, on a western fishing trip I was accompanied by a saltwater fishing guide who had weathered countless tropical storms and was a superb boatman. Booming down the haystacked rapids didn't appear to impress him, but he hung up his fly line on a midstream boulder and lost it as we slid down the big river in a johnboat. Dan Bailey, who was at the oars, pulled ashore fifty yards below the boulder and eyed the line, which was plainly visible. We had no spare, so Dan calmly announced he'd wade out and get the one on the rock. Dan—in his sixties and a fairly small, though athletic man—simply walked in a little above the rock, danced out to it through what appeared to be overpowering current above his waist, picked up the line, and danced back to shore, landing a bit below the boulder. It was a feat of skillful wading, fully appreciated by my 230-pound friend. After that, Dan was a hero.

Unless there is very deep water immediately below, and as long as there's enough depth to keep you off the rocks, you aren't likely to get worse than a wetting in fast water. The best way, once you've been ducked, is to feel for a sure footing and refrain from thrashing about until you get it. When you feel a fall is probable, you can steady yourself by using your rod as an emergency oar. Good waders move so as to present as small a surface as possible to the current, taking short steps, and they are sure of the next footing before leaving the first.

Wading staffs are a great help in crossing tough places, although they can be in the way for fishing. I once used a telescoping model that tended to collapse at critical moments, but most commercial models are good. For emergencies you can often find a suitable stick along the shore. I hesitate to advise about use of a staff because I always plant it downstream from my feet, in the belief I can thus push my tottering frame against the current, but although I have several friends who do it that way, there are veterans who say only a fool would plant the staff downstream. Since my efforts at setting it upstream from my course have failed awkwardly, I am going to let it go at that. Figure it out for yourself, and I am sure you'll do it quickly when the gravel washes from under your feet and icy water laps at your wader tops.

If you expect to wade near very deep water that you feel is actually dangerous, the little cartridge-activated life preservers are worthwhile. The U.S. Coast Guard isn't exactly counting on them, but they're a whole lot better than nothing. In cool weather, flotation vests and jackets are highly satisfactory.

AFLOAT

The "floater bubble" is simply a circular inflated doughnut with a place to sit in the center, and it will take you over deep water. It's excellent in slow streams or small lakes. Many fishermen improvise with a truck inner tube, simply attaching a canvas seat, but one of the best is a zipper cover of heavy canvas that takes a truck tube. Others are plastic with no canvas over the outside and somewhat less expensive.

I use these things frequently when there's little dry-land walking to be done. My chief objection is that I can't seem to keep my sleeves dry when the water's cold. You can get fins for

Using a floating bubble, Ray Donnersberger, of Chicago, fishes a slough just off Silver Creek near Sun Valley, Idaho. Although water is shallow, a soft bottom makes ordinary wading impractical.

your feet and Ping-Pong paddles work if you don't have to move too much. I believe the fastest propulsion comes from ordinary swim fins, with which you can push yourself backward, but it's hard to get these on over wader feet. If you're traveling by boat and wading wet, swim fins pose no problem at all.

LANDING PROBLEMS

Large landing nets can be efficient if you're fishing from a boat, but the wading angler must make compromises. A conventional trout net is best, secured to your vest between the shoulder blades by a French snap or other gadget that can be released quickly when you reach over your shoulder. The elastic cord that comes with many nets is capable of delivering a stunning rabbit punch if you walk near some bushes and something hangs up. Your net handle hits you from the rear, from as far as six feet, with arrowlike precision and effect.

Large landing nets will hold good-sized saltwater catches.
This one is a small tarpon that took a streamer fly.

A great many experts land fish by hand but sometimes wish they had a net, especially when there are numerous small ones to be released. I can hold an undersized trout more gently if I wrap him in the mesh. Larger fish can be drawn against the waders with your free hand, and if you really want him, you can then get him by the gills. Of late there have been some excellent folding nets, some of which are carried in sheaths, springing out into businesslike hoops when withdrawn. I have a dandy that can be opened with a flick of the wrist and requires no sheath at all.

If a fish is really tired, a surprisingly small net can be practical. You simply lead his head into it and sack him up. When a fish must be netted from below as he hangs in a current (don't laugh; this happens), a good-sized hoop is a decided advantage. Some of the finest nets have wooden rims and handles. They float when dropped and they look pretty. Their one disadvantage is that they stand out like submerged lighthouses when you slip them under the victim. If he's tired enough it doesn't matter; if he's a little green, he may well take exception to such expanses of varnish.

SEAFOOD TRANSPORTATION

The old wicker creel is disappearing, but it was handy for reel and line storage, could take a raincoat and lunch, and was well aerated for fish. Its smelly presence had long been a tradition of trout or panfishing, but some of the best tackle catalogues don't include it at all anymore; cloth creels are more popular now. The main thing is to let air get to the fish you keep. Stream-side cleaning is also a good idea. If you stay in the water once you get in, and there's little or no current, a stringer works well with a float tied to one end to keep the fish from between your feet. It's a poor policy, however, in salt water containing sharks.

BINOCULARS

Seldom seen on streams, but often needed by dry-fly fisher-men, binoculars can make insect identification much easier. Pocket glasses of six or seven power have been developed to a highly efficient point, and you don't need to be an entomologist to use them. When a trout is rising 50 feet away and you can't get closer, the glasses will show what he's taking if he's working on top. It's especially helpful when fish are selective and more than one kind of fly is drifting past. There have been times when a near-surface rise to nymphs was detected only by glasses. Without them, it would have been easy to decide it was a true dry fly rise.

FIVE

Black Bass

BLACK-BASS FISHING has changed, and although there are more bass and more bass water than ever before, the best fly-fishing areas have actually been somewhat reduced. It is a simple matter of the fly caster preferring shallow water and surface angling, while the new bass methods have been adapted to deep impoundments and bottom fishing.

Where the impoundments spread, many a meandering bass river has become only a groove on a lake bottom. Other shallow bass waters have been lost through pollution or drainage, but their loss has been little noted by users of highly productive new methods which work best with casting or spinning tackle. There may be more fishermen than ever before, but the percentage of fly fishermen among bass anglers is smaller than it was in 1940.

Strangely, there is much good fly-fishing water that goes begging these days and, in many sections, a lack of information about fly fishing for bass, giving the ardent fly-user the unique role of pioneer among thousands of bass fishermen on what appear to be well-known waters. Among the bait fishermen and those who manipulate plastic lures along the bottom, the fly fisherman is likely to be considered an unusual fellow indeed. On most of the bass waters I fish, the sight of a bug or streamer-caster is unusual enough to draw considerable attention, and comments heard above the drone of passing outboard motors usually refer to some other kind of fish entirely. A boatman will often tell his companion that the fellow over there is a bluegill fisherman, and I have heard the comment that "I didn't know there were trout in here."

Relatively speaking, I am sure the fly fisherman for bass was much more common back in the twenties, if old sporting magazines are any indication. Fly fishing came before baitcasting and spinning, and it was natural that it once led in bass fishing.

Careful students of bass in lakes have said that only 5 percent of the fish can be found along the shorelines. Although one fly fisherman told me those were the only 5 percent he was interested in, the general fishing public has gone strongly for deep-water tactics. Until a few years ago they didn't know that's where most of the fish are most of the time.

You can dredge with a sinking line and weighted lures, but fly fishing for bass is basically a shallow-water sport so you have special requirements for your fishing. A lake that reports the year's hottest fishing may have little to offer a user of the long

Ancient history. The author caught these bass in 1936. Tackle has improved since then, but the methods are about the same. This bamboo rod is still in service, although the reel has long since given up.

rod. The fly fisherman's first lesson is that he has special requirements in bass habitat.

First of all, let's be more definite about "shallow" water. For
surface bugs and for flies and streamers fished on a floating line
you'll usually want to be over water no more than six feet deep.
Along the shorelines, you're generally casting over spots that are
nearer two feet deep. Like most bug fishermen, I have seen a
smallmouth come booming up from twenty feet down in the blue
depths of a northern lake, but that isn't typical fishing for bass,
however wonderful it may be. You're basically a shallow-water
fisherman and you look for shallow water—with bass. If your
lake or river is shallow, you can throw close to your fish all year.
If you fish an impoundment, or other lake of great depth, you
must learn just when the fish will be on the shallow edges, a
matter governed by temperature to a great extent. You may not
be able to rely much on the general fishing reports put out for
bottom-bumpers and live-bait soakers, so you must be resourceful
unless you stick to familiar waters with established patterns.

There are many times when the fly rod will catch the most
bass; few times when it can be counted on for the largest. As
with outsize trout, very large bass tend toward deep feeding and
large meals. There is no bass lake or river I know of where fly
fishermen take great numbers of bass larger than five pounds.
I consider a three-pound bass a good fly-rod catch—largemouth
or smallmouth—and I have fished with great enjoyment in many
waters where the fish that went more than a pound was a prize.
Fly tackle can be adapted to the situation.

All of the freshwater basses are considered more advanced
than trout on the evolutionary scale. The basses are hard strikers
under many circumstances, often violent jumpers, and frequently
capable of digging very hard for any available cover when
hooked. They are not long runners and do not put up an extended
fight against adequate tackle. They seem more prone to fits of
rage than do trout, have considerable curiosity, and display great
ferocity, for fish without teeth; at times they will attempt to
swallow food objects almost as large as themselves. When com-

peting for baitfish they can appear foolhardy; at other times they are as easily frightened as brown trout. A highly successful fly fisherman for bass is likely to be a good caster of large lures under a variety of conditions and will be an expert judge of water temperatures and fish movements. He seldom needs the finesse of a dry-fly or nymph fisherman, and a delicate delivery is not often needed, although there are exceptions. Few bass fishermen delve into entomology and they often do not know the names of the baitfish their quarry feeds on. If this seems to be a derogatory summary it is unintentional, for I am a bass addict and have sought them in many places, nearly always with flies.

THE LARGEMOUTH

The largemouth bass (*Micropterus salmoides*) is known to live in every state except Alaska, and I like to think there are a few unknown colonies of them in southern Alaska, but can't prove it. Like the other freshwater "bass," it's really a sunfish. The color varies greatly, depending upon the water and bottom. Bass from dark swampwaters of the South are almost black themselves, and even their bellies have a dull hue. In the same latitudes, when caught from clear water over a light sand bottom, the fish have very contrasty markings with a very distinct broken line of blotches along the sides. You'll find that same color in the North where they may share a lake with bronzed smallmouths.

The largemouth's jawline extends past the eye, the most popular method of distinguishing it from the smallmouth and the spotted bass. Then, in addition to the usual differences in coloration, the hard spines of the dorsal fin are more nearly even with the soft rays in the smallmouth, whereas there is generally more of a notch between the two fin sections on the largemouth bass.

Although they often live together, the largemouth prefers warmer water than the smallmouth, with an ideal temperature somewhere near 70 degrees. Spring spawning usually occurs when the temperature gets well above 60. The male, usually smaller than the female, clears a nest and coaxes or herds the female over it. After spawning, the male guards the eggs and fry for a few days and may end his vigil by eating a few himself. Clean, firm bottom is chosen when available, and some obstacle such as a rock or root is likely to be used as a place for depositing the eggs.

Most largemouth nests are in fairly shallow water. Silt is an enemy of reproduction, and the male fish fans the eggs almost constantly to avoid their being covered. The eggs in a single nest are numbered in thousands, the quantity depending upon the size of the female, and several females may use the same bed.

The spawning process has caused controversy concerning fishing regulations. For many years it was believed wise to close the fishing season during spawning. Biologists have now concluded that closed bass seasons are unnecessary in most states; that plenty of fish will be hatched, given proper habitat; and that hook-and-line fishing cannot harm the bass population. There is disagreement about fishing over the beds themselves. Such fishing is remarkably successful at some times and places, and almost fruitless at others. A popping bug has proved very good over shallow bass beds in some lakes, but some of the best fishing is to be had in the spring, just before the bass go on the beds and are engaged in heavy feeding. At that time, both streamers and bugs work well. Big, showy patterns are at their best then.

There is a qualification about the premise that hook-and-line

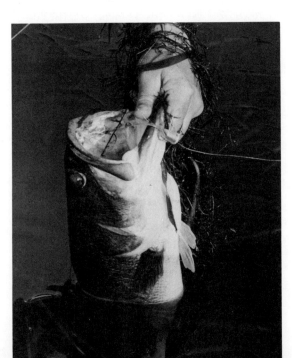

A big bass that struck on an eel-grass flat and was landed after becoming entangled in underwater growth. When wading such water, the fisherman must learn to feel gently for the lip hold that immobilizes the fish.

fishing cannot harm bass populations. It is quite true that natural reproduction can offset the fisherman's efforts as to numbers, but it is equally true that heavy fishing pressure can remove the fish that are eager to strike and make subsequent bass catching very difficult. It is also possible to decimate the numbers of really large bass by fishing over the spawning beds. I repeat that this does not materially affect the overall fish count—but it does make fishing tougher.

Largemouth bass have often been fished under well-controlled conditions and it is known that certain individual fish can be caught many times, while others are never caught at all. Some seem to become wary after being caught once or twice; others never learn. When fishing becomes poor on some waters and the population is assessed by electric shocking, it often shows that large numbers of big bass simply are not caught by fishermen.

Feeding habits of bass vary greatly, often tied in with the aging of lakes, and although the black bass, especially the largemouth, is tolerant of a wide variety of conditions, the balance is delicate.

Vegetation is desirable as bass cover in shallow water, but if it becomes too thick it can provide too much cover for baitfish. Bluegills are a favorite bass food but can crowd bass out under certain conditions. Most of the bass lakes that go downhill do so as a result of pollution that provides an oversupply of nutrients, a consequent overgrowth of algae, and thus a lack of oxygen. This may be an oversimplification, but it is a good start in understanding the problems, and serious bass fishermen should become acquainted with fishery biologists in their areas.

The largest largemouth bass are found in the South, but latitude is not the whole story. The big Florida fish (biggest of all in central Florida) are considered a distinct subspecies. Transplanted to California, they seem likely to grow just as large there, despite the warning of some ichthyologists that their size would gradually regress to the normal weights of native California bass.

Largemouth bass, wherever found, are likely to jump when hooked, although the really big ones may do it sloppily or not at

Good bass water in a Louisiana bayou. Obstacles along the shore are good holding spots for largemouths.

all. The bigger fish are likely to jump more when hooked with plugs than when caught on bugs or flies, a simple matter of trying to shake out a heavy tormentor. It is often said the largemouth is more of a surface feeder than the smallmouth, but I feel this is a matter of locale rather than inherent nature. Where found together, they behave very much the same most of the time, but we must remember that the smallmouth prefers cooler water, which means he may be deeper to begin with and will try to get back down when hooked.

This comparison between the two fish was especially interesting in a clearwater northern lake where my wife and I fished with popping bugs and hair bugs. When we found the fish on a shallow flat of fairly even depth over a gravel bottom, there was little difference in their behavior, the length of their fight, and the number of their jumps. When we moved out to deeper, bouldered water only a few yards away, we caught only smallmouths, which tended to dig for the bottom and jumped very little. I believe most of the largemouths were living in the shallows at that time of spring and that the smallmouths were trading back and forth.

One summer evening, on Lake of the Ozarks in Missouri, I found bass fishing good along a very steep shoreline. The largemouths were lying in only two or three feet of water, very close to shoreline vegetation, and were striking a hair bug hard and then jumping along the edge, with little inclination to go deep. I had caught five such fish when, after being hooked, the sixth rushed the boat and plunged downward in what must have been more than 30 feet of water. A little surprised at this turn of events, I put a creaking bow in my bamboo bugging rod and pumped as hard as I thought the leader could stand. Then, without jumping, a good smallmouth finally came up to the surface, completely exhausted from his digging.

My nontechnical explanation is that the largemouths had been living along the shoreline in fairly shallow water. The smallmouth had simply moved up with the cool of the evening and when he got into trouble he headed back for more familiar territory. It is such maneuvers that establish reputations which are not quite justified.

My conclusions are that the smallmouth is a somewhat more powerful fish and probably jumps a little less in the larger sizes, but that the differences between the two fish are minimized when they are in the same waters with temperatures satisfactory to both. I believe the reputation of the largemouth for harder surface strikes is largely a matter of his big mouth making more noise as it comes down on a top-water lure. Many smallmouths jump a fish-length into the air and come down on a bug. You can't try much harder than that.

Where food choices are concerned, there are minor differences between largemouth and smallmouth, but they are largely a matter of chosen habitat. The smallmouth is a lover of crayfish, especially those in the softshell stage, and that's probably his number-one food choice. He also feeds a great deal on large nymphs. Both varieties of bass are frog-swatters, but it may be the largemouth lives where they're thicker. There's probably no largemouth food that would be refused by a smallmouth, and vice versa. The very young of both species begin their feeding on microscopic water life and tiny crustaceans. As they grow, both have an eye out for small baitfish (and some not so small).

SMALLMOUTH BASS

Early ranges of the smallmouth bass *(Micropterus dolomieui)* were mainly along the Ohio River drainage and Lake Ontário, but widespread introductions have confused the whole picture during a hundred years of transplanting. They have taken my bugs and streamers in swift tributaries of the Sacramento in northern California, as well as from clear lakes in Maine where Down-easters never quite accepted the bass, even though it has been there for several (human) generations. New Englanders, staunch

Fishing smallmouth bass in Arkansas. Smallmouths often use water that appears more suitable for trout but is warmer, with numerous quiet eddies. Willow banks are good spots for either streamers or bugs.

in their allegiance to brook trout, simply don't follow the bass much and seem unable to understand why the tourists love them.

Smallmouths place a higher premium on clear water than do largemouths and prefer lakes with fairly deep areas. They spawn on gravel if possible, and, up to a point, the clearer the water the deeper the bedding area, which may be as much as twenty feet down. Ideal spawning temperature is between 60 and 70 degrees. The male prepares the nest but doesn't supervise it much once the eggs are deposited.

Rocky streams are smallmouth water, and when in the same

rivers they generally hold to more current than largemouths. They are between the trout and the largemouth in habitat preference, but where marginal conditions exist they tend to take over from trout. In turn, the largemouth will take over from the smallmouth when the water is a little too muddy or a little too warm. In the Ozark mountain rivers, where johnboat or canoe-floating for bass was a major sport before the big dams, an experienced fisherman could almost call his shots, even when using exactly the same tackle for both fish. Where the current was brisk and broken by boulders, or sweeping over large gravel, most of the fish were smallmouth. Even when the current pushed against shoreline willows the strike was likely to come from a smallmouth if water moved rapidly. But as he approached a clay bank or a miniature cove of dead water, the caster would bet on largemouth action. Then, when a floating party stopped for lunch on a gravel bar, an energetic fisherman would look for largemouths in quiet sloughs, often lined with weeds.

The colorful local names for black bass are descriptive but confusing. In some areas the smallmouth is called a "black bass" while the largemouth becomes a "lineside." Largemouths are called Oswego bass and green trout in some parts of the South. In the Ozark country, when I first fished there in the late twenties, I never heard the term "brownie" but that became a common name for the smallmouth later on. The smallmouth has an all-over bronze shade in most of its range, broken by irregular dark splotches and a streaky, smoky belly. The dark splotches may be latent in some areas, bold in others. On a stringer, both largemouth and smallmouth bass tend to show their dark markings more plainly. The term "bronzeback" originally referred to the smallmouth but I see it used to describe largemouths too. Generally, there's more green and less brown in the largemouth. The largemouth jawline comes past the eye, the smallmouth's does not.

Probably the big impoundments have the largest smallmouths of all, but they are generally taken with deep-going lures. In some creeks and rivers the fish run very small, not much larger than the rock bass, green perch, and bluegills, and the fun is with

A perfect point for small-mouths in New England. The larger fish are often found some distance from shore, among sunken granite boulders.

very small bugs and streamers. These little darters are frequently ignored in trout country, even though they may average as large as the trout. Some of Pennsylvania's brooks, for example, have busy little smallmouths that are almost completely ignored by fly fishermen. The smallmouth and the brown trout have deeply overlapping ranges, but the bass will dominate in most cases if temperature is suitable, a fact deplored by many New Englanders. Once the planted smallmouth is established, the die is cast. Bass introduction was made carelessly many years ago, too early for even today's advanced biology to change.

The Kentucky, or spotted, bass has its own scientific name, *Micropterus punctulatus;* it is somewhere between the two major types. It has a smaller mouth than the bigmouth, but much of its coloration seems to be a cross of the two more widely distributed fishes. It likes faster water than the largemouth, but slower water than the smallmouth. It likes more mud than the smallmouth, but less than the largemouth—and so on. It is found in swift southern rivers, many of which are hard to reach.

Regardless of whether it affects total numbers, heavy fishing will skim off the larger smallmouths in easily accessible streams. Some of the midwestern rivers I fished long ago produced good-size bass that have lately been replaced by more numerous but smaller fish, an easily explained biological process. Fly fishermen who like very light tackle can have entertainment where users of larger lures will be disappointed.

River conditions fluctuate rapidly in most smallmouth areas. Fishing is usually best in spring and fall, and the ideal situations occur just before the water clears up fully after a period of rain. Coarser lures are at their best when there's a decided color to, the water. Careful fly fishermen who are willing to adopt long, fine leaders and a cautious approach can be in business during low, clear periods. In localities where commercial floating concerns cater to smallmouth fishing, regular reports on river conditions are an important part of the operation.

Much of the floating for bass has given way to trout fishing below the big impoundments that have blotted out the small-mouth rivers. Cold discharges from the great spillways are more favorable for trout, although lower reaches far below one dam and above the next can still provide bass. The most ardent promoter will confess that this type of bass fishery has been greatly reduced.

BASS EQUIPMENT

Typical bass rods nowadays are 8 to 8½ feet long, taking 8 or 9 lines (GBF or GAF). By far the majority are glass. As in other fly fishing, the trend has been toward shorter sticks, and nine feet was standard until after World War II. The bass rod needs power to turn over big bugs and streamers, and some of the old bamboos were real wrist-crackers. When fishing big lures in heavy weeds, a big saltwater-type rod is helpful. When fishing small streams a trout rod is more fun.

More bass have been caught with level lines than with other designs, but a weight-forward is better if you intend to do more than flop-cast. There isn't too much place for the double-taper, although it works when trout equipment must double for light bass operations. The best floating bass lines have a short forward taper, such as the "bug taper" and the "saltwater taper." The short, heavy section brings out rod action on short casts, often essential in shoreline coverage. For most bass fishing, the leader length isn't important. A good choice is one about the length of the stick and tapering from something like 30-pound test to around 8 or 10-pound test.

You will hear there is no need for long casts in bass fishing, but this comes from fishermen who use the fly rod only under optimum conditions. The hard-nosed fly man who takes them as they come had danged well better learn to get at least 60 feet if he wants his share over clear shallows, from nearly inaccessible lily-pad pockets, or from fast-drifting boats. The man who doesn't believe in long casts simply can't fish in such areas.

Except for the dictates of tradition, there is nothing wrong with the automatic reel for bass fishing. It keeps excess line out of the way and lines last much longer if kept from underfoot,

Using short casts and an automatic reel to keep his extra line from fouling in the weeds, a bass fisherman wades a shallow lake in late evening.

and bass are not long runners. I can't recall ever giving more than 30 feet of line to a running bass, and there have been few occasions when I've given twenty; no reason why a good automatic can't handle that situation. The frank truth is that the single-action has become accepted as the master's reel, and many traditionalists wouldn't tether a dog with an automatic. I preach the automatic, but seldom use it. Of course, if you're going to employ the same outfit for long-running fish, especially in salt water, there's reason for insisting on a manual model. You won't need much backing for bass fishing but it will keep the fly line from getting into tight coils on the reel. It acts as a spool-arbor and gives a faster retrieve.

A landing net is a help when a boat or canoe is used, especially with smallmouths. It's practical to land a fly-caught bass by grabbing his lower lip—that immobilizes all varieties. But the smallmouth's lip is a smaller target. I never carry a net when wading, but it's good insurance if it has a generous opening. Bass live well on stringers, preferably held by puncturing the lower lip, or both lower and upper lips, rather than by stringing through the gills.

Since fly fishing for bass was an outgrowth of trout and salmon fishing, the traditional trout and salmon patterns were simply tied in large sizes and offered to bass. Spinners were added to the wet flies, but when spinning came along it proved a better way of casting such heavy stuff. The fly rod plugs and spoons seem to me to be a matter of edging into the spinning department. Certainly, spinning equipment is more efficient for such fishing.

Standard wet-fly patterns have largely given way to streamers for bass fishing. Bucktail, calftail, polar bear, marabou, and a variety of feathers are used in bass fishing, many streamers being sweetened by the addition of Mylar or tinsel. They are simply better lures than ordinary wet flies. It's seldom that bass anglers try to represent true insects. In recent years I have found the Muddler Minnow highly productive, fished either dry or wet.

Bass bugs have almost entirely replaced the big dry flies for bass fishing, generally doing a better job since this fish wants action and seldom looks for hatching insects. Even when smallmouths are taking mayflies, they will strike bugs in many cases. Smallmouth bugs are generally on numbers 2 to 4 hooks. Largemouth bugs go up to 3/0. A few bushy dry flies can come on strong in the streams. Get some loud popping bugs, a few that work more quietly, and some hair bugs. And public opinion dictates you should have a bug or two striped in black and yellow; otherwise, use your own judgment in colors. Have some bugs with rubber legs, and have something in frog shape.

THE METHODS

Fishing a shoreline with a surface bug or fly can be very simple, but there is a whole vestful of tricks. It's usually done from a boat or canoe, and where there's little or no current the lure can be controlled at the caster's whim. Getting close to the cover, or shoreline obstacles, is usually important and, if the shoreline is fairly even, fly casting is a simple way of doing it; once the length of cast is established an attentive boatman can hold the range. Then, even if your windage isn't too good, you can at least keep your trajectory adjusted.

In fishing fairly even shorelines that drop off rather steeply, a single boat fisherman will cover the fishy area better by keeping the boat almost against the shore and casting ahead of it. Thus, instead of striking the productive zone only at intervals as he goes by, he'll be able to rake the whole thing with his bug or streamer. The perfect solution? Well, not quite.

If the shoreline has numerous small indentations, the fisherman can't get back into them without casting across patches of land or vegetation unless he waits until his boat is too close. If he is using a boat operator, there is a danger of hooking that valued friend, as the backcast can be nearly parallel to the boat's keel. If the bank is brushy, the boat, motor, paddle, or oars will often become entangled, with resultant inconvenience and noisy warnings to any fish up ahead. If the bank slopes very gradually, the motor, oars, or paddle may strike bottom. If the wind is exactly right, however, all but the first of these disadvantages can easily be circumvented as the caster can keep close to shore, with the

Largemouth bass caught on popping bugs in brackish water. Rod is typical bugging stick, taking a number-9 line.

boat drifting while pointed at right angles to the land. However, this system doesn't work with two casters operating from the same craft, as the man behind is pretty well blocked out of action. There is one other disadvantage, which varies with the situation and the size of the fish. It's a matter of the hooked bass being able to reach bank cover by simply swinging on the leader. If you hook him from offshore you can put instant pressure in that direction. In special instances the fish may be lying considerably away from the bank, and that distance is best ascertained by working the lure at right angles to the shore.

Most fly fishermen, especially those using bugs, work a shoreline too rapidly. They move the bug too quickly and they skip large sections of bank because of boat speed. This too-fast habit is the key to some of the unexplained successes of rank amateurs who experience all sorts of foul-ups and hence leave bugs lying motionless for considerable periods. One of my larger smallmouths was hooked while I untied a wind knot in my line. He did it himself, with no help from me, and was jumping with my hair bug in his mouth before I could tighten up.

But some experts vie with each other in advocating slower and slower bug fishing. It doesn't seem such good policy to let it sit for a full minute before twitching it when you actually count off sixty seconds. It is true that many fish are caught that way when conditions permit, and it may be a top method if waves or current add motion. But there's a limit to slow fishing, and you can get diminishing returns—you cover much less area and get very few casts per hour. Although slightly faster fishing may miss some fish, it will find many others that hit within a few seconds.

The fish don't like a bug to act the same way every day, and your chief danger is falling into a routine sequence of twitches and pauses that is almost mathematically the same on each cast.

A good basic bug program goes something like this:

As the bug strikes, move it very gently for two or three inches. I fondly believe that a fish seeing or hearing it alight will accept the little movement as proof that it is alive and not simply a bit of random debris. As he watches it, the feathers, hair, and/or rubber legs move helplessly. Next, leave it immobile for five to ten seconds, then pop it lightly, strip a little line, and pop it again. Now let it lie stationary again and complete the retrieve with a loud pop. This retrieve doesn't take very long, but there are reasons for the various stages. The first long pause is to give a fish time to approach from a considerable distance, even if he goes cautiously. The second pop is likely to goad him into a strike if he happens to lie watching the bug, and the next pop has the same purpose. Finally, the loud pop should give him all the noise he may want on those special days when he loves explosions. But this loud pop is saved until last, for there are many times when it would scare the fish away. Now this program may be unscientific but it was arrived at after watching bass and bugs in clear water and it's a pretty good gamble for openers. Once you find a striking pattern, you may alter your entire process. I'm talking about an exploratory approach that gets the most out of the bug.

In very shallow water I work a cast for a shorter time than I do over deep water, on the theory that fish able to see it will be quite near and won't need long to reach it. My most extended retrieves are over deep and fairly open water where a fish may come from a long distance. The same is true when using a streamer, and it can be allowed to sink for some time before stripping begins, providing there's deep water. When starting surface fishing, a popping bug is a good choice because it can be worked both loudly and softly. If it's obvious a quiet retrieve is best, you can change to something else.

Most floating fly-rod lures can be pulled gently through considerable grass or weeds without hanging up seriously. It's the hard jerk that causes the barb to penetrate instead of being deflected. In very heavy stuff some sort of weedguard is called for, and I go to a heavy rod that will take a No. 10 line. On some of the wide weed flats of shallow lakes you can thus get results comparable to those of the plugger's weedless spoon, but this becomes hard work and is a game for the dedicated fly specialist.

Surface fishing produces strange reactions in bass, and the

missed strike deserves examination. If it's a loud splash, the chances are it was a sincere effort and the caster invariably took the lure away. The best follow-up is to slap it right back where it came from, and I have watched some dramatic demonstrations of that in clear smallmouth water.

My wife, Debie, cast a hair bug over fairly deep smallmouth water on a northern lake and received a loud strike after a short pause. Having missed the bug, which Debie instinctively picked up, the two-pound smallmouth continued at top speed toward the boat, evidently having been headed in that direction when he made his pass. Debie instantly returned the bug to the spot of the strike and twitched it gently. In the meantime, the fish had slowed and stopped quite near the boat and, still unalarmed, made a leisurely turn, going back to where the bug was quivering. The second time he took solidly and was landed.

I have seen good-sized largemouths that would approach a bug quietly and suck it under with hardly a ripple. Detection was simple, especially on one placid canal, where each slow bulge could be seen coming several seconds before the bug would disappear. The fish were in the two-pound class and never rushed all evening, while a rain squall built overhead and finally came down hard. Once hooked, the bass fought normally, but not a one hurried to the kill. At the time, I thought it was just a condition of that particular day, but a later visit to the ditch produced the same sort of strikes.

Knowing their choice in temperatures, it is possible to make educated guesses as to when bass will be in the shallows of deep lakes. If food and oxygen are available in desired quantities, the fish tend to seek their ideal temperature levels. Generally speaking, the largemouth likes temperatures around 70 while the smallmouth is satisfied with somewhat cooler water.

Temperatures change quickly in shallow water and this is a major reason for the popularity of morning and evening fishing in warm weather. In very hot weather, shallow water usually makes poor fishing for bass except early and late in the day. There are some exceptions, of course, and if there are enough obstacles to provide shade, bass will sometimes spend the day in very shallow water, even when the depths are easily available a short distance away. It is easy to say that they do not like bright sun, but it is not unusual to see them cruising about in two feet of clear sunny water at noon in the summertime. That's not where I expect them, but sometimes they are there. Generally, the shady areas are a better bet, and fish that seem to be loafing in shady spots will sometimes strike if a lure comes close enough.

In early spring and late fall, the bright part of the day may offer the best fishing in the shallows because that's when the warmest water is available, and midafternoon is likely to mean the warmest water of all.

In the shallower lakes a major part of the feeding occurs along shorelines, and in warm weather this happens mainly in evening and early morning. The morning may be the best time, for the water has had all night to cool. However, the fish may

A small cartop johnboat is a great aid in fishing the edge of a swamp, where the laregmouth catch is supplemented by bluegills and warmouth perch. Run-ins from the shallows are especially good spots.

have moved and fed all night, and the morning spree might be very brief. It's generally more convenient to fish in the evening, so early-morning angling is badly neglected on many lakes. On evening fishing trips I fish right up until dark, but I find that I catch more bass an hour or so before sundown than just as darkness falls. I have found bluegills active just at dusk, after the bass seemed to have quit temporarily. Night-fishing for bass is highly productive on many lakes, but I find there's usually a lull shortly after nightfall, with feeding likely to resume a little later on. There are few fly fishermen who ply their trade after dark, but a noisy bug can produce some startling events on a summer night. Night-fishing and very late evening or early morning operations are especially effective on some of the crowded resort lakes, where boat traffic is heavy during the daytime.

Most natural lakes in fairly level country have gently sloping bottoms, gradually changing from shallow to deep water. Unless there is a surface, or near-surface, vegetation to be covered farther out, nearly all of the fly fishing is done right at the bank. It's true there are fish to be had in the open water, but blind fishing there is a tiring and generally unrewarding effort. Those who use electronic fathometers can locate productive dropoffs and ridges, but most of these are farther down than the fly fisherman wants to fish. Most of the bass lakes with considerable vegetation are not clear enough for likely casting targets to be located unless they project above the water. The situation is quite different with some of the rocky natural lakes of hilly northern sections.

A typical mountain bass lake in smallmouth country has some precipitous dropoffs from rocky cliffs, but around much of its perimeter it has a clearly defined belt of shallows. The shallows are formed as the lake ages naturally and are gently sloping flats bottomed by the earth and stone that have gradually weathered away from the shoreline through the centuries. These shallows are often excellent fishing, but it is easy for a veteran of other waters to give up if the immediate shoreline doesn't produce. He should try offshore boulders and the dropoff where the shallows end and the water turns blue. As in other kinds of fishing, the fish are most likely to be found at the edges—edges of dropoffs, edges of large boulders, and any "edge" where one kind of water changes to another.

In a Maine pond near Lake Sebago, two of us ran quite a gamut of bass fishing in a few hours. Although such a capsule experience won't happen every day, the story illustrates several points.

It was early June and there had been hardly any fishing pressure so the bass could be counted on to be in normal loca-

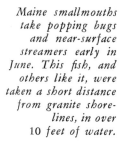

Maine smallmouths take popping bugs and near-surface streamers early in June. This fish, and others like it, were taken a short distance from granite shore-lines, in over 10 feet of water.

tions. Strangers to the pond, we ran the outboard to what appeared to be a likely point. It was early evening with a very light breeze. As I got the oars into action I was disappointed to note that the water was shallower than I had expected, no more than three feet deep, with the bottom gravel showing plainly for a considerable distance around the boat. That meant fairly long casts, and catching sharp-eyed smallmouths over shallow gravel bottom is not exactly my specialty. A series of casts against the shallow shoreline produced nothing, so I rowed as quietly as possible toward a single large boulder sitting on gravel bottom well out from shore. It threw a deep shadow, and although I couldn't see it at the time there was a little pocket of deeper water against the base of the rock. My companion made a fairly long cast with a rubber-legged popping bug, struck the boulder with it, and let it plop softly into the shadow. A smallmouth came clear out of the water and down on the bug almost instantly. Another cast in the same place brought a second fish. A third fish missed. Here were fish taking advantage of a small depression and a little patch of shade in the midst of a sunny gravel flat that had appeared fishless.

I simply rowed around the flat while my friend cast to a few scattered boulders after that, and nearly every big granite chunk had at least one smallmouth. By moving only 30 yards these fish could slide into blue depths, but they seemed to prefer the little patches of shade. My guess is that the water temperature of the flats suited them but they wanted shade so they concentrated about the boulders.

The next morning there was a flat calm, a problem for fly fishermen in clear water. A stretch of shoreline failed to produce, so we tried an area several feet deep, with chunk rock on the bottom and occasional boulders that nearly broke the surface. We went to long leaders tapered to 2X, we used hair bugs, we fished slowly, and we made long casts. Any loud pop seemed completely out of place in a silence broken only by the buzzing of blackflies and the whine of a distant power saw. We fished the hair bugs with dainty twitches and let them lie for long periods without picking them up. It was discouraging to see slab-sided smallmouths moving away from the boat, but we hoped the casts were long enough to find fish that hadn't been startled. We made a special effort at casting to the larger submerged boulders and we caught some fish, probably specimens that hadn't been able to see us because of their positions behind rocks. That's an important thought when you're in very clear water with no surface ripple.

About ten o'clock we got some breeze, and fishing picked up with long casts no longer necessary. There was just enough ripple to break up the fish's vision, and we began to gurgle and pop the bugs around the submerged granite chunks. That worked on two two-pound smallmouths, so we went back to the shoreline to see if it would change things there. Evidently, fish had moved out there under cover of the ripple, because business was good and we caught a pair of largemouths as well as a number of their bronze relatives.

Later in the summer, as the water warmed, that midday fishing probably wouldn't be much good unless you got down deep. A sinking line, cast out over the dropoff and retrieved slowly with a streamer, can work then, the lure coming up the dropoff slope but staying near bottom all the way. This is a prospecting method often used to locate the proper depth and it's a lot easier done with something besides fly tackle. But if the action is no more than ten or fifteen feet down, streamers can get in their licks.

Shallow and heavily weeded lakes generally call for surface fishing which means a weedless or semiweedless bug to most fly fishermen, generally worked slowly whether the individual jerks are hard or gentle. In such circumstances, lure contact with grass or weeds can be a help. The fish can't see too far from its position down in the shrubbery and is likely to investigate anything that shakes the stems a little. A bug that climbs a blade of pondweed, falls off the tip with a gentle plop, then twitches spasmodically, can get violent attention.

But there is a situation when weedless streamers can be the best choice. Some of the best bass fishing in eelgrass lakes comes just before spawning time, in early spring or late winter, depending on the latitude. Three of us fished such a spot one year when "lazy" was the only word to describe the fish. The big plugs that had caught fish there for years produced only some gentle swirls. The weedless spoons that had so often succeeded got nothing, although we detected the wake of an occasional following fish. I confidently used big popping bugs, but nothing happened. Now there have been many occasions when short strikers, or shoppers, that have stayed off the barbs of plugs and spoons have preferred

Eel-grass flats, with the vegetation just under the surface, make good bass cover, but it's no place for ultralight tackle. Weedless lures are almost a necessity and many fish are landed after exploratory probing in a gooey tangle.

something smaller and taken small bugs or streamers, but that didn't seem to be the answer this time.

With scant enthusiasm, I tied on a giant tarpon streamer, more than six inches long, and began fishing it very slowly. It seemed to crawl through the weeds in a soggy daze, looked like nothing any bass had ever seen, and made only a minor disturbance, but was so supported by eelgrass that it stayed near the surface and actually made a trace of wake. A four-pound largemouth took it in a resigned turn, and I had another fish a few casts later. The streamer was mostly white, but I doubt if color was important.

I wish I could say it was a revolutionary discovery and the certain answer to fish that move slowly, but like most such one-day wonders, it has since enjoyed only intermittent success. I have modified some of the big streamers with the addition of weed-guards and I have also made them into "dry" streamers with the addition of a little band of cork around the hook shank. There arc days when they work well in the grass and weeds but they're not revolutionary; just worth trying when things get slow.

Lily-pad water is made for the fly rod, up to the point where the fish is hooked. After that, landing procedures can be undigni-fied and often disastrous. The fly rod has the advantage of allowing you to cast into completely bordered pockets and then lift your bug for another cast without hanging up. Dropping a bug on top of a floating pad and twitching it a few times before pulling it into the water can cause a series of underwater vibrations that sometimes bring out the best in a bass, but pad fishing can turn into work because of hangups. Even a nonweedless bug can generally be pulled loose from the flat part of a lily pad, but if it gets caught in the notch at the end of the stem you'll probably have to go after it. Hooks with light wire are more adept at cutting through pads and weeds.

Many roadside canals are excellent bass fishing, and the fly rod is admirably suited to them since a fly line can be worked over the trimming of brush that generally edges such a ditch. Some of the best such fishing is to be had where the road borders a weedy marsh, and such terrain is likely where a wide ditch is dug for the roadbed. The little run-ins where marsh water comes into the canal are likely to be full of bait and deserve special attention, especially when the water level is falling during dry weather and much of the marsh water is draining out. While these things are pretty obvious, they are often missed by a fly fisherman. Since other tackle does not work so well, he may be misled into passing up dozens of good spots because he sees no one fishing them.

BRACKISH WATER

It has gradually dawned on me that some of the best and most neglected bass fishing in the country is to be found in brackish water. Although, like other bass fishing, it can be temperamental, there are certain patterns that make it partly predictable. It is likely to be shallow water, with fish that like their food on top. Since it is generally near saltwater fishing and saltwater fishermen, it is often ignored by lovers of surf and sea.

I believe the best known brackish-water largemouth bass fishing is in Currituck Sound, North Carolina. Although it is an ideal situation for the fly caster, I suspect there are similar conditions that have never been discovered on many coasts, and I have run into fly-chewing blass bass in several coastal spots where they've had no publicity at all.

Let's look at Currituck. The best times of year for fishing are similar to those of shallow lakes in the same latitude, with the spring peak coming around the last of May in most years. During the summer, the fishing is usually an early-morning and late-evening proposition, but the all-day fishing comes back with cool fall weather.

The salinity of the water varies greatly, but it remains fresh enough for the fish to reproduce and live happily. Until a few

Fishing for brackish-water largemouth bass on Currituck Sound, where guides pole their skiffs from amidships. Currituck fish are caught from the rushes along the shorelines, from open patches in elodea, and from the shelter of duck blinds.

years ago, most of the bass that fell to flies were caught around the innumerable duck blinds, and the Currituck guides, many of whom steer duck hunters in the fall, would simply motor from one blind to the next. It was not unusual to take half a dozen bass from a single blind, which was usually made with a log or plank framework and had a raised floor. It was natural for bait to congregate around such a spot, and there was always shade. Many of the blinds were almost against the low islands and points, most of which have no trees but carry thick grass, rushes, and low bushes.

But some years back Currituck Sound was invaded by milfoil, a persistent waterweed that has choked many bass lakes. There had always been beds of native grasses in the sound, but there had never been the quantity of cover that came with the milfoil. That meant the bass could find shade and cover almost anywhere, and it complicated the job of the local guides. Yet it's possible there are more bass now than ever before.

The fishing pattern is similar to marsh fishing in many other lesser-known areas, and the well-established guide corps can initiate a tourist at moderate cost. We went with Cecil Whitson on our first trip, and he used a small cabin cruiser for crossing the sound, then poled a skiff for the casting. The duck blinds are still productive at times, and the marshy shorelines, sometimes covered by a film of water, make excellent casting targets when the water is high. "High" and "low" water in the sound are a key to the fishing. It's far enough from the open sea that daily tides have no measurable effect, but a steady wind for a few days can blow the water from the flats until much of the shoreline is too shallow to fish. If the wind comes from the other way, the marsh can be so flooded that the bass will scatter everywhere, and these goings and comings add to the complications of the guide's job. But it's usually highly productive water.

Whitson took a quick look at the shorelines on our first day and announced that the water was too shallow there, so he poled to a deeper area with only a few pockets in the milfoil, which was matted on the surface. That's where the first bass came up to take a popping bug and go storming across the surface. In that kind of water it's wise to keep his head up and give him nothing.

That night the wind changed, and where the water had been too low it became just a little too high. But now the bass were along the marsh shores bordering dozens of sluggish creeks and rivers that moved only with the wind. They came out from the duck blinds to take the bugs and they made false strikes and threatening swirls tight against the grassy banks. Perhaps the best bet of all would be a small clump of grass just a little out from shore, an unexplained vagary of bass reasoning. It is probable that the little clump of grass gave him hiding and yet put him out into the path of moving bait that preferred to stay a little offshore.

Currituck Sound is great fishing and seems likely to continue to be so, but I think its greatest importance to us is that it indicates the possibilities of brackish-water fishing for black bass. There are similar spots known to very few fishermen and possibly none. I recall my surprise when I saw a smug angler bring in a string of largemouths from a marsh off San Francisco Bay, in an area I thought was strictly striped-bass country.

In quite different surroundings, I have had some of the best bass fishing of my life on the lower west coast of Florida, far up some rivers of the mangrove coast in an isolated area beloved by saltwater anglers and virtually unknown for its bass fishing. Ted Smallwood, an Everglades guide, announced that there had been good rain in the saw-grass rivers of the Everglades for some time, and that now dry weather had forced the largemouth bass down into the heads of the tidal rivers. Good water levels for reproduction and growth, and now the drought had come to make the fish vulnerable.

More than fifty miles from the nearest dock, we reached a mangrove-lined section of river that was almost filled with fresh-water vegetation. Along each shore was a narrow strip of open water. My first cast of a streamer fly brought at least four bass to the attack. This is a perfect streamer or bug situation of hungry, shallow-water bass and it can occur at almost any time of year. Perhaps the least likely is in midsummer when heavy rainfall will flood the saw-grass marsh and allow the bass to go back upstream. If a drought lasts long enough, there will be a fish kill, as the rivers become too salty for bass, but when rain comes the survivors will go back upstream and reproduce. This business of fish kills of coastal bass is a part of the natural cycle, and old books describe them as they occurred long before civilization imperiled the tidal swamps. In southwestern Florida I have found this exceptional bass-fishing in the Broad, Lostman's, and Shark Rivers, all within Everglades National Park.

Southern black bass fishing with popping bugs over an eel grass flat works well for a fisherman "wading wet" near shoreline.

THE IMPOUNDMENTS

Although I have bewailed the fact that much impoundment fishing caters to bottom-bumping and natural baits, there are times when the fly rod is most effective of all, especially in spring and fall, as well as early and late on summer days. The best fly fishing, of course, is on new impoundments, where an exploding bass population crowds the shallows. I have been present during this period on a few occasions and I was particularly happy with Lake Shasta near Redding, California, when it was still spreading into the mountain canyons. The water was clear and the fish would come up from great distance to take surface lures, sometimes in areas where the submerged mountain vegetation was still green, not yet killed by rising water. I found the same sort of fishing when Lake Mohave was new, and caught lively bass among Nevada cactus plants in shallow water.

But after the easy fishing of a new lake has worn off, the fly fisherman will get in his best licks far up the coves, especially those that become shallow flats. He'll also do well to explore the mouths of creeks. Sometimes these areas are ignored by bait fishermen and trollers who are working the deep ridges and channels.

Bass fishermen do not need much technical information regarding thermal stratification of deep lakes, but they should understand that the depths are warmer than surface water in winter, and colder in summer. Water is heaviest at about 39.2 degrees Fahrenheit, so when the surface of a lake freezes or approaches freezing in winter, the warmer and heavier water is found at considerable depth. Then, when the surface begins to warm in spring, it becomes heavier and leads to a general mixing or "turnover." A similar turnover occurs in fall when the warm surface water cools and begins to sink. All this mixing, usually aided by winds, is essential to the maintenance of adequate oxygen levels.

The *thermocline* sounds mysterious but is simply the strata of water where temperature changes rapidly from surface to depth. In summer, when the surface is quite warm, there is likely to be good fishing in the thermocline zone, which probably begins fifteen or twenty feet down—usually deeper than the fly fisherman wants to probe.

Although he can make the most of edge fishing in spring and

fall, the temperate-zone fly fisherman is usually better off on natural lakes than on impoundments. Some fine bass rivers have been ruined by dams, although in all fairness it must be admitted that some productive impoundments cover areas that had little or no fishing before they came.

SCHOOL BASS

Few fly fishermen have tried to fish the unusual performers known as "school bass," "jump bass," or "bar bass." These are simply bass that school up after the fashion of saltwater predators and strike bunches of bait on the surface. It's not unusual on large impoundments and it happens in some southern rivers as well as on a few natural lakes.

Anyone who has observed bass either by sight or with electronic gear knows that they often congregate in pods or in large schools. Generally, the schools are fairly loose, but jump bass are likely to attack in close formation. Sometimes they are excited enough to hit almost anything that moves in front of them, but there are times when they are highly selective, especially when the bait is small. Most of the schoolers are largemouth bass, but Kentuckies and smallmouths have gotten into the act from time to time. The white bass, a close relative of the saltwater striper, is a noted schooler and is a true bass, while our other "basses" belong to the sunfish family.

When bass school in rivers it is usually a result of a bar or current feature crowding bait into an accessible pod. The fish simply wait near the bottom until the quarry is at hand, then boom to the surface and churn things wildly. The best schooling occurs when the bait is migrating, thus moving up or downstream in a predictable pattern.

Nearly all school-bass fishermen use casting or spinning tackle. If the bait is large enough, they endeavor to match it with plugs or spoons. If it is very small, they may resort to trailers— flies, bugs, or miniature plugs trailing behind heavier casting weights, usually plugs that float. Most "rallies" are brief, so it's essential to get into the striking fish in a hurry, a necessity that eliminates most fly fishermen. However, one who is experienced in throwing with no more than one false cast can do business. If the bass continue to stay up, the fly caster who has his line working can continue to belabor the spot until the fish go down or one of them takes his fly.

When bass school on the surfaces of lakes it is necessary to pursue them with boats, a process that sometimes become ridiculous but can be fun. For some time I fished a small lake that had schooling bass in midsummer and I used a bright red boat with considerable acceleration. With my fishing partner, I'd rush to a series of splashes, get in a cast or two, and then wait until the fish came up again, possibly 300 yards away. Then it was throw the motor in gear and speed to the attack with the fisherman trying to false-cast as he went.

One day when I didn't fish I visited a fish camp operator located on the shore of that little lake. While I talked to him, a pair of fishing boats began to dash about the place, obviously chasing schooling bass. I remarked that it was a funny exhibition.

"If you think that's a bunch of nuts," commented by friend, "you should see that damned fool in the little red boat that was out there yesterday."

The fly rod is usually slower to get into action but it can handle tiny stuff that doesn't work well with other tackle. I once found a bunch of good-size bass striking very small minnows against a shore, and a plug caster anchored at the spot told me he couldn't get a strike with anything in the box. In what proved to be one of my rare strokes of fishing genius, I rigged a series of number-10 trout streamers on a leader and danced my whole "school" of bait across the surface where I figured the bass were lying. The result was soul-satisfying, violent, and confusing, for I frequently had more than one fish on at once. It has worked occasionally since—but not always—nothing *always* works on bass.

RIVER BASS

Most bass rivers are slow-moving enough to be handled the

same as lakes, but there is a heady business of smallmouths in brisk mountain currents—a form of fishing that is rapidly disappearing. The only bright spot in the picture is the fact that there is so little of it left that smallmouth stream fishermen are getting scarce and there's practically no competition.

A smallmouth stream is usually a little warmer, possibly a little slower than a brown trout stream. In fact, many a trout stream has been taken over by smallmouths. Often the same river accommodates both, with the trout living in the upper reaches and the smallmouths present lower down. Then the smallmouth water may give way to largemouth habitat, with overlapping all along the line.

Most of these smallmouth flows are rocky, with deep, slow pools and quick rapids. Those who fish with boats or canoes seldom give enough attention to the fast water. However it may foam and roar, there are likely to be dead spots where a bronzeback can rest. When warm weather increases the oxygen complications, bass often congregate in the rapids. I became a fishing hero very briefly one summer when I waded into the fast water and scored with streamer flies while most of the boat fishermen drew blanks probing the deep pools where they expected fish to be sulking in hot weather.

Bass have the same current problems as trout. A good spot is one where the fish can rest in comparatively dead water and watch swifter current for bait. That means the eddies just off heavy plunges of fast current, the protected areas at the side of rocks and below them, the cushions of water above boulders, the deeper pockets on the bottom, the undercuts below the willow roots.

A fast-water bass will take the same things that attract him in quieter water, and although there may be a rise of bass to a mayfly hatch, most bass fishermen are using lures instead of accurate imitations. In really swift water I prefer a streamer, in the belief it may be whipped down into the bottom pockets. Where the current is moderate and fairly smooth I have used big, bushy dry flies and even small trout patterns. The small trout flies were taken by bass all right, but they were generally small fish. I must

A mountain stream empties into Lake Shasta in California.
Above the falls is trout water. Below the stream's mouth are
largemouth bass.

admit that I have never caught anything very large on anything
that can be called a dry fly; the bass bugs definitely produce
bigger fish for me. However, when the fish run small, a large dry
might win in numbers.

Although I have caught smallmouths in a dead drift just as
if the target were trout, I have found bass less sensitive to drag
and I am not above twitching a big dry fly now and then if the
current isn't giving it much action.

In late evening or early morning, smallmouth bass, and
largemouths as well, tend to tour the quiet tails of large pools,
sometimes in water barely deep enough to cover them. This is a
time for long light leaders and a careful approach, as such fish

are easily frightened. A long series of casts over such water doesn't seem to help. If you don't connect after two or three tries, the chances are anything that was there has already left.

An opportune time for bass is just as high water goes down and the river clears. However, the small streamers, bugs, and flies are productive after the water is too low and clear for larger lures.

BASS AND BAROMETERS

Because bass are stay-at-homes and seldom make migrations of more than a mile or two, most bass fishermen know they are casting over fish, whether they catch them or not. It follows that the bass has been carefully studied with relation to moon phases and barometer movements, but most studies of such factors have been inconclusive, although there are some documented performances. Abrupt rises and falls of the barometer have frequently produced exceptional fishing. A steady barometer usually means steady fishing, with the bass following similar patterns through the settled period. Violent weather changes tend to produce changes in feeding patterns, meaning very good and very bad fishing. I have seen busily striking bass stop almost instantly at the sound of distant thunder and I have seldom had good fishing during rainstorms, but these are personal observations rather than general truths.

One fly fisherman who specialized in hair bugs on northern Michigan lakes told me he consistently found the bass on the shorelines during dark moon phases, and farther out when the moon was nearly full. Some night fishermen will try only when the night is dark; others have caught more fish in bright moonlight. Tide tables which indicate major and minor feeding periods are good for endless arguments, but most fishermen feel tidal movements do have an effect although it is blunted by other factors. At best, bass habits are erratic, especially where near-surface feeding is concerned.

SIX

Fly Rod Bugs

As FAR as I know, the first fly-rod bugs were used for pan-fish and freshwater bass; certainly they had been popular for those fish for a long while before any extensive use on others. At first the name "bass bug" was used even when the target was pike or mackerel, but it was gradually shortened to simply "bug."

Although many of the "dry flies" used long ago for bass may have been more nearly bugs than flies, Ernest H. Peckinpaugh is generally credited with making the first cork-bodied bugs, and Peckinpaugh bugs are still made in several styles. For a time, the Wilder-Dilg bug was well known. It was one of the earliest feather minnows, named after two early bug fishermen. The well-know Callmac bass bug evidently got its name from the man who sold it, Call J. McCarthy of Chicago, and I have found it advertised in a 1921 issue of Forest and Stream. Its most popular form had swept-back wings. The fly-rod bass bugs began appearing in the tackle catalogues about 1913.

There has been little attempt at establishing patterns and colors, and almost anything that is cast with a fly line, floats, and does not resemble a freshly hatched insect in form is called a "bug." Most manufacturers have their own catchy names. At present, most of the hair mice are similar, the "slider" or "bullet-head" is the same as what was once called a "feather minnow," and anything with a cupped or flat face is simply a "popper." The "bream killer" has a sponge body with rubber legs, and bugs with wings that stick straight out are frequently christened "dragon-flies." That's about it. There are hundreds of models but they fall under a very few general types, which greatly simplifies discussion.

BUG CASTING

There is nothing difficult about casting well-designed bugs with the proper tackle. True, there is a slight change of timing as a result of the increased wind resistance, and ultralight gear is unsatisfactory with heavy models, but the laborious flop-casting that so often goes with bugs is completely unnecessary.

For the largest bugs to be used in either fresh or salt water the line should be at least a number 8, with a rod to match. The forward taper is essential for any sort of distance—the short, fat "bug" or "saltwater" tapers are ideal.

Since bug fishing seldom involves a delicate presentation, there is little need for a long or extremely light leader. Many bug fishermen use them as short as four feet, but a tapered leader about the length of the rod is convenient to use and makes a smoother cast for most of us. An extralong leader is a decided disadvantage if the bug has a cupped face and is fished very slowly. The leader will often sink deeply, and when the pickup comes the sunken leader will tip the bug down and pull it under, producing a stentorian blurp and ruining the cast. So if the bug

Popping bug works on saltwater species as well as on bass. This is a brackish-water snook that was hooked near a mangrove island.

is to be left on the water for a very long time on each cast, the leader should be short, or doped with line dressing so it will float. When cup-faced bugs are fished, it is very important that the line float high so that the lure can get a good smooth start before the violent part of the pickup begins.

The bug pickup should be started very slowly, with the rod tip quite low, and the caster should watch the bug begin to slide smoothly on the surface before he flicks it clear of the water. It is a slight exaggeration of other pickups but becomes second nature after a little trial. You can jerk a small streamer or tiny fly and still get it into a respectable backcast, but a big bug will stand for no nonsense and must be picked up with a fluid motion. Keep the backcast high.

Many good casters despise bugs because they are careless with them. Aware that they are using a method commonly considered a little crude, they simply flail away, get poor results, and wear out their arms. Actually, bug casting requires as much finesse as any form I can think of.

Bug fishing sometimes requires considerable casting distance, but a good caster can throw a big bug to within a very few feet of where he can get with a small streamer—if he will use care. A dropped backcast simply ticks the surface if you're using a small fly, but a big bug will produce a startling pop back there, and your forward cast will have had it.

BUG DESIGN

Good bug design is essential for decent casting, and smooth-flying bugs will catch as many fish as the arm-breakers.

Since bugs often compete with larger surface plugs, there is a tendency toward bulk for bass, pike, and saltwater fishing. Great length may be desirable; extreme diameter is seldom of any help and can make casting laborious.

The noisiest bugs have either cupped or flat faces, and some have a diameter as great as $7/8$ of an inch at the front, a handicap in both pickup and casting. My favorites in big popping bugs have faces no more than a half-inch in diameter, although they may be as much as five inches long (including bucktail or feathers). This is as long as many ⅝-ounce casting plugs, and I have used some bugs with much larger cups but only three inches long. I believe the huge cups are working in the wrong direction, sabotaging the cast, and are unnecessary for noise-making. There are some simple tricks for making noise with a much smaller head.

Most of the bugs on the market today are fairly efficient, but for years many of them were built by people concerned mainly with the quality of construction and fish appeal, and not with the problems of casting. Bug-making requires a minimum of equipment and is a part-time project for many. Thus, there are numerous local manufacturers producing bugs under their own trademarks. Their products range from excellent to good to poor.

The most annoying design is one that "hooks" or dives on the pickup. In the water, such a bug may be attractive in appearance and action, but when the pickup starts it will tend to dive underwater and block the cast. The defect is not always apparent until fishing starts. Then, if the head has a very wide cup that rides low in the water, diving is likely. The hook eye should be at the bottom, of course, as the lure floats, and a loop connection with the leader can sometimes remedy the defect. Some bugs that dive when the leader is snubbed up tightly will pick up smoothly when the hook eye is attached with a loop.

If the bug rides with the tail low, it seldom gives diving trouble. Some of the best designs sit in the water with the nose pointed quite high. When twitched, the nose dips down, throws a little flick of water from the surface, makes a little pop, and then returns to its nearly vertical attitude. Such a construction generally employs a rather short body and a moderately heavy hook. This action is called "bobbing," which it does in addition to darting and popping.

To avoid the diving tendency, many builders make the popper's nose on a slant with the upper part projecting forward, so the tendency is for the bug to push upward when pulled forward. Some get considerable noise with a plain flat surface, but I have heard shoppers complain that such bugs would not be noisy

Typical saltwater bugs, including a slider, or "bullet-head," and two poppers. All have stream-lined shape to present as long a silhouette as possible without greatly increasing casting effort.

enough. I can't see a great deal of benefit in the cup, but it certainly sells bugs.

I have no preference in material for the bug body, or "head," having used excellent bugs made of cork, plastic, or balsa wood. Solid plastic is generally toughest but sometimes tends to be slightly heavy. Foam plastic is more fragile. The ones I've made were done with cork. For the tails, bucktail or nylon is more durable than feathers.

Durability becomes very important when bugs are used for pike and saltwater fish or in heavy weeds. Good bugs are expensive, often costing well over a dollar each, so a school of destructive bluefish can make fishing a very expensive hobby. But more often than toothy attacks, clinging weeds, and twisting lily pads, it is the fisherman's fingers that wreck most bugs, in the simple process of unhooking fish. Instead of grasping the hook, the angler grabs the bug's body and twists. That loosens the hook in the bug's body and it comes apart after a few casts. A bug fisherman will save money by keeping needlenosed pliers handy for gripping the hook.

The bullethead, or slider, rests fairly flat on the water and has no popping surface. When jerked briskly, it darts, usually to one side. It picks up smoothly, has a streamlined silhouette, and slips a little more easily through weeds or grass. Smallmouth bass generally like its lack of surface commotion. There are days when it is very effective for many saltwater fish—for anything that takes a bug, for that matter—but I use poppers more. The popper

A "bumblebee" popping bug with rubber legs caught this 8½-pounder for Ray Donnersberger, of Chicago, during cool weather preceding spawning time.

comes first because it can be worked quietly when need be, and popped—on the same retrieve, too. No pops with the slider.

I am convinced that rubber legs add a great deal to many bass and panfish bugs, splayed out from the sides and continuing to writhe long after the motion of the bug itself has stopped. When a bug is worked fast, they help little, but add to the catch when the bug is moved slowly.

Rubber legs are not very durable and some deteriorate rapidly in storage. Ideally, rubber legs should bend back along the bug's sides during the cast and then spread out again on the water. They must be slender and supple enough to continue moving for a while after the bug is twitched. Having too many legs can cause a light bug to land upside down and then dive when it's picked up. Usually, three to six on each side of a large, bass-size bug are enough to create the effect without interfering with casting and attitude on the water.

Sponge-rubber spiders or "bream-killers" are true bugs in that they float, however soggily. The rubber legs are a major part of their attraction; slow-taking bluegills will nibble on the legs and then suck in the entire bug, generally taking sponge bugs more gently than poppers. I have had indifferent success with bass on rubber bugs, and most of what I did catch were small.

Hair bugs, mice, or "powder puffs" are generally made of deerhair twisted about a hook. The finished product is a bushy apparition which can be trimmed to the desired shape, usually that of a mouse. Some of these mice are quite expensive, with eyes, ears, tails, even noses. However beautifully constructed, I doubt that the lifelike details add much, and sometimes they contribute to casting and floating difficulties. I have used some excellent hair bugs trimmed into frog shape. A fairly effective weedguard can be made by leaving a few strands of hair long enough to shield the barb.

If the hair is put on very thickly, it is essential that it be trimmed away on the underside or it will make the lure fishless, as well as weedless. Many amateur hair bugs refuse to float upright. My wife ties some pretty good ones but had a rough time at first, and some of the added frills I insisted on were nothing but a nuisance. Some hair bugs are made into very lifelike mice by leaving the hair long on top, smoothing it back to be tied at the hook shank, and allowing it to extend into a lifelike tail. The underside is trimmed short.

The hair dragonfly is simply a small, streamlined body with hair wings projecting at right angles from either side. Another type has a cork body with hair wings and tail. It is one of the most effective of all bass bugs, but one of the harder ones to cast. It has considerable wind resistance, and many such designs twist the leader in the air. They also land upside down much of the time. I use them less every year, scant gratitude for all the fish they have taken for me.

One of the older solid-bodied types is beetle-shaped with wings folded nearly flat against the back, presenting a compact silhouette, usually with a flat or cupped face. It casts well and catches fish, but I feel that it presents too small an outline to be good for large saltwater fish, though it is fine for black bass.

Hooking qualities have been ignored in some bugs. I have seen some with 3/4-inch faces, carrying little number 2 hooks with such a narrow bite that a fish would have to be extremely cooperative to get hooked. If a fish took hard and clamped down on the bug's body, there would be very little chance of his getting stuck, no matter how viciously you struck back. Bug-strikers are not especially easy to hook at best, for several reasons, so you need plenty of hook-bite. The classic test is to attempt to hang the bug on a piece of wire screen. If the hook can't be stuck into the wire, it's too small for the size of the bug's body. I have checked dozens of models that flunked miserably. Sometimes the bite can be opened up with pliers; I bend the hook shank slightly on a large percentage of the bugs I use.

WEEDLESS BUGS

A wire weedguard is the most certain protection for a barb, although stiff monofilament helps greatly, and very light hair bugs can be made weedless through extension of stiff hairs. Other guards have been made with loops of heavy monofilament, or with specially shaped hooks whose shanks are bent into a keel shape and ride with the barb upward. The latter hook can be adapted to small-bodied hair bugs. Any weedless arrangement wards off some strikes, too, and I have run some tests showing that hooks with weed guards hooked only a fourth as many fish as those without protection. It depends, of course, on the way in which the fish strikes.

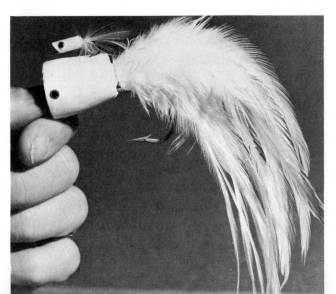

Popping bugs come in all sizes, from the panfish lure, shown on top, to the salt-water monster constructed by Bill Gallasch, of Richmond, Virginia.

Most cork-bodied bugs can be made weedless very simply with a piece of stainless steel leader-wire, about Number Five size. Using pliers, push the wire through the cork body from the top or "back" of the bug, being careful to run it a little off center to miss the hook shank and the glue around it. When enough of the wire has gone through the body to form a hook-guard, cut the wire a little above the body and bend it into a small U at that point. Now pull the wire on down until the little U is embedded in the bug's back, bend the guard to shield the hook, and cut it to proper length. This wire will not be as springy as the material used in factories but it is highly effective, and once a fish has bent it out of shape you can repair it instantly. It's a convenient stop-gap.

For some years I have been using a factory-made frog that is fished with the hook riding up. It has a large body, is oval on top and quite flat on the bottom, and its "legs" are made of hair. Most of the time it lands right side up and has proven to be a good hooker even when fished through some of the thickest large mouth cover. On the occasions when it does land upside down, or is overturned by contact with grass it hangs up—like anything else. Its manufacture involves a delicate job of balancing, and I'd rather not try to copy it at home.

FISHING SURFACE BUGS

There is an old saying that you can't fish a bass bug too slowly. Like most other flat statements about fishing, it isn't true. But there are times when it's almost true.

Years ago I used to fish an old railroad pond at Farlington, Kansas. It gradually filled with more and more water growth, until there was little room to move a bug. You'd simply cast to small open pockets and shake your bug a time or two, then pick up gingerly and look for another opening.

I arrived on the scene late one hot summer evening, just in time for the best bass-bugging, and met a stranger on the shore. He announced that he fished the pond regularly and I noticed that he had a tiny, homemade boat and a fly rod with a dragon-fly bug knotted to a short leader. He paddled out for fifty yards, anchored, cast the bug into a tiny pocket, and sat back to relax with his pipe. He never moved the bug after it struck the water. Never moved it at all. A few minutes later there was a gentle swirl and he hooked a two-pound largemouth. He cast to another pocket and after a few minutes he caught another bass. Although I used what I considered to be much more advanced methods, I didn't catch nearly as many fish as he did. My (rather shaky) explanation was that there was a brisk breeze and the ripple kept the bug bobbing around against the restraint of the leader.

Stillfishing has worked for me on many occasions, but I seldom leave a bug for more than a couple of minutes without some movement, however slight. If the fish seem to take best with very slight movement, it is possible to cause a lifelike quiver by tapping the rod butt or shaking the rod tip gently. There are times when bass want brisk movement and plenty of noise, and other times when they want very gentle movement, or none at all, for long periods. Generally speaking, you need little bug action on a calm surface and can use loud plops when the surface is riffled. If the water is extremely shallow, I fish faster since the striking fish doesn't have far to go. Over deep, clear water, a slow bug may get much better results. When California's Lake Shasta was first filled, I had wild-eyed bass come charging up from blue depths for a slow worked bug after it had been in the same position for half a minute. The fish would appear as indistinct shadows that grew rapidly, and it was difficult to wait for the banging strike that sometimes brought the bass clear of the water.

Most saltwater fish prefer louder noises than do bass, and generally they prefer faster bug movement. There are exceptional days, however, and the rule that no bug is too big or too loud for a striped bass may be suspended from time to time.

On very calm water I favor hair bugs, for both large and smallmouth bass, and the plain mouse is as good as any. If there is ever a time for dainty presentation of a bug, this is it. You can use a moderately light leader to good advantage when the surface is flat calm, the thunderheads high, and the evening bullbats dive for insects. Cast it lightly and work it slowly, bringing it along

A variety of bugs intended primarily for freshwater bass and panfish. Hair bugs and those with rubber legs are especially effective when worked slowly in quiet water.

with gentle stripping of the line hand and long pauses. Strikes may not be loud, often coming as ominous swells and gentle smacks. Under such conditions, a five-pounder can take with little more commotion than a nymphing brown trout. Hooking is usually easier with the hair bugs because the soft body encourages firm holds and deep takes.

The hair bug does not require a bug rod and is the tool of the ultralight fly fisherman for bass. A tiny six-foot bamboo will work a sizable bass bug on a five line as long as the bug floats high. Treat it with line dope or use dry-fly oil and it will skate like a thistle. But there are other times when you want it to gurgle, pop, and sputter, and for that a heavier rod is better. Put the dope only on the top of the bug and allow the lower half to soak up water. Such a bug rides low in the water, makes a healthy wake, and can be popped to suit. If the hair is too water-repellent when untreated, apply "leader sink" to the lower part.

I knew a bass and panfish guide who encouraged his clients to keep surface bugs moving slowly at all times. It wasn't that he felt the motion was necessary to attract fish, but that by doing it that way the fisherman always had a tight line, and the percentage of hooked strikes was much higher. The way to do it is to keep the rod pointed almost at the bug and retrieve the line very slowly with the stripping hand. When you pop the bug, do so with the rod tip and then take up the resultant slack instantly. For strident popping of big bugs for big fish, you will need a little slack for the rod tip to work with, but you can recover most of it immediately after each pop, using your line hand. Resist the tendency to lift the rod tip higher as the lure is worked.

At best, there is a large percentage of missed strikes on bugs, especially those that are worked hard. It is a simple case of the fish knocking the bug away with his wake, or misjudging its location in the splash and sputter, plus the likelihood of slack line due to lure manipulation. The hook should be set with a quick lift.

Not all missed strikes are easily explained, and there are days when everyone has them, even when the fish seem to be taking with a rush. Sometimes they are false takes, possibly by angered or curious fish that are not feeding. The likelihood of this occurring is greatest with black bass, fish that are believed capable of many lure responses in addition to hunger.

Most bugs are impressionistic lures, not closely resembling living creatures, but exciting by action, color, or sound. However, on some occasions the bug does closely resemble natural foods. I once had very fast bass fishing on a central California lake when there was an invasion of toads during their breeding season. After seeing dozens of toads moving about in the shallows, I dug up a feather frog, worked it next to the weeds in short tugs, and caught a limit of bass in short order. They struck wildly, even though I couldn't see any of them taking the live toads. In that case, the bug was a fairly accurate imitation of a natural creature present in considerable numbers.

Of course, the hair mice are also quite accurate representations of the real thing, but although bass will take mice all right, it's hardly a staple of their diet, and it's doubtful that the bass really takes the bug for a mouse; it's more likely simply a fuzzy, crawly thing that looks alive. Some effective fishing lures are built on shaky premises. I have heard that a bass takes plastic worms for snakes and some fishermen believe snakes are a common part of the bass's diet, but a biologist told me that in the thousands of bass he had dissected he had found the remains of only four small snakes. Maybe they're all looking for snakes and just can't find them.

Some of the small bugs I have used for smallmouths, on both lakes and streams, did resemble food items. I have caught many smallmouths on a goofus bug, a popular trout item, which is fished dry. Since it has a solid body, I consider it a bug. I moved it only slightly on New England lakes, just enough to make tiny wavelets in a silent cove, and then jumped when the fish came roaring up from the rock and gravel bottom, through eight feet of water.

With the smaller lures, it is hard to separate dry-fly fishing from bugging. Perhaps the main difference is that the dry fly is usually drifted in a dead float with a current, while the bug is moved as if under its own power. Some very large trout have been caught on popping bugs, but I've had little success at that. I have done well with both trout and smallmouth bass on large muddler minnows, doped with dry-fly oil and fished with a few twitches on quiet water.

The color of the popping bug is usually a minor matter, but there are isolated instances when bass show decided preferences. The bumblebee color is one of the most popular in both the Midwest and the South, whether for scientific reasons or not. Yellow, white, and combinations of the two have been the leaders for more than fifty years over much of the largemouth country. Frog finishes are standard in most lines.

There is conflicting testimony about hair-bug color. Personally, I have found little difference anywhere I have used hair

"Bite" of popping bug hook is tested on a piece of screen wire. Unless the barb can be stuck into the mesh, the bug's body is interfering with its hooking ability.

bugs, and H. G. Tapply, who ties the most artistic ones I have ever used, says the color has made no difference for him but that he uses bright and harmonizing tints just to make them pretty. Except for Mr. Tapply's, most of the hair bugs I have used were either white or brown, and that is true of muddler minnows too.

I know of only one case in which hair-bug tones were found important in a careful test, and that was back in the thirties. The late Russell Francis operated a fly-tieing shop at that time and sold many of his creations in Michigan. He and V. M. Gowdy tested what Francis then called a "buck hair floater" (simply a powder puff or hair mouse), intending to keep careful records of the results on northern Michigan lakes. Fishing in early summer, they found the smallmouths consistently ignored the brown lures but took the white ones. They stopped the scorekeeping as no contest.

In less convicing tests, they found that the largemouths farther south seemed to prefer the brown bugs, but I got into that one myself and couldn't find much difference. For some time, I used brown and red hair bugs, simply because I had them, but I believe plain brown would have done just as well.

When it comes to saltwater bugs, you're generally trying to make the things appear as large as possible, so I tend toward light colors. We sometimes sprinkle silver and gold metallic particles on the bug bodies and use Mylar in the feather or hair tail sections. Some of them are painted with metallic aluminum paint, and I have used Mylar strips glued to the bug bodies as well as tied into the tails.

A dropper fly or nymph, fished along with a large bug, is a potent accessory, especially when the fisherman is after both bass and panfish. The theory is that the bass will go for the large bug and the panfish will take the dropper fly. Such a combination isn't the easiest way to cast and tangles frequently, but it can be deadly. Many of the larger fish take the dropper fly instead of the bug, and the assumption is that they are attracted by the popping, which resembles a feeding fish, and then notice the easily taken nymph or wet fly. The combination of a popper and a trailing streamer fly works well on saltwater weakfish.

While freshwater fishermen are almost too persistent in the use of bugs when streamers might do better, saltwater fishermen neglect their bug fishing, partly because they dislike casting such large items, partly because streamers are more consistently successful. As a result, it is difficult to find good saltwater bugs for sale in many coastal areas. The fact is that most saltwater fish that will take streamers have their days for bugs, and on a bug-taking day the streamers may be completely out of it. A saltwater fly fisherman should have bugs in his box.

BUG MAKING

The commercial manufacturer of saltwater bugs has a dilemma about construction. If he builds his bugs strong enough and salt-resistant enough to withstand corrosion and crushing jaws, they will be too heavy for pleasant casting. If he makes them with light hooks and bodies for good casting, they won't last long enough to justify the price, which is likely to be more than a dollar.

Although I don't make freshwater bugs anymore, being dazzled by the array of good ones at the tackle stores, I still use homemade saltwater ones. They're lightly constructed and expendable, but they have both a lengthy silhouette and good casting qualities. If I tried to sell them commercially I'd probably

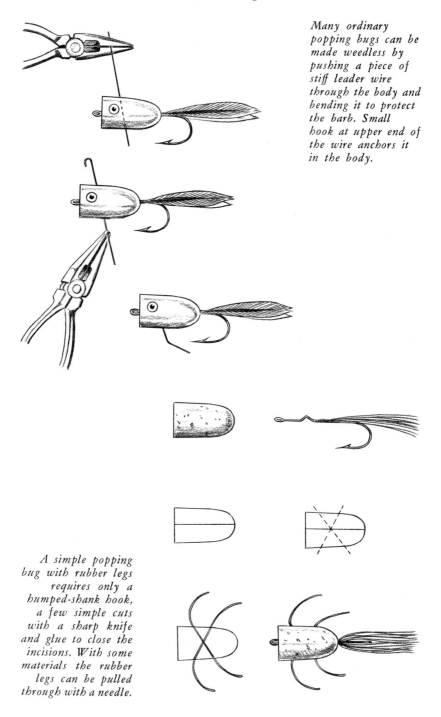

Many ordinary popping bugs can be made weedless by pushing a piece of stiff leader wire through the body and bending it to protect the barb. Small hook at upper end of the wire anchors it in the body.

A simple popping bug with rubber legs requires only a humped-shank hook, a few simple cuts with a sharp knife and glue to close the incisions. With some materials the rubber legs can be pulled through with a needle.

be investigated by the Better Business Bureau, for the light hooks rust promptly unless thoroughly washed and dried after each use.

Construction is simple. Bullet-shaped cork heads, ½ inch in diameter, are available from tackle supply houses. You can use foam-plastic bodies if you prefer, but I like cork. We use hump-shanked 2/0 hooks on light wire. The dressing is usually bucktail, but feathers will work too.

Simply take a sharp knife, wet it for easy passage through cork, and cut a slit lengthwise in the head, with a slightly deeper cut where the hook hump goes. Tie the tail of bucktail, nylon, or feathers to the afterpart of the hook, as if building a streamer fly. Insert it in the slit so that the hook eye is at the edge of the cup if it's to be a popper. If it's to be a slider or "bullethead," the hook goes the other way, with the eye at the small end of the cork body.

Fill the slit with a good waterproof glue. Generally a second application will be necessary after the first dries. Use spring clothespins to hold the slit shut, and keep it upright to prevent glue from seeping out. After both applications of glue have dried, the bug is ready for painting. If you want to improve its appearance, you can use filler on the cork before painting, but it won't catch any more fish.

If you want to add rubber legs, insert them in deep cross-cuts in the cork before inserting the hook. Use long strips of rubber (these too, are available from tackle supply houses), so that one piece extends through and forms two legs. I see no use for legs on saltwater bugs, but they are an added attraction for bass or panfish.

If you want to make smaller bugs there are all sorts of cork sizes and shapes. The instructions given here are for crude and expendable lures, and I make no effort at producing a bug-building manual. With the big bug just described, you have a long silhouette with little wind resistance and tail enough for satisfactory planing through the air.

There's more to bug fishing than most fishermen bother to learn.

SEVEN

Trout and Grayling

It was trout and grayling that started fly fishing as we know it. They are the fish that feed on insects, even after reaching considerable size, and flies were tied to deceive them before any sportsman knew that we would someday cast huge streamers to imitate smelt or shad. The first flies were imitations of insects, and a purist might go so far as to say that anything else is a lure.

Trout and grayling are coldwater fishes by definition, even though some of them can live in water of more than 80 degrees. No matter what his personal preference, almost any fisherman will agree the trouts are glamour fish, a fact which enables hatchery rainbows to draw high prices in a restaurant. It also causes New England sportsmen to despise bass, simply because they have taken over from the native "brookie."

The Atlantic salmon is part of the trout family, but you're on dangerous ground if you argue that any fly cast to a salmon is actually a lure since salmon don't feed on flies (or anything else) while making the spawning migration during which they are caught on fly rods. The salmon-lover will immediately respond that the salmon strikes flies from memory of his youth, and he will ignore your argument that most salmon flies resemble no insect that ever lived.

Even now, with bass striking popping bugs in abandon, and the corps of saltwater fly fishermen growing steadily, you'll find most of the fly fishermen north of the Mason-Dixon line (which has also been called "the fly-rod line," although there are trout in some of the southern states).

Almost any trout man will readily rank the species as to fighting qualities. If you don't count the Atlantic salmon, he'll usually place the rainbow, or steelhead, first, followed by the brown trout, with brookie and cutthroat bringing up the rear, largely because they don't jump. He probably won't mention the Dolly Varden, or bull trout, at all, and the lake trout, or togue, doesn't come to the fly except under unusual conditions. Even though he may love the grayling and acknowledge that it jumps, he won't class its dainty habits with rougher trout tactics.

This ranking is approximately correct, although the exceptional fish must be reckoned with. A pellet-fed hatchery rainbow could be towed upstream backward by a wild brown trout of equal size. When the fish come from the same water with the same food they are more nearly equal in fighting qualities unless the temperature favors one or the other.

There are some other trout which aren't too important in the

A productive stretch in Vermont, where trout have a choice between deep shade and an aerated riffle in the sun.

overall picture, including the golden trout of both West and East, and a whole list of offshoots from the main species.

All these trout tend to be migratory to some extent, although most of those caught by fly fishermen stay in fresh water. Rainbow, brown, brookie, cutthroat, and Dolly Varden all go to sea in some parts of their ranges. The seagoing rainbow, or steelhead, is best known except for the Atlantic salmon, which is a closer relative of steelhead than of Pacific salmon. Brown trout that go to sea are called seatrout, and so are cutthroats when they cross the tide line. Brookies are generally dubbed "salters." Evidently the steelhead and Atlantic salmon go much farther than the others we've mentioned. We'll put the Pacific salmons, which die after spawning, in a different classification.

All trout are good fly-takers when they are small. The brown trout has the best reputation as a dry-fly fish because it continues to take dries after it becomes quite large, even when most of its diet must be smaller fish. It also has the reputation of being more selective than rainbows or brookies. This gets a little hard to prove in some cases when a dry fly catches browns and doesn't score so well on rainbows. Nevertheless, the brown makes a fine wild fish, and planting programs are unnecessary where habitat is proper. It takes care of itself.

Warmwater fish populations take less management, and trout populations aren't too hard to handle in deep lakes. But stream fishing has the greatest appeal for flyrodders and here we have big troubles. For a trout stream has rigid requirements which cannot be bypassed, and tampering with the stream bed and its surroundings is touchy business.

For one thing, a trout stream needs its bends and crooks, even though it changes them in the course of time. The natural meanders provide the undercut banks, the eddies, and the sunny riffles essential to good populations. The stream needs shade, but not too much, so a slow stream in a mature forest can be a poor one for trout. The riffles are almost always homes for insect life because they are reasonably constant and are not covered by the silt that comes with flood waters.

A brushy New England creek where fisherman must hunt for room to cast his fly. Such fish are seldom selective, but must be approached carefully.

If all of the timber is cut, the land erodes and the sun warms the water too much. If a stream is straightened, much of the insect life is destroyed in its aquatic form, water runs off too fast, and the good trout lies disappear. If a stream becomes broad and slow as a result of bank erosion, it becomes warm and its insect life suffers. It may get too warm for the trout, too. There have been successful experiments in establishing bank shrubs that hold the soil and provide shade, but these things take time.

The degree of warmth tolerated by trout varies with the species. The brook trout can live in water up to 75 degrees, the brown trout to about 81, and the rainbow to about 83. As upper tolerances are reached, trout have been known to bury themselves in gravel.

Richard Vincent, fisheries biologist for the Montana State Fish & Game Commission, ran an electronic survey of a stream that had both natural meanders and a section widened by land practices, all within a short distance. The weight of trout supported by the natural section ran more than four times the amount found in an equal area of widened flow.

In most small streams, the heat of summer is nearly as dangerous as the cold of winter, and the removal of only a little shade or the elimination of a few deep runs can make the difference in trout survival. As water temperatures near the critical point, seemingly minor factors assume major importance. For example, dry air increases evaporation and causes a stream to be cooler than it would be in a humid climate.

But these are technical things and the trout fisherman is likely to leave them to fish-management experts. It is the complete elimination of running trout water, by dams or excessive irrigation demands, that poses difficult problems. Damming of trout streams for irrigation or power has removed a large share of our fishing waters, and fights against such interests have been largely losing ones. Even in the field of recreation, the dam-builders get prime support for a reservoir that accommodates boating, water skiing, and trolling, for it will afford amusement for more people than can wade a trout stream. It is true that this entertainment is casual and brief for most of those who visit reservoirs, but that's a rather subtle point.

One specific type of trout water is especially treasured by expert fly men. There never was much of it and it's getting scarcer with private leasing becoming more and more prevalent, even in the United States. It's the cool stream with a constant flow only slightly affected by rain or runoff, and it's exemplified by British chalk streams, such as the revered Itchen and Test, some of the limestone brooks of the East, and the spring creeks of the West.

Very little direct runoff water enters these streams. The flow comes either from springs, or through porous soil in such a way that the streams seldom get noticeably colored. They have extremely heavy insect populations, heavy submerged vegetation, and large populations of insect-feeding trout. Because of the constant flow, the insect hatches are likely to be reasonably predictable. The fish are less so but can be seen working at regular intervals, and they provide the kind of challenge sought by the best dry-fly and nymph casters. Remember, there are some who have little interest in "blind" casting and prefer to fish only to individual rising targets.

Leasing such water is expensive; the price surpassed only by that of beats on Atlantic salmon rivers. Since polished operators who appreciate difficult trout streams are truly a minority group of the fishing world, there aren't too many fishermen who are capable of being effective on these streams. Therefore, the government hasn't spent much in an effort at keeping them public. In at least one case, conservation organizations and private firms have united in leasing such water and holding it open to all as a public service.

The trouts have been so widely distributed through introduction that a history of such efforts is impossible. Most trout fishermen are surprised to find that the majority of their fishing is for introduced species. And before man took a hand there wasn't the mixing there is now. Cross-breeding has produced all sorts of combinations, most of them good adaptations. Although trout waters are constantly reduced by development, land uses, and pollution, there's trout fishing in more places than ever before— thanks to introductions. They produced high-quality fishing in many waters, though some eventually fell off because of human population pressures of one kind or another. In many instances, we're whittling away at what we built ourselves.

For many years, the hatchery was believed the answer to all trout problems, and enormous sums of money have gone into this kind of production. Although the hatcheries served an original objective in providing trout for suitable waters that did not have them, they finally reached a point of diminishing returns. When fish managers saw the problem had turned into one of habitat rather than stocking, there was a period of loud debate and costly misunderstanding. Sold on the idea that the more fish you introduced, the more there would be to catch, the public wailed loudly at talk of closing hatcheries and diverting funds to stream improvement. That argument is still with us, although in somewhat milder form, the whole thing tied into a matter of conflicting concepts, even with modern knowledge of what makes a trout go.

It comes down to quality fishing versus quantity fishing. One view is that the trout fishery should exist for the millions, provid-

Ben Williams lands a brook trout from an old beaver pond after approaching from below the dam. He used a small dry fly.

ing the most possible fish for the most possible fishermen. This evolves into put-and-take planting of fish that can be caught with even the crude methods of beginning or casual fishermen. It has reached the absurd point where people actually follow a hatchery truck and, when it unloads, yank out limits of naíve trout, fresh from concrete pools and completely befuddled in their new surroundings, but still hungry. Marshmallow and canned-corn fishing may not be very esthetic, but it entertains people who are incapable of more difficult efforts. One angler developed what he called a "pellet fly." He wanted to fish with flies but knew that the hatchery fish wouldn't have much interest in natural insects they'd never eaten, so he dressed one to look like hatchery food. And it worked.

Fish management is supported by the public, its source of revenue being the fishing license. In return, it must provide fish that can be caught by the public. If people are happy with hatchery trout, they'll keep coming back. Closely linked to the public's desire for recreational fishing are those whose income derives from the tourist trade; the motel operator can't rely on the occasional expert angler for a living. Easy fishing attracts crowds, swells the ranks of fishermen, and boosts the economy in that area. It may in fact be that hatchery trout have an economic value greater than that of wild fish.

The initial purpose of the hatchery was to produce very small trout that were expected to reach catchable size after being planted, but that took a long while. Then came the era of catchable fish, which were dumped into rivers or brooks to compete (unsuccessfully) with wild trout. They didn't look much like wild fish, with their hatchery pallor and the streaks and scars of crowded hatchery life, but many of them were a foot long and they were easy to catch.

When these fish are introduced to a large watercourse, they tend to stay very close to the release point, which is usually near a highway bridge or automobile access area. I have found them holding in the same thirty feet of water for several days. Sometimes they are ridiculously easy to catch with flies or lures. It may be heresy to confess it, but I have worked them over a number of times on days when the wild trout were too smart for me. We also used them for motion pictures on a large western river since it was possible to start the camera before a cast was made, with reasonable assurance a fish would strike each time. I've found them less cooperative in hatcheries, when experimenting with hookless flies. My explanation is that the fish in the river had missed a feeding or two and were in a more receptive mood. Also, the current was a little broken and tended to obscure the fisherman and his activities.

The survival rate of such unfortunates is very poor, and the number that actually make it for a year in wild waters is so small as to make the operation appear impractical. Of course, the objective is to have them caught immediately, and biologists simply don't count on much of a carryover. Once there is a successful introduction, however, the supply is then largely controlled by the carrying power of the range, unless fishing pressure is excessive.

The survival of hatchery trout usually depends on the individual hatchery. If its conditions approach those of wild waters, the fish are more likely to survive when planted. But the nearer the hatchery approaches wild conditions, the more expensive the project becomes. The ideal hatchery would produce "wild" trout. Reared fin-to-fin in placid pools, most hatchery trout are short on survival instincts. Tests show that such fish don't bother to hide from predators, have little instinct for safe holding water, and are chased from good feeding spots by wild fish.

What species to produce in hatcheries was also a problem at one time. The rainbow is now the most popular and the easiest to raise in quantity, and that's fine with the casual fishermen who find rainbows easier to catch than brown trout. If the water is suitable, brown trout populations will hold without help from plantings. Evidently an increase of fishing pressure increases the brown's wariness, so the brown is a favorite of the master angler who prefers difficult fish.

Fisermen place great importance on the size of the fish to be caught, but very large fish, especially in smaller streams, are of questionable value. Some fly fishermen advocate the removal of the bigger specimens to make room for fish more likely to take flies. It's more a matter of very large fish preferring something more solid than an insect diet, than a matter of wisdom growing with age. A 10-pound trout taking a number-16 fly from the surface probably expends more energy than the insect is worth to him. He'd rather use that same energy to go after seafood. So the big fish is a cannibal, and this fact gets the brown trout into trouble with some people. A buster brown is no more fish-hungry than any other kind of big trout, but giant fish in small streams are most likely to be browns, simply because of the cagey nature of the species. Some fish biologists who took an annual stream census of a small brook, using a shocking device, turned up the same old female brown in the same area every year and told me she was seventeen years old. The remarkable part was that the water seemed more conducive to 10-inchers. Most of the fish caught in that brook measured less than a foot and it was hard to believe that anything over 10 pounds could live there. When only a few very big trout are found, the immediate conclusion is that cannibalism has created the condition. But there are too many other factors to consider before making any assessments.

The ideal condition would be to have trout of all sizes, indicating regular propagation and growth, but overcrowding in some lakes has led to fish that simply never grow very large. Generally, the little ones are almost too easy to catch, and chances are there will be a few very large ones that are too tough. The same thing happens with black bass, and even the most astute fish manager must admit that "further study is indicated."

There is another interesting factor in trout propagation: Some of the waters that will allow fish to reach great size are not conducive to reproduction, the trouts being highly particular about where they lay their eggs. Some interesting trout fishing is had in the cold waters below large dams—a case of bass water being turned into trout water, as the spillway discharge is too cold for bass. But in some of the best of these rivers the trout reproduction is minimal. In many cases, of course, there were no trout before the dam was built. The cold discharges have produced the float fishing for trout in the Ozarks, usually over what was formerly smallmouth and largemouth bass habitat.

Many misfortunes can befall a fingerling trout, but predation is a natural part of balance. Trout spawn is ideally deposited in gravel and covered so that large predators, such as other trout and sculpins, get very few eggs once the spawning is completed. With minor variations, the procedure for the various species is the same. The spawn is discharged by the female in a nest which she has scooped out with her body and tail, and during the spawning act the fertilizing male is alongside. For a very brief period, there is a chance for another fish to dart into the nest and snatch a few eggs, but the female chases them away when possible and quickly covers the nest when spawning is finished. She brushes the covering gravel in from the sides, mainly from upstream so that the current helps her. After the eggs are covered, the larger predators leave them alone. The gravel-covered eggs can still have their problems though, sometimes being attacked by fungus, or smothered by silt. Some youngsters fail to find their way out of the gravel after hatching, and there is always the chance that a second female will scoop out her own nest in the same spot, thus allowing the first spawn to wash away. In any event, the eggs from a single female may run from a hundred or so into the thousands.

RAINBOW TROUT

Rainbow trout *(Salmo gairdneri)* were native only to the Pacific slope when man got into the act. The original range ran from California to Alaska, but because rainbow eggs are easily transported and because the fish is quite adaptable, it has been planted successfully in every state that has water cold enough to keep it going. It's also found now in Europe, Asia, South America, Australia, New Zealand, and Africa. The water doesn't have to be very cold; the rainbow tolerates more heat than any other trout and can live in temperatures above eighty degrees. Spawning temperatures are always considerably lower.

The steelhead is a rainbow that spends part of its life at sea, and the rainbow is very closely related to the Atlantic salmon, separate evolutions apparently having gotten underway back when the northern part of the continent separated the habitable part of the Atlantic from the Pacific. The Atlantic salmon is more closely related to the steelhead than to the Pacific salmons, which die after spawning.

As either a steelhead or a resident rainbow, this fish has a preference for faster water than other trout. In some cases the preference is so marked that a veteran fisherman can make a good guess as to what kind of fish you'll hook in a given spot of a large river, even though browns, cutthroats, and rainbows live there together. Of course, there are other waters where they all mingle in the same currents as a matter of food selection, but I've seen a few runs in which the feeding stations, too, were almost mathematically predictable.

I've always been deceived by current speed and, like most observers, tend to think it's much faster than it really is. A dry

Home of rainbow trout in Alberta, this coldwater lake is high in the mountains of Jasper National Park.

fly doesn't come down a roaring slot as fast as we expect it to, and some of the foamiest flows can conceal patches of slow water down below.

When we say the rainbow is a fastwater fish, we mean that it prefers to stay in the proximity of fast water and will chase food through fast water. That doesn't mean a rainbow, or any other trout, is going to beat its scales off against a cataract if it can hold where things are quieter. Edward R. Hewitt, probably the most quoted of all trout authorities, conducted an experiment that indicated trout prefer water which moves less than 50 feet per minute, or a little more than one-half mile per hour. Even in the wildest rivers there are places where current is almost stationary. One such spot could be a pocket formed by an underwater boulder with white water roaring over it. From such a lie, a trout can drive out into the main current for very short periods of time, but no fish can swim up a falls all day. The rainbow's maximum effort is actually very short, but possibly it can breast heavy current longer than the other trouts. If so, it must be a stronger fish. That would substantiate a claim that it fights harder than brown trout and in fast water where it keeps in top condition, I believe that it does. I hope a few brown-trout lovers will stay with me anyway.

All fish are individuals, but I believe the rainbow is even less consistent in its fighting qualities than most other fish. I'm not referring now to steelhead in the various stages of their upstream journeys, but to resident trout of fast water and apparently satisfactory temperature. The wildest rainbow that I ever hooked was in the Madison River, near Ennis, Montana, during the annual salmon-fly hatch. Fishing had been wonderful and I had caught a number of big browns during the week, using large dry flies, when just at sundown a rainbow slammed my sofa-pillow pattern and ripped across stream, then jumped an unbelievable distance, roared off again, and finally broke me off. In all honesty, I doubt that he would have weighed three pounds and I blush to confess that the tippet was no cobweb by any means.

It was a week later that Debie caught the sleepiest rainbow I ever saw while she was fishing in Rock Creek, near Missoula. Although we had caught no big ones, the rainbows had shown plenty of steam, offering an opportunity for a beautiful photograph of a leaping fish. I was taking a picture of her casting into fast water against rock bluff when she had a strike, told me it was a good fish, and warned me to be ready. The line went taut and the rod tip bent, but nothing else happened. She then tried to provoke a jump by alternately giving slack and jerking. The fish simply tooled about a small area, so she led it over to shore and it seemed relieved to be scooped up. It weighed three pounds, was brilliantly colored, in excellent condition, and had been living in fast water. It was normally hooked in the jaw with a number-10 Royal Wulff, and was apparently a lover of peace and quiet and confident of being released, which it was.

There is no catalogued physiological difference between the steelhead and the stay-at-home rainbow, but even when the sea is available, some strains of fish don't go to the salt. It is believed all rainbows are descendants of sea travelers. The steelhead seem more active than other rainbows when fresh in from their salt-water tour, but that's true of all ocean-going fish; growth is much more rapid at sea and fresh-run steelies have extra vitality.

Young steelhead go to sea when they're two or three years

old, and return as adults when four, five, or six. Some of them stay close to tidewater for their entire careers; others travel as much as 2,500 miles from their home waters. They've been caught as far west as the farthest Aleutians, and a tagged fish from there was a resident of a Washington river. Two or more returns for spawning can occur, but the dangers of migration and ocean life stack the chances against more than a single return.

As in the case of the Atlantic salmon, the fisher of steelhead deals in a romantic business. He seeks a fish that has run the gauntlet of silted creeks, polluted rivers, the perils of the open sea, deadly commercial fishing, then the pollution again, and a return to an unmarked home by instincts completely beyond present-day science. Most of the Alaskan and Canadian steelhead rivers remain only slightly changed, but father south the big dams have stopped many runs and will stop more. The steelhead that once crowded the streams in southern California are gone.

The steelhead, like the salmons, returns not only to the same coast, but to the same river mouth, to the same creek, and pos-

Dead trees and windfalls make tough fishing in this forest pond. The fish are rainbows.

sibly to the same yards of gravel after years at sea in another kind of life. What is it that leads him to the river mouth from thousands of miles? With eerie precision, returning salmon have been selective even to the very last tinkling fork of the final mountain stream. And when low water has caused an estuary to be blocked by sand and mud, the steelhead have waited in tidewater for a freshet to give them passage. Even when no water trickles through they have waited. There is the possibility they could taste something from underground seepage; a man's hand in the water can change the movements of salmon a hundred yards downstream.

There's strong evidence that taste or odor is the main guidance. Migrating salmon near the heads of streams have been taken down-current and then released, some with their nostrils plugged. Those with plugged nostrils were uncertain about which fork to take as they went back up. With their nostrils open, the other fish chose the same fork they had taken before. Some tests have shown fish can set courses by the sun's location. None of this helps catch a steelhead on a fly, but these marvels are hard to ignore.

Steelhead travel a long way up the rivers. For example, there's excellent steelie fishing in Idaho where they've entered the Columbia River system and come up on the Snake and into lesser known branches. At sea, the steelhead begins to look a great deal like his cousin, the Atlantic salmon, and its bold freshwater spots disappear almost entirely. The pink or red stripe that distinguishes the rainbow in rivers is almost totally absent in the returning fresh-runner and it is in this condition that he is at his violent best on a line.

Then as the fish fights the current it uses some of the fat of its free-feeding ocean days and much of the steam goes out. Far from salt water a steelhead can be a bit sluggish, but that's not the entire story. Given some time to rest, some of the fire comes back, along with the natural red stripe and a darker back.

There are summer steelhead and winter steelhead, but spring is the spawning time for the majority of rainbows. The summer steelhead simply comes in early. Some rivers have easily defined runs of fish. Others have trickles of entries in every month of the year, in addition to heavy runs. It appears steelhead are more inconsistent than either Atlantic or Pacific salmon, adhering less rigidly to schedule. It seems to me that they do more dallying, and it's accepted that they may take a little food now and then. The freshwater fasting of Atlantic salmon, on the other hand, is fairly strict except for a few foreign juices in his stomach, possibly from squeezed insects. The summer steelhead, who is going

Rainbow trout hold in the boulder water of a mountain stream in North Carolina.

to be around for a while before spawning, has a reputation for acting more like a resident and often takes dry flies. Water conditions are likely to be better for that kind of fishing in summer anyway.

There are races of especially large steelheads, not necesarily caught in the largest rivers. For years the Kispiox River in British Columbia has produced contest winners on the fly, and the Babine River seems to have fish that are just as large. Both are part of the Skeena River system and only a few miles apart, and it would seem the main reason for the outstanding record of the Kispiox is that it's more easily available and has been fished hard for years by a corps of dedicated fly anglers. The Babine hasn't been worked by so many competitive fly casters. But the main point about these rivers is that others of the system can't compete in steelhead weight. I guess both the Maurice and the Bulkley have more fish, but they don't run in the same size category. The first time I visited the Kispiox, I fumbled around until the water got dirty (the Kispiox goes up and down like a yoyo) and then went into a sweat, fearing I wasn't going to catch any steelhead at all. The Bulkley was clear (and much prettier, I thought) and we got Helge Byam, of Houston, to take us fishing on his outboard riverboat. I'd come from the modest and murky Kispiox where people were talking about 20-pounders, and here I was on a big, gleaming watercourse of shining riffles and blue pools, with Helge talking about five and six-pound fish. I caught a 10-pounder under his almost occult guidance and then went back to the Kispiox. Two days later it finally cleared enough to give me one big steelhead weighing more than 20 pounds. Helge's eyes got big when I told him about it, for he just hadn't been catching that kind of fish, even though the two rivers were only two hours' drive apart.

Even on a given river there are special years when the fish run larger than usual, apparently the offspring of the hatch of a particular year, and students of the subject can make some sort of prediction about what's going to happen in a given season. When they used to say that "this will be a year of big fish," I didn't listen, but they're frequently right. A good or bad season for the hatch will have its effect five or six years hence, you must remember.

But there's a special lesson in the trip with Helge. He ran his boat for several miles, clearing the shallow rapids with a motor jack. He then beached on a gravel shore where the water ran deep from a pinched-in pool head and spread out into a wide stretch, trimmed in gleaming fall-tinted hardwoods. Fishy as the place looked, it seemed little different from half a dozen such places we'd skimmed over. Helge stood back and gave me first crack at heavy current, so I worked out my fast-sinking shooting head and let the fly swing around, feeling it bounce now and then on the rocky bottom.

"Watch yourself when it swings opposite that dead tree," Helge said. The tree was clear across the wide river, far out of range for any fly caster, and the water between it and my shore looked just like the rest of the pool. It took me twenty minutes to work that far down. And then I felt the nudge down there on the bottom, and the steelhead came up and lunged on top, to be scooped ashore after a few minutes. It had been a matter of forecasting a strike in a certain five feet of two hundred yards of water; if you count the distance we had come by boat it was five feet out of about five miles.

There are obvious reasons for some steelhead lies, but some hotspots can be learned only through experience. On strange water, even a veteran can be wrong about steelhead and he may be better off if there are plenty of other fishermen around. At least he'll know where to fish.

Helge's next demonstration was positively spooky. He ran the boat some more and put me into another pool, one where the rapids came in at an angle and created deep eddies.

"Now, here," Helge said, "you should get a strike, but you'll probably lose him. I can't seem to land fish out of this spot. Hook pulls out after a short run."

Such pronouncements smacked of soft-sell showmanship, but that didn't fit in with Helge's quiet modesty about everything he did and knew. Anyway, after several casts, I had a strike, set the hook hard, and never saw the fish. The hook came loose after a very short run. My only explanation is that the fish lay in some sort of position that made it impossible to hook them solidly. I still try to visualize what goes on down there.

Steelhead tend to lie in heavy water below really steep flows, and the theory is that they're waiting to go on upstream. Somehow, a 20-pound steelhead can find a haven anyplace where there are boulders a foot or more in diameter, and some lies are used year after year. Often the hotspots are just as they were on Helge's Bulkley, only a short piece of a long run that seems about the same from end to end. That's where knowing the water is essential. While you're fishing one pool, the local veteran has hit the hotspots of a dozen.

With all of the talk about fly fishing for steelhead, the feather merchant is in the minority, and in recent years bobber-type lures, on long steelhead rods with spinning or casting reels, seem to be the choice of most experts. They use a lure that bounces along downstream, pegging along just a little above the bottom, with a pencil sinker trimmed to fit the current's speed. Some steelhead flies are tied and fished in frank imitation of the weighted casting lure.

When asked what a certain fly of his was made to represent, Carl Mouser, one of the most successful of steelhead fly anglers,

In an ungraceful but successful landing operation, this fisherman puts a big steelhead on a rocky bar. Most experienced fly fishermen prefer to beach steelhead whenever practicable.

simply said, "A cherry bobber." What does a cherry bobber imitate? Well, drifting salmon eggs, I guess. Anyway, steelhead flies needn't be fancy. We'll look at them in Chapter Nine.

Chances are that the fly fisherman arriving upon a strange steelhead river will take his cue from fishermen using weighted lures. But he should remember one thing that didn't soak into my head for quite a while: the sinker bouncers are working heavy water for the most part, and there will be productive shallower, slower stretches they can't operate in. After I had gone to heavier and heavier flies, in an effort to get my hook clear to the bottom, I found that some of the best fly fishermen for steelhead were using slow-sinking lines and bearing down on the tails of some pools I hadn't even bothered with. Low, clear water is the best for fly-fishing steelhead. In some of the muddy torrents of winter steelheading, the fly fisherman is playing a losing game.

Because the fish were big, I first used a nine-foot saltwater rod and 10 line for steelheading. You need lots of backing, but I think that's more rod than is usually necessary. Distance is more important in this than almost any other kind of fly fishing— simply a matter of getting past the main current. I find most experts are equipped with something like an 8½-footer taking an 8 line. If the flies are very heavy for deep, fast water, you might prefer something a little more potent. It's nice to get a hundred feet with a shooting head and monofilament line, but careful wading and stream study can give much fishing at shorter ranges.

Giant rainbow trout, fish that often resemble steelhead, are caught in lakes. Generally, these big fish are from deep water and fall to trolled lures, but there are times when a sinking line and giant nymphs give fly fishermen their innings. Some of the deep lakes have histories of wild fishing which has fallen off because of some subtle change in the trout's food supply. Rainbows take drys during shoreline hatches on some of these lakes, but most of the fishing is fairly deep, with slowly worked sinking gear.

Regardless of the fly or streamer used, remember the rainbow as preferring the faster water of most trout rivers.

BROWN TROUT

The brown trout *(Salmo trutta)* is the dream fish of thousands of fly fishermen—a trout that moves in the difficult streams of waving water growth and a thousand kinds of insects. The brown is a fly taker and looks upward at the surface when other fish are grubbing on the bottom. It grows large amid a forest of waders and clumsy lures.

A good stretch of brown-trout water in Michigan. Logs at upper left will dig a holding pocket as current gouges at gravel bottom.

Its liking for a dry fly is perhaps the most important of the brown's characteristics. Much of its appeal, however, comes from the knowledge that small and gentle streams hold giants that are seldom seen, but which might accept a fly if the hatch is matched, the float perfect, and the angler cautious. These old cannibals may take their share of lesser fish, but there is something about their presence—the giant bulge at dusk, the bulky shadow against the rotting stump, the heavy splash in darkness. . . .

It's seldom that a record fish will rise to a number 16 dry fly, but three-pound browns take them frequently. It's safe to say that the brown will generally take floating insects later in life than will other trout. But the brown is the hardest of all trout to catch because he is the product of centuries of selective breeding that enabled browns to thrive in Europe, where they developed the fly fishing we know today largely with that one species in mind. When the German brown trout (or Loch Leven—depending upon where the plantings came from) was brought to the United States almost a hundred years ago, it took to the wilderness streams with enthusiasm. It made an even better showing in the hard-fished waters of populous communities, and it brought finesse to America's fly fishing.

The brown's love for submerged hiding places, such as deeply undercut banks and log jams, places a premium on casting ability, and once a fish is hooked there's likely to be a tackle-tearing plunge for hiding. The big browns are strongly territorial when living in small water. I don't know how long an individual will live against a given bank, through flood and drought, winter and summer, but some big ones have been seen for years and they do break a lot of tackle. Sometimes you come to the dilemma of only getting a rise with a tippet that has no chance of stopping the quarry.

The big brown in the little brook can become an institution. I used to fish a little cow-pasture creek with plenty of 10-inch trout and apparently nothing bigger. You could step across the brook in most places and you did your casting well back from the ten-foot pools to keep from being seen; wading created too much disturbance. Long after I thought I knew all about the creek, I happened to notice a shady pool a little farther upstream than I'd ever gone. It was deep on one side, where tree roots overhung an undercut, and several dead limbs had jammed there.

I made my first cast a full 10 feet from the tree roots, and a brown trout larger than any I'd seen in the creek came out so fast he was a blur of yellow-bronze. He struck in a quick turn, broke me off, and was back under the bank almost instantly—a clear case of a fish leaving what he knew was security and wanting back there in a hurry. That's a far different performance from the usual take of a small fly by a large fish, but it must have worked well for him. Evidently it was his feeding routine, however unusual. I saw no other trout in the pool.

A week later I came back, stalked the pool with great care, and put a dry fly in exactly the same place. The fish flashed out in the same way, and this time I landed him, although he almost made it home against rod bend and leader stretch. I'd like to say he weighed four pounds, but it was less than three—a good fish, nevertheless, in a creek noted for nothing larger than 10 inches. It's unusual for a fish to come that far and fast for a fly, but he was a special fish or he wouldn't have been that large in that puddle. I could reasonably expect him to do nearly the same thing a second time.

Brown trout spawn in the fall or early winter, for the most part, and large fish, both males and females, are extremely active when the water takes on an autumn chill. The best bet for large browns on a fly rod is on good-sized rivers in the fall. Because many fishermen have adopted steelhead equipment for this fishing, complete with sinking line and monofilament backing, the scores on large fish are much better than they were a few years back. It is only during the past ten years that the sinking line has been widely adopted for streamer fishing, but now the fly users are getting big fish that formerly fell to bait or hardware. On large western rivers the water is at good fishing level when brown trout make spawning moves, and it is still warm enough then to fish comfortably.

Of late, deep fishing with big streamers has become such an attraction that a lot of good dry-fly water goes begging at that time of year. Dry flies work in many streams as late as Thanksgiving, even as far north as Idaho, Wyoming, and Montana. For that matter, there are some hatches all winter long.

Brown trout go to sea in many parts of the world, are then

Fishing a big streamer in late fall, Red Monical lands a big brown trout on the upper Missouri River, near Helena, Montana.

known as seatrout, and evidently return, salmonlike, to freshwater streams for spawning. They do not seem to have a wide range in salt water, however, and it appears many of them go no farther than the estuaries of their home rivers.

Like other trout, the browns travel upstream for much of their spawning, but do not insist upon the very small streams that brook trout prefer. They like spring-fed tributaries and will spawn in water from six inches to two feet deep. The incubation period is about a month in typical water, where temperature ranges in the upper fifties. Thus their spawning time and incubation period are similiar to brook trout. They can live in water slightly above 80 degrees (slightly cooler than the upper limit claimed for the ubiquitous rainbow) but they do not fare well in cold water and introductions in high lakes have not proved practical. In some such places, the introduction of brown trout has damaged brook trout populations; the browns though apparently unable to prosper in large numbers, were still capable of reducing a brookie population.

On some large rivers, the fall movements take large brown trout upstream from the deep impoundments where they have spent the summer, and the gravelly creek mouths are good places for large streamers. When a lake has small creeks, their mouths may be excellent spots as cool weather comes on. The big-streamer fishing of late fall is usually done in heavy water, but there is also a tendency for prespawning browns to busy themselves about wide and placid pool tails. Evidently they are prospecting for spawning sites, whether they actually leave eggs there or not.

When main streams are muddy with runoffs or heavy rains, the browns tend to seek clear water in backwaters and tributary creeks. The other trout do this too, but browns seem to go farther into sloughs and ditches. Many fishermen who do well in those spots in early season do not realize they are fishing the only water in good condition and drawing upon a supply of fish that have withdrawn from a muddy river. When the rivers clear, the creek populations will thin.

The brown does not always jump when fighting the hook, but he is capable of high and wide ones. He is more prone to hunt cover than is the rainbow, and big fish are especially good at nosing down behind a bottom boulder and shaking their heads violently. I suppose all trout do this occasionally, but the brown is master of the art.

I have always felt a fully colored brown trout, with bright red spots and golden belly, is as handsome as any fish I ever caught, but most writers consider it too drab to compare with brookies and rainbows. Perhaps affection for the fish and its temperament affects my judgment. Also, the brown is considered less desirable food. That depends upon the water it's caught in and what it's been feeding on. It's difficult to rank fish as to table qualities unless they all come from the same creek.

GOLDEN TROUT

Golden trout *(Salmo aguabonita)* strike no harder, fight no longer, and require no more skill than any other trout, but they are hard to reach and are associated with the creak of saddle leather and the thin air of the peaks. The remoteness of their habitat is, however, the greatest part of their appeal.

It is difficult to consider a golden trout as "just another fish" after you have trudged or ridden through a mountain thunderstorm, crossed a tilted meadow of high-country wildflowers, and watched a herd of elk melt into a timbered canyon in the process of reaching him. When you finally come upon his home—either a bouncing mountain brook or a bright lake reflecting the moods of a mountain sky—you are prepared for no ordinary fish. And when you gingerly work out your line at a lakeshore, looking apprehensively over your shoulder at the whorls of grotesque little white pines that seem to reach for your leader, and then lay your fly well out, just past the dropoff, you expect nothing ordinary.

Fishing a high, hike-in lake in the Rockies. In such areas of year-round snow, several states have planted golden trout.

The fish comes up out of blue water, past the shelf, and takes the fly like a burning blade, more brilliant than you thought he would be, and when you have him at the shore, you hold him as if he might shatter in the air, and wonder how long the color will stay if you keep him to have for lunch.

It is very satisfying to release a golden trout. But he *is* just a trout and, once you find him, in most of his waters he isn't particularly hard to catch if you can reach him with a fly or nymph.

The goldens were discovered when they were confined to a small section of the High Sierras at the head of the Kern River in California. They have since been introduced successfully to high mountain lakes over most of the western states. They're red, gold, white, and black, so there's little doubt of identification once you get to one. It's natural for almost any fisheries man to attempt to plant them at lower levels but, as far as I know, the colors are lost almost immediately. The golden hybridizes freely, so if you want to see him at his flashy best you'll have to climb the mountain.

They've been known to get quite large, more than ten pounds, but that's under ideal conditions which aren't often encountered. Most goldens are quite small because they live in places with short growing seasons and spartan diets, but even though the fish are small you may need considerable rod on high lakes. The wind can tear your shirt and the fish have a habit of nosing along just out of reach and in plain sight. A lake that supports trout at 10,000 feet or so has to be pretty deep. There are times when a sinking line and a woolly worm or a nymph can save the day. They usually take small dries and wets avidly, but I've seen them very shy after a little too much human activity around the borders of a lake.

CUTTHROAT TROUT

The cutthroat *(Salmo clarki)* was there to meet the pioneers of the Rockies and is the true native there. I don't know that the numbers have decreased so much since then, but the sizes have. There are so many documents concerning the native trout that

Cutthroat trout too big for his basket attract a fisherman on the upper Yellowstone River where the water is too fast to wade.

"averaged four or five pounds" that we simply cannot put it down as the exaggeration of the good old days.

Many cutthroats remain but they don't withstand the competition of other trout too well. Crosses between rainbow and cutthroat have both the pink stripe and a hint of the blood-red throat. The cutthroat will also cross with the golden trout, being adaptable to high altitudes and chill waters.

It takes flies well, and although it does not have the reputation of the brown trout for shyness, I see very little difference in their selectivity when found in the same water. I do not consider it a particularly active fighter as it rarely jumps, and even the rainbow-cutthroat crosses tend to stay in the water when hooked. Nevertheless, two trips of mine illustrate the charm of fishing for cutthroat which, like the golden, usually live in spectacular country.

In midsummer, three of us crawled into the Seven Mile Hole

of Yellowstone Canyon. The river was a crashing storm of water and we cast big dry flies wherever we could find a patch of surface calm enough to float them. It was a carefully chosen time; Johnny Bailey and Ben Williams had gauged the trip to meet a hatch of stone flies which had been moving progressively up the river for weeks and was about to peter out in the high cataracts. Our flies were cast from along the edge mainly—there was hardly any place to wade—and the fish took willingly. We kept them out of the heavy current, which had a visible slant and was largely white, and had little trouble. The fish went up to two pounds.

Williams had made the trip before at that time of year and said the fish were likely to be climbing small tributary streams to spawn. (The spawning times of the various cutthroats seem to vary greatly, and there are numerous subspecies.) While I stuck with the main river, I saw him climbing what appeared to be a waterfall—a series of pockets with vertical plunges of white water between them. When I heard him yell, I turned to see his rod bent and a fish plunging down through the series of pools. He stopped it in one of them and picked up his two-pounder in what seemed a completely impossible spot for anything more than a fingerling.

The next time I visited Yellowstone National Park for cutthroat it was well into the fall. My wife and I went with Don Williams, a Montana guide who has a preference for high-country cutthroats. This time it was big woolly worms, drifted near the bottom in a deep run beside a highway, and the fish took with slow pulls. Again they were averaging near two pounds. While we shivered a little in spite of our waders, wool, and insulation, a mountain snowstorm turned the whole scene to monochrome. There would be no action for half an hour, and then a series of strikes over a ten-minute period. Williams said that was typical of the spot.

Cutthroats go to sea but evidently stay close to their home estuaries. There is good reason why they are primarily wilderness fish since, except for the sophisticates of a few valley streams, they do not withstand fishing pressure well.

BROOK TROUT

No longer necessarily an easterner, the brook trout *(Salve-linus fontinalis)* lives almost anywhere in America that the water is suitable, but such water is getting hard to find, for it must be cold, pure, and preferably remote. Like the Dolly Varden, the brookie is a char.

Most of the fly fishing for brook trout is in small water, and most of the fish are small within the United States. However, there are still big fish in Canada, and possibly untouched populations in Labrador. Originally, the fish was distributed from the Arctic Circle south to northern Georgia and west to the beginnings of the Mississippi. Although it prospers in tiny ponds or creeks, the brookie population is hard to regulate. It is prone to explosions that create swarms of tiny fish that attack flies in squadrons. It takes severe predation to keep the numbers down and the size up.

Brook trout are deeper feeders than others of the tribe, and most of the real whoppers that come from Canada are caught on hardware; but big streamers have worked too. There is a charm to brookie fishing, especially in narrow brooks and aging beaver ponds, but fish of more than a pound are unusual except in nearly untouched water. If they are plentiful the fishing becomes a little too easy in most places.

Maine is the favored spot for the brookie, but some of the Maine waters are tiny, willowed brooks where a backcast is a disaster and travel is as much crawling as wading. But there are also the dark, boggy ponds where the fish have especially brilliant color. A brookie rise on a Maine pond can be thrilling, even when the fish is small, and Paul Fournier showed me a spot near Jackman where the evening show was as profuse as raindrops. Our canoe stopped the feeding only in a narrow path as we cast a number-16 mosquito over a shallow, muddy bottom and hooked fish that came in reckless charges.

Brookies spawn in fall. Those found in brackish water ("salters") evidently do not make long migrations and do not reach the size of the steelhead and the sea-going brown trout.

Water temperature is a severely limiting factor in brook trout habitat. Their upper limit is about 75 degrees, which is colder than the limit for any of the other trout.

DOLLY VARDEN

The Dolly Varden *(Salvelinus malma)* is not an important fly fish. It is a char with none of the glamour of its relative, the brookie. It is also a close relative of the Arctic char. It swarms in some Alaskan waters, has been accused of overpredation on the

Very narrow, but deep, brook is fished for trout in the West. Note that angler stands well back, out of sight of the fish. Both wet and dry flies are satisfactory, and patterns that resemble terrestrials are especially good.

more valued salmon and salmon eggs, and has even been the object of a bounty in Alaska.

Sea-run Dollies are plentiful along the Alaska coast. Its range includes the western coast from northern California northward, and it is also found on some parts of the Asiatic coast. It fights about the same as the brook trout when hooked but it's usually sought with coarse tackle. Wherever I have fished for Dollies, they seemed to prefer hardware to feathers.

LAKE TROUT

Lake trout *(Salvelinus namaycush)* are more likely to take deeply trolled spoons than flies. They are primarily fish-eaters rather than insect-takers, but they have provided good streamer fishing in some lakes in the far North, where temperatures are low enough to keep them near the surface. Just after ice-out, they are caught on streamers in some lakes farther south, but the time is critical and short.

GRAYLING

The grayling *(Thymallus arcticus)* is a novelty fish for fly casters. Writers turn toward poetry in describing its grace and beauty. Its scarcity adds glamour.

It is primarily an insect feeder, has a small, almost sucker-like mouth, and is a ready taker in most of the streams where it appears. Its colors are more subtle than those of trout, and the huge dorsal fin, larger in males than in females, is a delicately tinted flag. I want to go into this grayling business a little because my experiences are a little different from some of the reports I've heard and read.

The Montana grayling, the only one presently found in the contiguous states, is the same as the Arctic model as far as I can tell, and I've heard the same thing from fisheries men. If there are any differences, they don't affect fishing methods. The Montana grayling is present in more areas of the state than is commonly believed, due to successful plantings.

If you want grayling, the chances are a Montana fish biologist can direct you to them. When I first looked for grayling I made a couple of false starts, as a few plantings have strangely disappeared. The first ones we caught were near the beginnings of the Big Hole River. Historical accounts indicate they were thick among the trout and whitefish on numerous Montana rivers in 1886, but the whitefish have prospered and the grayling receded. Most fly fishermen now consider the whitefish as trash and the grayling as a special prize when caught among trout.

There's also a European grayling, which is found over much

of that continent—almost anyplace where the water is cold and pure enough, and a Michigan grayling, now extinct.

The Michigan story is strange. In 1882 a paper by Dr. J. C. Parker of Grand Rapids stated that there were no brook trout in the lower peninsula twenty-five years before that time and that

An Alaska grayling, hooked on a hairwinged dry fly, hangs in shallow current.

the fishing until then had been for grayling. When the grayling finally disappeared, it appears to have been replaced by brookies, but the barrels of grayling taken home by eastern fly fishermen probably didn't help the population. Anyway, brook trout and grayling have similar requirements in habitat.

There's no shortage of grayling in Alaska and much of Canada. They are a school fish and can sometimes be seen in shoals just offshore of deep, clear lakes.

Grayling jump freely when hooked but lack the power of

either trout or whitefish. I mention whitefish in particular because Rocky Mountain whitefish often feed on the surface in dimpling pods, the same as the grayling, and I've caught the two together. The whitefish pull harder but hardly ever jump.

Wherever I've made inquiry about grayling, I've run into what amounts to a wet-black-gnat syndrome. The local people nearly always say to fish a black gnat deep, but I've usually done better with dry flies on the streams. Pattern hasn't seemed important, although anything big is hard for the grayling to take.

I have also had innumerable missed strikes on certain days, a confession which has caused me to be viewed suspiciously by many good fly fishermen who obviously feel my missed strikes were whitefish. (Whitefish are hard to hook most of the time, probably because of their very small mouths and a sucking approach.) But I've missed grayling that I could see plainly, and I think half of the misses weren't true takes at all, simply a matter of a fish splashing around my fly in curiosity. The grayling has a distracting habit of following a floating fly while inspecting it carefully. There have been occasions when they've insisted that the fly drag sloppily before they'd strike—a disgusting situation for someone who has made a career of trying to get perfect floats.

On the very large Teslin River in Yukon Territory, Les

The late Mert Parks, well-known Rocky Mountain fisherman, employs a log raft to fish a mountain lake for grayling.

Allen, an astute river guide, took my wife and me to a small riffle out of the main current and told us to fish our dries in the broken water. We would get follows on nearly every cast, but the fish refused to strike until the fly dragged. A little later in the day he told us to try deep slicks because there would be some hatching flies. There we caught fish on conventional floats, the grayling coming up from blue depths, their big dorsals spread, and striking in plain sight.

On the Pine River in British Columbia, I had special difficulty with small pods of grayling which splashed around my drys but took rarely. I caught fish but certainly didn't cover myself with glory. In other streams I have had no difficulty at all, as long as the flies were small.

Grayling are exceptionally fine to eat. Although there have been specimens in the four to five-pound class, that's very rare. A 15-inch fish is a good one everywhere I've fished. The grayling is, as I said, a novelty and thus a sort of bonus for most of us, but there aren't many serious grayling-chasers in this country.

EIGHT

Dry Flies and Nymphs

DRY-FLY AND NYMPH fishing are not necessarily the most difficult ways of taking trout but they are studied more than any other methods of catching any kind of fish. Either can provide simple fishing in some cases, but the depth of study possible is virtually endless. If any fisherman thinks he has solved every problem of a specific stream, all he need do is go to another watercourse and start over.

Definitions are almost endless, but most dry flies are meant to float without manipulation from the rod. The purest form of nymph fishing follows the same principle, except that the nymph is under water and generally out of sight. The least technical of the dry-fly operations comes on broken water with big flies, some of which do not imitate specific insects. Perhaps we can say the simplest form of nymph fishing is drifting a large one along the bottom on heavy water, after casting into the current from the side. There is overlap between nymph fishing and wet-fly fishing, but while some wet-fly fishing is crude, some nymph fishing is the most delicate of all.

Most dry flies represent a fresh hatch of insects that have

discarded the nymphal shuck and are floating on the surface before flying away. Most nymphs represent the insect before it turns into a fly and, technically, a wet fly represents a drowned insect that has died after eggs are deposited. All of this is over-simplification, however, because dry flies can represent terrestrial insects that are in the water by accident, or a mature insect that has realighted on the water to deposit eggs. Nymphs and wet flies can even represent each other if fished in certain ways.

Fishing a dry fly to individual rising fish is more complex than blind casting. This is true not only because some accuracy is required, but because the object is to show the fly naturally to the fish, in a specific location, without scaring him with line and leader. The perfect presentation and strike would entail seeing a given fish taking a given insect, and then matching that insect in color, size, and appearance on the water. The fish would take it exactly as he had been taking natural flies.

If a fish has been taking natural flies with gentle sucking or mild plops and then takes yours with a "smashing strike" or a "wild rush," your triumph is sullied. He has obviously recognized your fly as being something entirely different from what he has been feeding on. You've made him grab something but you haven't fooled him in the classic way.

After endless arguing, it is agreed that fish have good eye-sight, can discern colors, and can hear sounds outside the water. Since fish have such broad peripheral vision, with only a little blind spot behind them, it becomes important to know just how they see things on the surface, where your fly and the natural insects are floating.

To begin with, because of the refraction of light through water, a fish sees objects on the surface only through a cone of vision. A fish can see a surface object at an angle of no more than $48\frac{1}{2}$ degrees from the vertical. Fly fishermen call this cone of clear surface vision the fish's "window." Theoretically, he can get a clear view of anything within his window. The deeper he lies, the larger the window. As he approaches the surface, the size of the window decreases. All of the surface beyond his window in

Perfect dry-fly water in a spring-fed creek where the constant flow permits shoals of vegetation. Such streams are extremely fertile, with very high insect populations.

any direction acts like a mirror and reflects the bottom, or anything between the bottom and the surface, providing the water is clear enough.

None of these facts is earth-shaking but they are the basis of many assumptions about why fish strike or don't strike. Many fly dressers place great emphasis on the fly's approach to the window and the period of time when part of the fly (wings or hackle) is visible above the window's edge and part of it is seen only as punctures in the reflective surface outside the window.

As he delves deeper into the business of fooling a trout, the fly designer usually proceeds on the assumption that the fish window is a place of perfect vision. The deflating truth is that the surface is hardly ever perfectly smooth and that many triumphs occur when the fish has a pretty wiggly view of your creation. Most of us know that, short of boiling foam and spray, the more distorted the surface, the better the chance of getting a strike. There is another disturbing fact: None of the successful flies really look much like the real insect, except as to size and color, and some really faithful plastic reproductions have made poor flies. So we have to confess that the obvious fakes must either pique the fish's curiosity and appetite, catch him in an unguarded moment, or arrive when, for some reason, he can't get a good look before he makes a fatal move.

The properly presented dry fly comes downstream, and the

fish rises to meet it. He may start up when all he sees is the indention or puncture of the surface film, caused by hackles (or body, if no hackles are used below the hook). I submit that he may strike without ever getting a better view of the thing. As he comes up, the window pinches down, and the fly may stay outside the zone of perfect vision right up until it's too late. I am sure of this in some circumstances when a fish is right at the surface, with his dorsal breaking the water, and taking several flies in a single rise. Remember that his eyes are practically in the film, and as he opens his mouth he's in a poor attitude to study something on top.

The classic dry-fly drift, on a completely calm surface, would first show him the little specks or "explosion" of light coming through the mirror of the surface, well outside his window. He would then wait until the fly was beginning to enter the window, or had entered it, before rising or refusing. This makes a good argument for wings or high hackle atop any dry fly. The wings would show in the window before the rest of the fly could be seen and they might tip the scale to a strike without much further examination by the victim. It's easier to fool a fish in shallow water, providing you don't scare him, because he has a small window. It's very tough on very slow, deep pools.

Most of the smaller dry flies are tied to represent mayflies, which sit with their wings high and dry in preparation for flight, but I've often hooked selective fish when the artificial wasn't sitting upright. Things can happen to a real mayfly, and many of the naturals taken are tipped over, half drowned, or otherwise imperfect.

The "no-hackle fly," successfully designed by Doug Swisher and Carl Richards (they wrote a highly perceptive book about it), presents a fairly solid body to the fish, unsupported by hackle legs. The theory is that the fish looks at a real body, instead of a vague and fanciful outline of hackles, and the flies are very productive. Some of the bushier hackles are primarily for the purpose of floating the fly, but no-hackle flies are dependent upon highly buoyant body material (often dubbing). Some of them have high and well-formed wings, which add to the illusion and increase visibility for the fisherman.

LONG AND SHORT FLOATS

The ideal cast shows the fly to the fish before the leader passes his lie. Most dry flies are cast upstream, above the fish, usually from well off to one side. This is where the battle of drag comes in, the object being to throw the line and leader so that intervening currents don't make the fly show the pull of the leader. The more confused the currents, the more confused the fisherman, and careful casting position is so important that the rule of never using the rod to replace the waders is a good one. After you've scared a fish silly with poor floats, it's too late in most cases, to get him with a perfect presentation.

Most casters endeavor to use the longest dragless float possible, but the longer the float the more chance of error, the more likelihood of too much slack line, and the more possibility of a sloppy pickup. If several fish are rising near to each other, the long float may get one that is far upstream of the one you're casting to, but many an upstream fish is scared by efforts aimed at one farther down. The best plan is to work upstream, taking the fish as they come as long as the risers, or their surface disturbances, are plainly visible. The ideal cast puts the fly down just above where the fish is likely to notice it. Fish that are moving about a great deal may have too much time to examine long floats. If a fish tends to stay up near the top in taking several flies at one trip, a very short float works better for me. And when he's in scant inches of water the ideal cast lands pretty close to his nose, like a fly that has taken off and then landed again. One very productive fisherman, Chester Marion, does not throw curves but depends primarily on accuracy and short, perfect floats.

There are three very important spots: The place where the fish first sees a floating insect; the place where he actually intercepts it; and the place where he lies waiting for his food. He may change his procedure now and then, and when the fish is invisible many a cast is directed near the widening circle of his last rise.

Boulder water makes long floats difficult. Here, current is about to take slack out of an upstream dry-fly cast.

Water does move, however, and the circle may have drifted downstream so far that the artificial lands below the fish.

Fishing with small flies to individual rising fish is one of the most advanced forms of fly fishing, so it may seem that we're setting the cart before the horse. But once you understand what such trout are doing, you'll subconsciously apply your knowledge to trout that are not rising. You'll do your blind casting to selected areas and with specific purpose and you'll have a long head start toward catching fish anywhere.

It's impossible to receive too much advice, but you must sort it out to fit your situations. It's possible to become bogged down in unusual methods practiced by successful veterans, and there is a pitfall in skipping basic approaches. Unfortunately, an expert who has spectacular success with a pet method is likely to be such a good fisherman that he could catch fish with freak flies, poorly matched equipment, and unconventional approaches. He may unintentionally give sketchy instructions and omit some of the most important things. If you develop a good presentation, you'll catch fish almost anywhere with slight adaptations to specific situations.

READING THE RISE

A trout makes all sorts of surface disturbances, and these have often been classified into rise forms by careful observers. The beginner usually assumes that any fish disturbing the surface film is taking dry flies. When I started dry-fly fishing, I nearly broke my arm trying to catch fish on dries when they were nymphing, eating fresh water shrimp, or even chasing minnows. I still spend a lot of time figuring out what they're doing.

Since all the rise forms have variations, I won't try to list them in numerical order but I may be able to help with some general observations:

A very small trout is likely to make a spattering strike upon even a small fly. To him, the prize is worth an all-out attack, and he hits it the way a bigger fish might take a five-inch frog. He may jump clear out of the water and come down on an insect that is matched by a number-16 fly. You soon learn to classify these fingerling charges and leave them alone if you're after bigger game.

A larger trout will often take a small dry fly by simply opening his mouth and letting the fly and a quantity of water come in, as he hangs almost stationary in the current. It is a quiet take and makes only a circle on the stream. The fly goes down his gullet, and the water goes out through his gills, in a separation process known only to fish. Any air bubbles are also discharged through the gills as the fly goes down. It is sometimes hard to tell if he has taken a high-floating dry or something in the surface film. Sometimes he sucks the fly in and, if he does it quickly, the roof of his mouth can produce an audible plop. Fish that are feeding rapidly make more plops because they are moving more when they take the insects. Sometimes their dorsal fins and tails show as they move along the surface. Such fish should be receptive because they must have a poor surface view of what they're eating.

The sucking business sometimes means they are "smutting" (getting very tiny stuff from a surface film). There are some fish, affectionately called "slurpers" in the West, which take large quantities of already drowned flies that are so small no one could match them with an artificial. When Gene Decker, of Colorado, was showing me how to catch them, he used a fairly large fly that looked nothing like the tiny targets.

"This fly," grinned Gene, "represents a clump of little flies."

It seemed to work.

A "bulge" is simply a hump of water that rises up as a fish comes near the surface, and it usually means he's taking nymphs near the top. He may not break water at all, but leave just a circle on calm water. If the water is very shallow, or he comes very close to the top as he takes, his tail may break the surface and look much like a dry-fly rise. Sometimes he'll "tail," with his tail actually sticking out for several seconds or longer, usually when he's grubbing nymphs from the bottom, or picking them from submerged vegetation.

A flash below a floating fly generally means an inspection and a startled refusal. A splash on the surface may drown a fly and be no take at all. Atlantic salmon consider this a pleasant pastime on some days. The fish may be playing. More likely it is excited, but unconvinced the fly is good to eat.

A fast V on the surface means a fish chasing something just below it. It sometimes occurs when there is actual competition for a floater. Such competition is not common in quiet streams, where the various risers usually have their own territories.

When there's a plentiful hatch of natural flies, a busily feeding fish usually establishes a rhythm in his rises. He will take a fly or two and then sink, with something of a wriggle. It looks like a little wiggle of ecstasy but it's probably got something to do with getting the fly down into his engine room for digestive purposes. He will then drop to his feeding station for a little while before coming up again. It is leisurely feeding, and I suppose the time spent between rises is for resting, as fish simply aren't built for long, sustained activity. "Coming up like clockwork" is an accurate description because the rises are almost exactly spaced in some cases. In other instances, the fish comes up in irregular patterns and rises only when the insect floats exactly where he wants to take it. It seems to me that the fish which rises at regular intervals is more likely to stay near the top for two or more flies. I firmly believe I have seen them head back toward the surface simply because it was time to take again, and with no particular fly in sight. This rhythm of feeding can be a deadly weapon for a good caster. When he figures it's time for his fish to come up again, he simply presents the fly at the opportune moment. When a fish is in plain sight (an uncommon but happy situation), you will notice he often shifts his position just before rising. As he shifts, you cast. Some fishermen are strongly against casting between the proper rise times because it gives the fish a chance to study a fly he has no intention of taking. That's cutting it pretty fine.

I know fishermen who have caught far more than their share of trout in lakes by careful time-and-distance operations. During a heavy hatch on a lake in Michigan, one fish biologist managed to have his fly in the right place most of the time. Fish were rising all around his boat, and he would pick out a worthy individual, mark its direction carefully, and note the distance between the rises (since lake fish usually move about as they feed). He would then estimate the exact spot where the fish should come up next, and cast his fly there. His friends thought he was lucky.

Angler works furiously to get tight line on a trout that has taken a dry fly and then dropped downstream in swift, shallow water.

In moving water, the fish generally goes forward to meet the fly and often slows as he gets close to it, evidently to make sure of his aim. By the time he has taken it, he has usually drifted back a little, so he then slides forward slightly to sink to his original station. Most of this is done with a minimum of effort, although there are more energetic fish that cover a wide area and will go off to one side for several feet after a particular fly. If the hatch is sparse, a hungry fish will cover a much larger area, of course.

During a heavy hatch, I have seen individual fish move to the very edge of the stream, where water barely covers their backs. Out of the heavy current, they are able to collect flies with a minimum of effort, simply tipping up and moving slightly to collect them. This water is often so calm that the fish don't even face upstream all of the time. Since their vision is very limited by their nearness to the surface, they are easily deceived by imperfect flies or nymphs but they feel insecure in so exposed a spot, and a poor cast may send them back to deep water.

A hatch of flies can be too heavy; you may find yours just one of a crowd drifting over fish that have no incentive to take anything which doesn't look just right. Fishing is often better near the beginning of a hatch than at the height of the action, simply because the fish are still looking for flies and not yet full. A straggling fish that rises when the hatch is nearly over may be an easy mark. It's tough when several kinds of flies are hatching at once and the one you match carefully isn't the preferred model. A fly the fish fed on yesterday may be ignored today because there's another hatch that tastes better. When this happens you may need binoculars to tell just what they're actually taking. And there is the really frustrating time when trout insist on taking near-surface nymphs, just before they hatch, and ignore the hatched flies. Your drys won't work there, but you may spend some time learning what's happening.

No one hooks all the trout that rise to a dry fly, even when they're good-sized fish and seem to take solidly. The angle of approach and the leader are prime reasons for these misses. For example, a fish that comes to a fly whose leader extends straight downstream can hit the leader with his nose and abort the strike. When a fly is drifted straight downstream from an upstream rod, it can be pulled straight out of a striker's mouth. The ideal situation is a take made a little from the side, so that the hook is pulled into a corner of the jaw.

Some of the most sophisticated trout have a weakness that wilder fish don't. Although your trout from heavily fished waters may be extremely selective, having been hooked and caught several times, he can learn to have little fear of fishermen and their waders. This means you may continue to cast over such learned fish long after a wilder one would be under a rock. I guess "forgiving" is the best word for it. On some of the toughest trout waters, a sloppy pickup or ploughing fly will put the fish down for only a short while. They've seen all these mistakes many times before and they're used to stumbling fishermen. On some such streams, you can stand for an hour in the same tracks and continue to have targets. Best of all, you can make a sloppy cast or two, and work fifty times over the same fish, and then have him take when things look just right. Not all choosy trout are like that, however, and I suppose it takes plenty of conditioning. By contrast, wilder trout may be more susceptible to a poorly dressed or presented fly but may call it quits for the day if you make a single really bad cast.

It's a deceptive situation when you wade into a heavily fished stream, locate a rising fish, and get a swirl from him on the first try. On the next cast he may follow the fly downstream until it drags. Then you change flies, and he shows interest again but won't strike. He simply goes back to feeding on naturals at his regular stand, and you continue to put casts over him without driving him down. The unhappy truth is that he knows you're there, is probably able to tell your flies from the real ones, but isn't disturbed enough to stop feeding. It can make for a tough trip, and you'd do better to leave him and find a new fish.

Many fine fishermen never cast where they can see fish plainly, but if you ever have an opportunity to watch fish take flies, don't pass it up. You learn rapidly and you can apply your experience to years of fishing when no trout is sighted before the strike.

When you do see rising fish and can get one to take your artificial exactly as he has been taking naturals, you are fooling him. If he does it differently, he's mistaken your fly for a "stranger," but his friends may not.

EASIER WATER

There are excellent trout streams where you'll never notice a concerted rise, either because there is none or because the water is too turbulent. The easiest dry-fly fishing is in broken water where fish are looking for targets of opportunity. Although in this case fly selection may be critical, the fly need not represent a specific insect so closely. Many of the most successful patterns represent nothing in particular.

Almost invariably, the dry fly used in rough water is larger than one used on quiet streams, partly because the fisherman can't see a little one and partly because the fish can't see it. Visibility for the fisherman is important, and some of the best rough-water flies, in addition to being very buoyant and having bushy hackles, have very bright wings or are nearly white on the upper side. Where the "small" fly of rough water may be a 10, the small dry of placid brooks may be as small as a 22 in special cases, and possibly even smaller. Most of us can see a 16, and that's the point where visibility gets rugged, especially if there's a heavy hatch of naturals. I go to anything smaller than 18 with reluctance, unless visibility is ideal. I have heard fine fishermen say they retire from the field if a 16 fly on a 6X leader won't handle it.

Brook fishermen are often appalled by the roar and rush of big rivers, convinced they'll need long casts and special techniques. The gimmick is to break the big river down to the size you want —by looking for splits, backwaters, tributaries, and long side channels. A bar that runs part way across a wide river often has breaks which provide little creeks within a big river, with deep eddies below them. The late Merton Parks, of the Yellowstone,

Dry-fly fisherman works a brushy bank on a placid valley stream. This water moves slowly, but currents can be erratic because of underwater vegetation.

was a master at making small water of big water and caught countless fish with short casts while less productive casters heaved for the middle.

Rough water doesn't require the finesse of the placid brook, but remember that the fish still lie facing upstream, that they don't want to fight a cataract all day, and that logical lies can be located easily. The fish is near the current, and the edges of anything are logical places—edges of heavy current, edges of the eddies below boulders, edges of the cover at the banks, and edges of the undercuts.

If it's harder in rough water to get a perfect float, remember it's also harder for a fish to detect a poor one. When working a choppy run from below, do so gradually. Don't lengthen line in order to fish the heads of runs before you've checked the water between you and the beginning of things. After you've made 15 casts up past a fish, dragged your line over him 15 times, and made 15 pickups under his nose, it's a little late to approach him with finesse.

Choppy water at the head of a pool doesn't mean there's no quiet water containing fish. Clumping approaches to shallow pool tails may leave you standing where the fish were before you tore things up. A common failing is to approach a strange spot with one ideal cast in mind and to ignore the less appetizing tails of the pools. Maybe there are good fish there. If there are only small ones, they may stage a frantic flight that scares the ones you want. A few casts at the unlikely spots take little time and will get you a lot of fish through the years. You can use your long casts on big water but you should save them until you've worked out a few short ones.

Fish in rough water usually feed on a variety of things, and some of the best flies can be taken for grasshoppers, spiders, or beetles that were hatched elsewhere and came to the water by accident. Examining the stomach contents of fish caught in some small but insect-rich flows may reveal great selectivity, but a fish in a big river will feed on anything from chubs to dragonflies. He's just not so particular.

The smaller a wild stream is the more likely its fish are to depend largely on terrestrials. The grass may hang into the water in long sweepers, and anything from a caterpillar to a field mouse can fall in. Terrestrial insects may swim frantically, so a little drag isn't necessarily the bugaboo it might be where the fish are picking and choosing among several kinds of mayflies.

If the open waters of wide spring and limestone creeks require caution, some of the very narrow and brushy brooks demand even more. It's not that the fish are more selective, but it's close-range casting, whether with dry or wet. The dry is especially difficult because it must be cast up and drifted down in the many cases where the wet or nymph can be paid downstream more efficiently. Remember this about those step-across brooks: The fish are especially attentive to what happens ashore, and a fish that was raised in the shadows of herons or minks will be alert to careless steps. In walking such trickles for brook trout, I've found the percentage of bungling approaches is high, and a little pool with a mud cloud or two on the bottom probably won't be productive. The brookie may be hiding in the mud, just below his cloud, but he isn't about to come out for a while.

Wrinkled water you can't see through hides you from the fish as well. Thus, if a beginning dry-fly fisherman is out to catch

Ben Williams fishes a big dry fly in the edge of white water during a stone-fly hatch. This stream is too swift for wading.

the most fish in the least possible time, he will do well to ignore smooth glides, backwaters, and sloughs, and keep his feathers very close to the broken runs.

Not all dry flies are floated with the current. On windy days, when natural flies are frequently blown about wildly, it is possible to give an artificial a lifelike skipping movement with a high rod tip and short line. One advantage is that any trout inspecting such a fly has to move fast and thus may be careless in his examination. There are flies especially tied for movement to be imparted by the leader. The skating spider is one of these. The "bump cast" is designed to make a fly bounce or hop, preferably just outside the trout's window. Seeing the flicks of light made by the bouncing hackle or fly body, he may chase the thing in the belief it is about to escape. But this is a delicate maneuver, best done only with very light tippets.

NYMPHS

Not many people can fish nymphs well, and those who can are unable to impart much information, for their success is made up of a number of rather intangible things they acquired through practice and can't describe. The most consistently successful trout fishermen are nymph users, and the explanation is simple: Wherever water-bred flies will hatch, there are nymphs—and an insect is generally a nymph for most of its life. The surface hatches may last an hour or so, but a nymph is present for months or years—there are always some down there somewhere—and the nymph is a basic food.

The upstream nymph is the tough one. It represents a stage of the insect that comes just before surface hatching. The idea is to cast it upstream and let it ride down in the current, possibly moving upward as if preparing to hatch on top. The beginner seldom hooks his strikes on such a thing. His line isn't quite taut, and he sees nothing happen unless his nymph is very near the top. The knack of setting the hook "just before he strikes" doesn't come easily, and nymph bunglers like me usually operate with numerous experimental lifts, one of which occasionally finds a trout with the nymph in his mouth. The bottom-tracing nymph will bump against rocks and other obstacles, and the man on the rod learns to feel all of these little tremors, setting the hook gently any time he thinks he feels a fish. On placid water, there are all sorts of schemes for *seeing* the strike, whether it is felt or not.

With a high-floating line you can see a little twitch as the fish takes. Some fishermen dress the leader with floating solution, except for the part very near the nymph, and can actually see the leader twitch with a strike. Some use a dry fly as a bobber, fastening it to the leader above the nymph.

Some real nymphs simply float free on their way to the sur-

face, some are mobile and move on the bottom, and others are
fast swimmers. Nymphs burrow into the bottom, cling to rocks
and vegetation, and, in the case of the caddis fly, build protective
cases from sand or debris. Artificial nymphs can represent any
of these forms, and some are probably taken for scuds or freshwater shrimp. Thus, it is possible that a nymph will be attractive
to a fish no matter how it acts. But a fish expecting something in
a dead drift, with possibly a slight, feeble movement, is not going
to be too eager for something that darts across the river. So the
requirements change with season and stream.

"Nymph" sounds more advanced than "woolly worm," but
the woolly worm represents all sorts of nymphs, usually large
ones. Impressionistic nymphs, with just a little dubbing and a
suggestion of feeler or wing case, are sometimes more productive
than exact replicas of known nymph forms. This is an embarrassing refutation of my theories about vaguely shaped dry flies that
work because they aren't seen clearly—trout certainly gets a good
look at a nymph. All I can say is that although the trout has been
proved very conscious of both form and color in scientific testing,
its rudimentary brain probably can't consider color, shape, taste,
and action at the same time, so it takes an impressionistic nymph.

More fish are caught on downstream and across-stream
nymphs than on upstream casts, simply because few fishermen
have acquired the upstream knack. Some say anything downstream is wet-fly fishing, and Mert Parks once asked me when a
wet fly becomes a nymph. He grinned widely enough that it
wasn't necessary to answer. In some quarters "nymph" and "wet
fly" have come to mean styles of fishing, rather than kinds of fly.

Ray Donnersberger, of Chicago, does not consider himself a
true upstream nymph fisherman, but he has had spectacular success with nymphs fished in quiet water where a dry fly was useless.
He is a tireless experimenter, being much more interested in
fish he can't catch than in the ones he can. He once gave me a
disconcerting lesson on Silver Creek, near Sun Valley, Idaho. It
was getting along late in the fall, and I'm afraid I wasn't thinking about trout since I was on a chukar hunt, but he got my atten-

tion pretty fast. I'd decided to give Silver Creek a lick and a promise and be on my way, but Ray took me to a quiet slough, well back from the main creek, handed me his own rod, and told me where to cast. I could see big rainbows tooling around the weedy, mucky bottom and I flopped a cast to where he pointed and brought the nymph back with a hand-twist retrieve. I hooked a fish almost immediately and had a so-what attitude for a minute, but it finally soaked in that he had developed that nymph with great effort and that it was about the only thing that would work.

Still water in a Colorado stream requires delicacy with dry fly or nymph.

Then he took me to the main creek, a few hundred yards off, and showed me that a completely different nymph was required there. This was a spot where my pet theory about manipulation of nymphs didn't work out so well. In this case the pattern was the important thing, and all you had to do was hump it along at almost any depth. Of course, flies and nymphs usually must be moved when worked in quiet water.

I see nothing especially complex about most lake fishing with nymphs, once the proper depth has been established. Sinking lines have simplified that process, and most retrieves are fairly slow.

There is no doubt that movement is essential in most cases—to attract the attention of the fish, as well as to make the fly lifelike. Call this wet-fly fishing if you like.

Among the most difficult trout are those living in nearly dead backwaters and sloughs, most of them interested mainly in subsurface feeding. On a few occasions I have caught such fish, when they were visible, by merely casting a nymph, allowing it to sink, leaving it quiet until a trout swam quite near it, and then giving it a little motion. This is a sneaky business, requires patience, and is a little like waiting for a rabbit with a hand-operated snare.

THE INSECTS

It is possible to live a lifetime of fly fishing without ever knowing where the natural insects come from, without ever identifying them, and without ever inspecting the contents of a trout's stomach. Entomology runs away with some fishermen but it may be just as enjoyable as the fishing itself. Matching the naturals can be so engrossing that some fishermen don't bother much with other essential techniques and are disappointed when less studious anglers catch fish with flies they wouldn't have in their box.

Somewhere between the extremes is the average serious trout fisherman who has a pretty good idea of what the hatch is all about. He looks at hatching flies and tries to match them with what he has in his vest. He may be a flytier but he usually copies commercial models, with a few little changes he makes for fun. He hardly ever takes a fly-tieing kit to the stream. He often checks the contents of a trout's stomach but he seldom tries very hard to catch insects, although he may kick over a stone or two to see what the nymphs look like. He probably has no net to catch the nymphs with, and binoculars are too much trouble to take along, being considered less important than the camera he usually forgets.

Many fishermen feel a little silly pursuing flying insects with a net, particularly if they are being watched by amused bait users or hardware throwers, but most of us have, at one time or other, employed a landing net in a full-armed tennis swing. The flies go through the mesh sometimes, but it's possible to make a kill with a little persistence, especially if the flies are big. A very small net can be carried especially for the purpose, however, and some of my friends are quick-draw artists on insects.

Nymphs can be collected with a little square of fine mesh. You fasten it to a couple of sticks, rummage around the bottom stones, and keep the net downstream from your disturbance, much as some bait fishermen collect small bottom fish.

The most important of trout-stream insects are the mayflies. There are more than five hundred different American insects in this class, varying greatly in size but having some common characteristics that suit the entomologist's classifications. Although almost any insect or worm that creeps, crawls, drifts, or swims underwater is frequently termed a nymph, I am told that the true nymph is a stage of only certain insects. That's not important to the fisherman unless he goes into the subject more deeply than I intend to here.

Briefly, the life history of a typical mayfly goes something like this: The eggs hatch into very small nymphs which may be classified as burrowers, clingers, or crawlers and swimmers. Feeding on tiny water life, largely vegetable, the nymphs go through a series of moults as they mature. Many of them live for about a year underwater, but some do not mature for two or more years. When finally matured, the nymph floats upward and moults at the surface, becoming a *dun* or *subimago.* It is the dun that usually brings about the best dry-fly fishing and that's the fly which floats downstream with its wings held vertical to the body, so most dry flies imitate this stage. Then the dun flies to a bush, tree, or other resting place near the stream, and spends some time before a final moult, often about twenty-four hours. In the final moult, the mayfly emerges as a full-fledged adult and is ready for mating and egg laying. This final stage is called a *spinner* or *imago.* As spinners, the mayflies go through a mating "dance of death" over the water, during which the eggs are fertilized and deposited on or in the water, and after which the spinners die. Through all of this cycle, the flight movement is primarily upstream. If they went with the current, the hatches would occur in the ocean after a few years, as the eggs would be laid farther and farther downstream each season. And, of course, they'd soon get into warm and slow waters, unsuitable for aquatic insects that require trout-stream conditions.

The mayfly hatches occur when air and water temperatures are correct. On a typical stream, this might be at the warmest time during early or late season and would be around noon. During midsummer it would more likely occur in evening or early morning, but usually in evening. In some climates the midday hatch continues through the summer. The midday hatch is most reliable on a sunny day of average temperatures and might not come off if there's a cold snap or hard rainstorm. Hatches can be stopped by high water, so we see why the streams of constant flow are the most reliable. Fluctuating streams are more prone to produce surprise hatches, some of which come off with no fishermen present.

Students of given waters can forecast the chronological order

A big brown that took a bushy dry fly in the Madison River, near Ennis, Montana. Fairly heavy rods are needed in the swift, heavy water with prevailing high winds.

of mayfly hatches, and elaborate tables are available for many localities. Some of the books on trout-stream entomology have excellent hatching tables that cover the entire country, although those on the eastern streams are more complete. This is partly because those streams have been more thoroughly studied, partly because the fishing areas are not so large as those in the West, and partly because the East is the cradle of American dry-fly fishing and for a long while contained most of the careful operators. In the Midwest there are some very carefully studied streams, especially in Michigan. I do not disparage the accurate studies of individuals on specific western water, but the information is less inclusive because of the thousands of miles of trout creeks and rivers.

The good caster with adequate equipment can often get his research done for him if he will make friends near a well-known mayfly stream. They will tell him which fly patterns the local experts have found successful, and I see no shame in having this information. You'll still have the business of applying the flies correctly; that alone is satisfaction enough for most of us.

Although there are trout streams—wonderful ones—where a local fisherman can tell you within fifteen minutes of when a hatch of some sort will develop (weather permitting), most of them are less consistent. The most learned way of predicting a hatch is to find some of the nymphs and examine them. If they're about ready to come forth as flies, the wing cases (those bulgy parts along the forepart of the nymph) will be dark and lumpy with the nearly matured wings. Nervous and attentive birds are a sign, for many birds take the emerging duns almost as readily as the trout do, and you may see a swallow dive for an insect before you're aware any are hatching. Occasionally, the trout are busy with near-surface nymphs before flies are in evidence.

It is easy to be confused about mayflies, with several varieties coming out at once. Some flies taste better to the trout and are more nutritious. A fly that attracted them yesterday may not work today because they are now exposed to something they like better. However, if our pattern matches yesterday's hatch, and the same naturals show up again, it is hard to believe that repeated rises are to something else. That's an opportune time for pocket binoculars. Just focus on a steady riser and see what he's really doing. Possibly a smaller fly is floating unobstrusively with the ones we matched the day before. There are unexplained days when the fish are catching the nymphs on the way up and pay very little attention to the duns on top, all of which is very exasperating, but is one of the things that keeps you coming back.

Mayflies appear on a wide variety of water, even very warm lakes a long way from trout country. Although such flies are different from those on clear, cold streams, they have attraction for warm-water fishes and there are mayfly rises on smallmouth-bass rivers. At such times, many of the most successful fishermen don't use mayfly imitations at all, but find that cork bugs are attractive to fish in the mood for surface striking.

On some lakes and sluggish warm-water rivers, the mayflies attract panfish and small black bass, both of which can be caught on mayfly imitations. Then there are the large bass that come looking for the off-guard panfish, and a popping bug or big streamer sometimes works well on these. They aren't interested in the mayflies but are happy to eat the next link in the food chain.

Mayflies, caddis flies, and stone flies are generally listed as the three insect groups of special interest to trout fishermen. However, the dobson-fly nymph, more frequently known as a hellgrammite, is also widely imitated by enormous woolly worms and slightly different concoctions that are called nymphs by their owners.

Dragonfly nymphs crawl out of the water before turning into flies, and so do stone flies. The caddis nymphs sometimes hide in gravel, but the types that get most attention are those which build cases from sand or debris and live loosely encased in their sometimes portable homes. Water runs through the cases and, like other nymphs, the caddis has gills. Nymph gills are located in various places and usually not recognized by casual observers.

Caddis nymphs are often scooped up, case and all, by trout,

Generally associated with swift rivers, the inflated boat is also an important aid in covering quiet backwaters. This slough requires small flies and careful casting.

and the presence of strange bits of debris in a trout's stomach is sometimes explained by this practice. When it comes time for the flies to emerge, some types swim up to the surface, others go to the shallows and crawl out. The adult, while resting, holds its wings folded back along its back or abdomen.

The stone flies, often called salmon flies, trout flies, or willow flies, are less important because they do not appear on a great many streams. But where they do, the hatch can be the fishing event of the year. The stone-fly nymphs crawl to the banks and climb out on bushes or nearby stones. When they mature, they indulge in clumsy flight and are seen floating down the stream with their wings folded along their backs. Some of them are two inches long and attract very large fish that might not bother with hatches of small mayflies. The stone-fly hatch, where it occurs, can be so dramatic that it deserves a little extra attention.

I think the best known stone or "salmon fly" hatch occurs on the Madison River of Montana, beginning in June and appearing first at lower locations, then proceeding upstream. At times, the riverside willows are sagging with these awkward flies which go bobbing down over the swift, shallow Madison by the thousands. Almost any very large dry fly, such as the Sofa Pillow (a big squirrel-hair pattern with bushy hackle), or any other of approximately the right color, will get enthusiastic rises since much of the Madison is broken water. In a good year, a great many three-pound trout are caught, and a four-pounder is not unusual. The Madison is usually clear fairly early in the season, so the hatch can be followed upstream as it moves. And herewith lies a bit of strategy that can be applied to much dry-fly fishing.

Since the salmon flies appear only once a year, and feeding habits are not yet established, they get little attention at first from the bigger fish. Later, at the height of the hatch (which may last for several days in a given area), there are plenty of takers, but your artificial may be competing with a few thousand naturals. But as the hatch moves on up the river, and flies begin to thin out, trout that have become used to easy meals must now look for flies—and the fishing is likely to be best of all.

Some big western rivers, such as the Yellowstone, are likely to be muddy from snow runoff when the salmon-fly hatch occurs at lower elevations, but when the hatch reaches high country, fishing may be good. The great stone fly shucks are extremely durable and a late fall fisherman will find them thick on stones and brush three months after the hatch occurred. Stone fly hatches are dramatic because of the size of the flies; it's a sort of fishing circus with everything just a little bit larger-than-life including many of the fish.

THE IMITATIONS

The dry flies used for trout can be roughly classified as bivisibles, hair-wings, spent-wings, skating spiders, no-hackles, and the orthodox dries. The latter have prominent wings, with feather or hackle standing fairly straight up and usually separated a little at the top. Some on this list are so small as to require very delicate casting and very light leaders, but there are big dries that need little more care than popping bugs and can be cast on 10-pound tippets if you want to.

On the large end are some of the imitation dragonflies (which sometimes have solid quill bodies) and the enormous bushy things that represent big stone flies. It is possible to buy dry flies with hooks as large as number 4 from most of the best fly dealers. Although these are pretty heavy, they are supported either by very thick applications of hackle, or by buoyant bodies. Such flies are easy to dope with fly-floating spray or liquid. Some fishermen actually use their line dressing on these big things, but it's easy to smear them out of shape that way. These big ones are a little much for ultralight trout rods, but since they are commonly used on bigger water you'll probably have your heavier tackle along. Some of the imitation grasshoppers are quite large —halfway between flies and bugs—some flies are actually made with cork bodies, although they're unusual.

The traditional dry fly is supported by its stiff hackles pressing against the surface film, the hook barely touching water, the barb riding down. If the fly has a tail, it supports the rear end. The bivisible fly is almost entirely hackle but may have a tail of softer stuff. It looks about the same, regardless of how it lands on the water. The bivisible is very convenient in rough water and usually floats well.

Hair-wing flies may have no additional attraction for the fish but they are very easily seen on the water. The Royal Wulff is an especially good choice, being a good floater and a takeoff on the standard Royal Coachman (which imitates nothing in particular but is the best known fly in the world, as far as I know). The big, white hair wings of the Wulff are highly visible in rough water, and the thing floats high if there's plenty of hackle.

Not many spent-wing flies are used. They are usually dries, although they can be fished wet, and are intended to represent a dead imago or spinner fly. The wings, therefore, spread out flat on the water, or nearly so. Some of them tend to alight part of the time with the hook up, but a dead spinner might be upside down, too, so there's no great problem.

Dry flies and nymphs
in patterns which demonstrate
general types.
Top row, l. to r.:
Royal Coachman hairwing;
Adams (hackle point wings);
Brown Bivisible
(fly that is "all hackle").
Second row, l. to r.:
Grey Wulff; salmon skater fly;
Wickham's Fancy
(wing made from separate
feather rather than from hackle).
Third row:
Woolly Worm
(soft hair or hackle);
Brown nymph
(typical nymph form).
Bottom row:
Paradun
(horizontal hackle);
No Hackle
dry fly.

No-hackle flies are supported by their bodies rather than by hackle, and, in the smaller sizes, it is especially important that the body be buoyant. It is generally made of dubbing (hair or other material that is twisted about thread and then wrapped on). The paraduns, as made by Swisher and Richards, have some hackle in parachute shape above the body to assure right-side-up floating. There are many other fly makers, but I mention these in particular as their work is quite recent and needs a little explanation.

The skating spider has very long hackle, mounted around the front part of the hook, and rides on the water with the hook "hanging down."

The best results are had when dry flies float, as they're supposed to, with the hook down and wings up—if there are any. Nevertheless, a large percentage of dry-fly fish are caught when the fly has fallen over on its side. This may be treason but it's true, and beginning fly fishermen whose flies tip over now and then shouldn't be too concerned unless the fish are being very persnickety. If it's completely upside-down, however, the illusion is badly spoiled. Now and then you'll drown a fly by slapping it too hard or throwing it into a breaking wavelet. Leaders catch in eddies and suck flies under too, but drowned flies sometimes catch fish, so the drift should be fished out. Natural flies often drown, too, so you're still imitating nature, however unintentionally. Picking up such a fouled-up cast is much worse than letting it drift over the fish.

The nymph ties can be very simple, or wondrously complex. I've caught many fish with simple, dubbed bodies of various colors, truly impressionistic things that simply rely on looking soft and squirmy. Since most nymphs must go down, they are tied on heavy hooks, sometimes with the addition of lead wire and body materials that soak up water. Leader-sinking solution is often dabbed on them, and they're sometimes rubbed in mud. If no one is looking, some fly fishermen "bend a little lead" on the leader.

The mayfly nymph, drifting up to the surface to escape its shuck, generally faces upstream since it has gills and uses the current the same as a trout, although it is drifting backward. To mimic this situation, some nymphs are tied on the hook "backward," with the head near the bend, and are fished upstream. It's a pretty fine point, though.

Dry flies and nymphs are seldom tied in sizes smaller than 22, although some fishermen use hooks as small as 28, or even tinier. Such small hooks hold better than you'd think—usually capable of outlasting the tippets they're used with. Dries smaller than size 20 are invisible to many of us on most casts, and even those who can usually see them will have trouble some of the time.

The smallest flies I have used are what I call "film flies," things so tiny they are seldom visible to the caster and are held on top by the tension of the surface film. Some look like flies, some look like nymphs, and they catch fish that are "smutting"— taking things too small to be copied, sometimes too small even to be identified. When we can't see what the fish are rising to, it's common to say they're taking "a midge that's too small to match."

Sometimes these things can turn an unsuccessful day into one of triumph. I once found some fish barely dimpling the surface of very deep, still water, on a river that had generally been productive with fairly coarse fishing. To reach the fish, I had to wade so deep that my waders had only two inches of freeboard.

I went down to a number-20 dry and got no attention from what I thought were very small trout. The spot they were working looked as if it had collected odds and ends of very tiny debris against a notch of backwater. With darkness coming on, and still fishless, I dug out something that had been given me by a man from California and which was called a "Moose Mane fly." It was just a few moose hairs on a tiny hook. I don't recall the size, but

Chester Marion releases a good cutthroat in western spring creek. Constant flow makes such waters ideal for dry flies and nymphs.

it was hard to tie on. I got it to the rather scummy spot where the tiny dimples were appearing, saw the leader twitch a little, and set the hook. When a two-pound rainbow went into the air I nearly drowned from surprise. But, having shipped only a quart or so of water in my waders, I played my fish around on the tiny hook—and lost it. I cast back to the same spot and landed another rainbow, this one about a pound. Then I caught a brown of about that weight.

Now, I've watched many dimpling fish of good size, but they usually give themselves away by an extra large bulge or an accidentally loud slurp. These never did. I don't believe the wonderful Moose Mane fly imitated anything they were taking, but it was in the size range they were thinking about and looked like something that was alive or had been alive.

Film fishing is a lot of trouble, and the worst of it is that you seldom see your fly unless the light is exactly right. Such fish are hard to hook, too, as the method is similar to that used with the upstream nymph—a matter of leader twitches, unusual swirls, or extrasensory perception.

THE FLIES YOU NEED

Nearly all trout fishermen acquire hundreds of flies, but the common mistake is to collect a wide variety of patterns before rounding out a basic variety of sizes and types. Some of the very best fly fishermen use very few patterns; a basic collection for a given area might include no more than a dozen. Without going into any specific patterns now, I'd say such an assortment should include some big and bushy dries in 12 and 14 sizes and some sparsely-dressed dries of fairly neutral colors in 16s and 18s. Then there should be some really big nymphs or woolly worms in 10s or even larger, and some olive, tan, brown, and black mayfly nymphs from 12 to 16.

Once having acquired flies to match the major hatches of his streams, the fisherman should round out the assortment by getting several sizes of each. Highly sophisticated fish are sometimes remarkably careless about exact shades and tones, but will insist

196

on proper size. Sometimes, their preference may be smaller or larger than the prevailing hatch. Veterans having poor success among rising fish will change fly size first; they begin to consider pattern only after two or three sizes of their most likely candidate have been ignored.

Most of the flies that do not try to match any specific insect (call them "attractors" if you like) are fairly large, with emphasis on their visibility to the fisherman. In big, rough water, the big flies are also easily seen by fish. We hear about the "big western patterns" and the "little eastern patterns." Of course there are different insects in the West from those in the East, but fly size is determined by stream size and speed. A small western creek and a small eastern brook are likely to require flies of a similar size, and a western hatch can be just as small as an eastern one. It is true, however, that there are more big, fast streams out west.

Any stranger to new waters is bucking the current if he insists on his own fly choices without consultation with local fishermen. An investment in some local favorites will be worthwhile, even if only to get the free advice that usually comes with them. The local expert can, of course, become wedded to certain flies and simply stop experimenting and the newcomer occasionally has spectacular success with something else. Still, he's foolish not to try what the locals recommend. If his collection doesn't include the local preference, he should try to come close to it, and then branch out a bit.

Some years back, we fished Hazel Creek in North Carolina. It's a sizeable stream, opening into Fontana Reservoir, and is mountainous country. The spot we fished required a considerable boat trip and then an uphill hike of several miles.

We had been bass fishing, had only a skimpy collection of trout flies along, and little inside dope on the situation when we met a really astute fly angler who was just leaving.

"It takes an Adams," he told us, "but I think you'll do better with a male Adams than with a female."

We thanked him and went on to a likely spot. There we

opened the fly boxes and found no Adamses at all. With scant confidence, we tied on Light Cahills and were catching trout before we had really worked out our lines. The Cahill proved deadly although it didn't seem to match any of the naturals we saw, and the Adams couldn't have done much better. But it doesn't always work that way.

CREATING A HATCH

There has been a great deal of talk about creating a hatch by simply floating a certain pattern over the fish in a single small area. The trout decide a hatch is in progress and start rising to the persistent fly you're casting. I have had indifferent success with this device but I do know that a fish will sometimes take a fly, after showing on initial interest in it, when he sees it re-peatedly.

In South Dakota I once fished a small stream that was partly underground but appeared at intervals as glassy pools with faint current. Fish were rising to something I couldn't even see, and I failed miserably. I finally abandoned serious fishing to indulge in trout watching after I found a big boulder overlooking a deep, quiet pool filled with big rainbows. I lay on the rock and watched them make repeated rises to something tiny. I'd had no idea there were fish of that size in the creek. I cautiously flipped a big, bushy thing over them, and although they paid no attention to it, they didn't seem to be frightened. After 20 casts, I lost interest in my fly but continued my nature study. Finally, I just left the big fly on the surface, convinced my introduction of a "stranger" was a waste of time.

One of the largest fish rose fairly regularly, and I strained my eyes in the dusk to see what he was taking. Then, after one take he seemed to act strangely, retired to the bottom, and gulped uncomfortably. Something big came out of his mouth and floated up to the surface. It was my fly, which I'd completely forgotten.

Such performances will never enhance my fishing reputation, but it was an experience impossible to forget. My only excuse is that it was getting dark and I must have been hypnotized.

NINE

Streamers and Wet Flies for Trout

THE DISTINCTIONS become rather finely drawn. Dry flies, generally presented in a dead drift, are sometimes twitched with the rod tip. Nymphs, usually accepted as dead-drift attractions, are often manipulated and swung in the current. Wet flies are fished in dead drifts, but more often with some manipulation. When we come to streamers, we can speak a little more definitely and say that most of them represent small fish instead of an insect stage. Hence, they are generally fished as if they had mobility of their own. This is about as far as we can go with definitions.

The conventional wet fly has probably caught more trout than all the other ties put together, but fishermen still argue about what it represents. The fact is, it represents different things at different times. Technically, I suppose, it represents a drowned insect—probably a spent mayfly that has already mated; possibly an emergent dun that was accidentally drowned in a riffle. But these things are a little uncertain and it becomes embarrassing when I try to tell what it is that I hope my wet flies are doing.

Most beginners fish first with wet flies because much wet-fly fishing requires very little casting ability. It is true that, in many

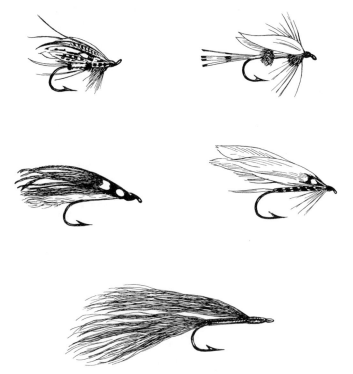

Typical patterns in wet flies and streamers. Top, l. to r.: Jock Scott (typical wet pattern for Atlantic salmon); Royal Coachman. Second row, l. to r.: Red and White bucktail; Black Ghost streamer (using feather instead of hair). Bottom: A double tie of the Blonde series, showing how overall length of streamer can be increased by tying hair in twice.

waters, a few fish can be caught without much skill. But the difference between the beginning wet-fly fisherman and the polished performer can be measured in many ways, and most dramatically in the number of fish caught.

WET-FLY GEAR

The conventional wet fly may be tied on a heavier hook than the dry. The wings usually lie back near the shank, and the hackle is soft and pliable since it has no mission in holding the fly high on surface film. Many of the wet-fly patterns are the same as dry flies except for these characteristics, and some flies can be fished dry or wet with the addition of either floating or sinking solutions.

The wet-fly rod is now generally the same as that used for dry-fly fishing. There was a time, however, when wet and dry-fly actions were considered so different that the expert always used different rods. Wet-fly action is softer and slower than dry-fly action, and, although it is seldom mentioned the very soft or "weepy" rod is best of all for very short casts. In other types of fishing, we might scornfully call these presentations "flop-casts"; in wet-fly fishing they can be a very important tactic. Even the very long rod of 9 or 9½ feet is used in some kinds of wet-fly fishing. The method is almost the same as dapping, a European system of using extremely long rods to barely touch natural flies on the surface. Although we talk of 100-foot casts, a large percentage of fish taken on wet flies are hooked with no more than 15 feet of line working. Some expert small-stream fishermen seldom have any more than a short leader in the water.

In shallow water, the floating fly line is usually best, and the various grades of sinking lines are a help in different speeds and depths of current. Many wet-fly fishermen use two flies at once, and a few use three.

WET-FLY METHODS

A wet fly can represent several things during the various stages of a single cast. The most generally productive moving-water method is to cast the fly slightly upstream and try to get a natural dead drift for some distance. As the fly reaches a point nearly opposite, the fisherman can release some extra line to obtain more dead drift. However, there will almost certainly be some dragging movement in that transaction. Then he allows the wet to be stopped on a taut line and swung across the current, in almost exactly the same maneuver used with a streamer. Up to the point when the fly starts to swing, it resembles a drowned insect, and many fish take it then. But the hot spot is at the point where the free drift stops and the quick cross-current swing begins. I don't know what the fly represents then, and I doubt if anyone else does—it would be highly unusual for a drowned mayfly to suddenly dash across a fast current. At any rate, many strikes come at the beginning of the swing, so I assume the fish is following the fly and automatically strikes when it seems about to be taken away from him.

Once the fly is almost directly downstream, there are all

sorts of possible manipulations: It can be retrieved for several feet and then allowed to drift back; it can be played with short twitches in the current; it can be retrieved by a "hand-twist" retrieve (a maneuver first named by Ray Bergman); it can be retrieved rapidly upstream by hand-stripping; it can be worked back and forth in the current by moving the rod tip left to right, a stunt that can cover some 18 feet of stream at a right angle to the current. In short, on a single retrieve, a wet fly can pretend it is a drowned fly, a living nymph, a quick minnow, or an active scud. Whichever maneuver succeeds is the one to concentrate on.

Many fishermen use two flies on their leaders. The three-fly cast isn't as popular as it once was. Multiple flies can be rigged so that one rides much deeper than another, revealing fish preference as to depth. Generally, two patterns are used, one of them considerably larger than the other—at least until something can be learned about the fish. When a short line is used, the dropper fly is sometimes danced along the surface.

Most wet-fly fishermen work downstream, and some of them actually employ shorter drifts than dry-fly users. They flick their flies to likely pockets while moving along rather rapidly and casting downstream. They give short dips of their rods to allow free drifts, then retrieve jerkily or gently. Whatever else you may think of the conventional wet fly, its user can display it in a tremendous variety of ways.

It is difficult to beat the wet fly in very small, brushy creeks. It can be drifted, nymphlike, under obstructions and undercut banks, and its effectiveness is not ended when a drift ends, for many fish take while the fly dangles. Many a brookie has been caught with only part of the leader hanging from the tip, and the fisherman so entangled in brush that his rod was used as a probe rather than a casting instrument.

The roll cast works well with wets on a small stream. As most of us throw it, the cast goes a little slack at best. Thus it is possible to give the wet flies a few feet of free drift, manipulate them for a few seconds, and then roll them again. I have known some small-stream fishermen who said they could catch more fish

Not all steelhead can be beached easily. It was necessary to play this one until it was on its side before it could be landed.

by wading constantly and briskly, making innumerable roll casts, and constantly showing the flies in new water. Of course, such methods are out of the question when there are many fishermen on a stretch of stream.

The wet-fly fisherman working downstream should be a careful wader because the trout are facing him. Since he can't often see the fish he is after, he frequently becomes careless— more careless than he would be if the fish were rising to drys. He doesn't get the advance information given by most rising fish, so he must figure the good spots by knowledge of what trout water should look like. A man who fishes wets over the same stream all season will generally do much better than any visiting expert. If it's a matter of fishing to rising fish, any experienced angler may do a good job because he can see where they are. But when fish are not visibly rising, knowledge of the particular water at hand takes on special importance.

It's been said that the dry fly will nearly always win if fish are seen taking drys, but that the wet will be much better if there is no apparent hatch.

In very quiet pools, or in ponds and lakes, depth of fishing becomes critical, the correct depth sometimes producing instant success. A counting method can be the solution but requires patience. The fisherman begins by simply letting his fly go all the way to the bottom on each cast, until he gets a strike. If he has counted while all his casts sink, he will have a good clue to the depth the trout are using. At any rate a sinking fly in quiet water is an attractive thing whether it is manipulated or not.

The two most popular retrieves in lakes are a very slow one that keeps the fly at what the fisherman hopes is the ideal level, possibly quite near bottom; and an intermittent retrieve in which the fly is retrieved rapidly for a short distance and is then allowed to sink to the bottom, or nearly to the bottom, after which the process is repeated.

BOTTOM-BUMPING

Fishing bottoms of large rivers for steelhead and large trout involves a strange combination of relatively coarse tackle, long casting, and a delicate feel for unseen bottoms. We're involved in classification trouble again, but I suppose the procedure most resembles deep nymph fishing, although the flies or streamers are seldom so classified. There is no doubt that bottom-bumping got its impetus from steelhead fishing, where fly fishermen tried to compete with bait and lure anglers—and did a pretty good job of it.

The idea is to get the fly all the way down but keep it light enough that it will move in the current. It literally sweeps the bottom, and that's what you feel in your rod hand. The delicate tip vibrates and dips from sinking line, leader, and fly washing over gravel stretches and rounded boulders. The mortality rate of flies is high, a large share of your hangups coming when the line catches between two rocks and pulls the hook into a crevice as you retrieve or pick up. But, as Johnny Walker, sage of the Kispiox, once remarked, "If you don't lose flies, you're doing it wrong."

Most of the steelhead bottom-bumpers use sinking heads, with monofilament or very fine fly line as running line. A "whole line" of sinking material is just as productive if extremely long cast are not needed. Most of the flies are slightly weighted, and heavy hooks are used. You need a whetstone or distributor-point file at hand, for the hook dulls quickly. A short leader is a help in keeping the fly down and it usually doesn't need to be very fine, as bottom trout are seldom tippet-shy.

There is disagreement about the tippet material, and some experts feel stiff monofilament is a help in keeping the fly from becoming entangled in the leader. It also prevents twisting as the fly is washed along the bottom. Others say the fly will move in a more natural drift if the leader is pliable. I agree with both these opinions, but I like the stiff leader because I am lax about checking my terminal tackle, often getting an overhand knot as the fly drifts erratically in bottom currents.

If the current is right for it, you may cast straight across or even downstream. If the water is too swift for that, you must cast progressively upstream, until you can feel the telltale vibrations of the fly and line tickling the bottom. It is possible, when fishing a constant current, to tie up a combination that will allow the line to sink and the fly to stay a little above bottom. But that's cutting it pretty fine.

Most bottom strikes feel like bumps, indistinguishable from those caused by boulders. Yet you must set the hook, regardless of how many rocks you have snagged. If you don't, the fish will

Steelhead caught on bottom-bounced fly in British Columbia. Note that fisherman is casting well upstream in a fast run to allow fly to get down.

have plenty of time to spit out the fly before anything comes tight, since it is extremely unlikely your leader and line are anywhere nearly taut. When I first fished the bottom in this way, I had an idealistic dream of everything proceeding in orderly fashion along the river floor. But when I watched from a bluff, I learned that the line and leader may be well ahead of, or well behind, the fly, and often going downstream in slack curves.

I believe the nearly dead drift is most effective most of the time, but there is no objection to a little manipulation as the fly goes along. A little mending of the line will help you to extend the period of dead drift. Once a sinking line has gone well down, mending is difficult, but there is a trick that works just as the line strikes the water and before it can sink. Simply make a quick mending motion, throwing a little slack upstream, and you'll get your fly down quicker. Then, after the fly is bumping along the bottom, you can gain some slack by a quick pull and then feeding line. Not only does this increase the length of time your fly is actually dead-drifting, but it multiplies the number of "swings" you get. The swing, as the fly starts to rush around below you, is a productive part of many casts, and if you can make several such starts during the drift you should be ahead of the game.

When fishing heavy water, be very attentive to just when you first feel bottom on each cast. The fly may be getting down sooner or later than you think, and attention to this detail will prevent you from missing much water. If you get a strike, try to remember just where the fish took and the exact position of your line and fly, for this kind of fishing is usually done in big water and the same holds may be good season after season. You might be surprised at where the fish actually picked up the fly, since it may not be where you expected it at all.

Bottom-bumping is used most of all for steelhead, but exactly the same technique has served me for brown trout, saltwater weakfish, and shad. It is only slightly different from big-streamer fishing for trout in large rivers. The streamer catches steelhead, too, but a fly of shorter silhouette has been much more popular.

Unlike the ornate dressings of Atlantic salmon flies, the steelhead attractions can be extremely simple. Bodies of fluorescent yarn, with tinsel ribbing and skimpy hackle, have caught many fish in recent years. Every river has its own steelhead flies, but there is a leaning toward orange yarn. Sometimes it's combined with yellow or light green, with tinsel or Mylar ribbing. Sparse hackle, or none at all, leaves the thing looking pretty simple, which it is. And it's good that it is, for many steelhead flies are lost to hangups. The general appearance is often decidedly woolly-wormish. There are also all-black steelhead flies which certainly do not resemble salmon eggs, but big nymphs instead.

Before the popularity of light spinning, many fly casters used small spoons in exactly the same way that the bottom-bumping fly is handled. Few of them used sinking lines, however, since the spoons were generally heavy enough to get down by themselves. That combination was used for inland trout and for shad, but I doubt if it was used much for steelhead. Few of us like to cast spoons, and most of them should be reserved for spinning tackle.

TRUE STREAMERS

True streamers are, for the most part, intended to imitate small fish. Their overall length is considerable, many of them tied on long-shank hooks, and most trout streamers are fairly lightly dressed. Although there is a frequent distinction between "bucktails" and "streamers," it's just a matter of hair versus feathers. The use of polar-bear hair, or calf tail, complicates the whole thing to the point where I simply call them streamers and let it go at that.

Conventional streamer construction includes: a body; feathers, which lie close to the body; a tail, which is relatively unimportant in dry or conventional wet flies, but can add considerably to streamer appearance and to visibility in the water. Tinsel or Mylar ribbing adds to the flash of streamers, and any feature which adds a headlike front contributes to the lifelike appearance. Many streamers have eyes painted on. Feather and hair streamers often have a dark streak along their sides, due to a "topping" of

Large streamers employing both hair and feathers. Streamer third from left shows silhouette of fly when wet.

peacock herl. In most minnows, this lateral line is fairly distinguishable, making the thing look more fishy to the caster, if not to the fish.

Most standard streamer patterns are altered by the individual flytier, and many of the variations do improve performance under special circumstances. The chief disadvantage of personalized patterns is that, eventually, two fishermen can't discuss any streamer without an example in hand. I am not saying continual alterations and adaptations of the patterns aren't desirable from a fish-catching standpoint; simply that they make it difficult to order a streamer and know what you're getting.

In the matter of innovation, I'm among the most guilty. I have an irreverent attitude toward conventional patterns, and have encouraged my flytier (who also does the cooking at our house) to throw together all sorts of fish-catching but nameless things. They're very nearly one of a kind, but my pride in her originality is not unmixed. If I lose one, I don't know what I lost and can't even describe it half the time.

What I call a Silver Outcast is a good example of deviation from the standard. Dr. Ralph Daugherty of Pennsylvania once gave me a variation of the Silver Doctor streamer, for saltwater use. It worked so well there that we made smaller ones for trout, and caught some big browns. Dr. Daugherty's original was not quite a standard pattern, and I believe we made a change or two because we didn't happen to have exactly the right materials—but streamer patterns aren't critical, so what the heck? When we'd had considerable trout success, I showed the streamer to Dan Bailey, the fly manufacturer. He sadly commented that "it isn't quite the way we tie Silver Doctors." It finally dawned on me that if Bailey made a different Silver Doctor for every fisherman who showed him one, he'd soon be out of business. We still use the streamer and call it a Silver Outcast, but I'm the first to admit it probably has little advantage over a standard Silver Doctor in most circumstances. Adherence to standard streamer patterns may be a little stuffy, but it's the only way we can discuss things without a sample of everything.

There is, of course, an understandable joy in having a special fly with a special name, particularly if it's named after you. Nevertheless, the new trout fisherman who wants something named for him after his fifth cast is doing us no favor. Trout-streamer confusion is bad enough, and it's even worse in salt water, so let's confine ourselves here to the traditionals.

Hair streamers have a crawly appearance that's advantageous when dead-drifted or worked very slowly. I doubt if the crawliness shows to much advantage when a streamer is worked rapidly, or is whipped by violent current. Polar-bear hair has a special gleam, and calf tail is kinky enough that it has a special action. Bucktail is straight and makes a streamer easy to cast with a light rod since it has little wind resistance. The buoyancy of hair, quite important in dry flies, is of little importance in streamers.

Mylar is a flashy addition to streamers. It is fairly tough and doesn't become dull with use. As body material, it can be bought in tube form and slipped over hooks. Strands of it add flash to either hair or feather streamers, although the strands must be quite narrow to prevent fluttering during the cast. The tubes which cover hooks are simply the piping used for some clothing decoration. By fraying out the tubing, a tier can secure strands 1/64 inch in width. He can straighten out the kinks, if desired, by applying a little heat. Any width greater than that will interfere seriously with casting. Some fishermen who don't tie their streamers from scratch occasionally add a little Mylar to standard patterns.

STREAMER OPERATION

Many fishermen use streamers only when the water is too high or too dirty for other flies. Some trout anglers use nothing else regardless of water levels. I have had very poor success with streamers in slow streams when water was low. I have done well with them almost everywhere water is fast, and, although I am careless of pattern, I have found size to be critical in many situations. It's beyond me why a quarter-inch of length should matter to a fish chasing something as long as your little finger, but sometimes it does.

In slow water, most fishermen give the streamer considerable movement with rod tip and stripping hand. In swift current, the dead drift—followed by the familiar swing across current—is the most practiced method. When a floating line is used, frequent mending will cause the streamer to go downstream, making for more dead drift, as well as numerous turns and darts. In theory, the broadside float will show the full silhouette of the streamer to the fish, rather than giving only a tail-end or front-end view. This presupposes that the fish is lying almost immediately below the streamer when he first sights it, and I think this is generally the case. There is another theory, however, that head-on or tail-end view will arouse enough curiosity for the fish to take a better look. It has been suggested that a vague glimpse is more likely to be effective than a full-scale examination. The truth is that there is no set rule and that varied presentations will generally get more fish. Undoubtedly, the broadside float encourages the striking fish to take the fly from the side and thus be hooked in the corner of the mouth.

Anyone who has cast large streamers in big rivers has seen indications that the fish are following for considerable distances, whether he gets many strikes or not. There are two distinct kinds of follow: one in which the fish keeps pace with the streamer but stays close behind it; and one in which the fish goes around, over, and under at high speed. I think the fish that follows close behind is trying to smell the thing. The one that circles it is trying to get a better look.

I have repeatedly hooked trout by throwing slack in the line when I saw they were chasing a streamer. Of course, a streamer that suddenly stops and then goes with the current when pursued does not act like a normal minnow, but I don't think our streamers are meant to represent normal minnows anyway. They represent a little fish with something wrong with him. Anyway, when fish are following, the rule is to change something. If the streamer is drifting, give it a twitch. If it is being retrieved, give it slack. It has been proved many times that a trout often reacts violently to a change of pace. And there are so many strikes that come as a streamer is being reeled in that it cannot possibly be put down to coincidence. However, the steady retrieve should be tried, even though it may seem unnatural to the fisherman.

Streamer targets are much the same as dry-fly targets, except that the "blind" dry-fly cast usually covers only one potential lie. The streamer can be worked with a long cast, often nearly across a large stream. For example: A fisherman standing on the shallow side of a curving pool may throw his streamer clear against an undercut bank, then bring it into the edge of the full-bore current, allow it to dead-drift briefly, then whip it across the main flow, and finish his cast by working it in slower and shallower water

Big streamers are effective in swift, heavy water where angler is attentive to any obstruction that can shelter a trout from the current.

on the inside of a stream curve. When no fish are seen, it is easy to get into mechanical casting. But careful retrieving often makes it possible to show the streamer to several selected spots on a single presentation. It will pay off in fish if you watch where the thing is going—or rather—coming.

Fishing a streamer against undercut or willow-sheltered banks can require extreme accuracy. This is especially true in midday, during warm weather, when it is often essential to throw within two inches of a deep bank. I am sure the fish can see the fly when it lands two feet away, possibly even better than when it comes down almost directly above him, but two things enter in here: Perhaps the fish is unwilling to follow anything that already has a two-foot jump on him; or perhaps his view of it is *too* clear. A streamer that lands immediately before his snout is an irresistible surprise, appearing suddenly at close range and triggering his striking instincts. Remember, too, that a terrestrial insect or animal would probably fall very close to shore. This necessity for very close casting has arisen many times, and I can cite numerous instances where very tight shoreline casting was absolutely necessary.

It is difficult to be extremely accurate with any sort of a slack cast, but when there are eddies or boils near a shore it is often possible to throw additional slack to the streamer just after it strikes. This will allow it to be sucked into an undercut, one of the deadliest approaches in streamer fishing, or in conventional wet-fly angling for that matter.

I fondly recall a highly successful streamer session on a medium-sized brown-trout stream that flowed swiftly, but with few breaks, and was about 40 feet wide. It was late fall and nearly spawning time for the browns, but the fish we took were certainly not on spawning gravels. Instead they hung very close to steep banks, some of which were undercut. At that time I felt the main thing was simply to show the streamer to the fish. I had no particular desire to hit the bank with it.

Two of us started wading down the center of the stream, heading back to our car after a rather poor session with dry flies, and casting streamers as we went. Since I was second in line I had little hope of doing much good, so I amused myself by trying to see how close I could come to the bank. It was brushy and willowed, liberally sprinkled with grass sweepers in some sections. I began to catch fish, but my friend failed to score. We matched our streamers but I continued to do the damage. It finally dawned that the difference of a very few inches in the shoreline coverage was the difference between good brown trout and no fish at all. When my buddy began to throw at the bank, he scored, too.

Bank combing is especially productive in streams with fairly smooth bottoms and few midstream obstructions. The best lie is against a bank where water is slowed and there is protection from sun and predators. There's also the probability of terrestrials, such as grasshoppers and spiders, and an occasional frog. Admittedly, such fish may move to midstream during a fly hatch.

Some of my most arm-breaking trout fishing has been in trying to hit a riverbank with streamers, when fishing from a boat or canoe. Frequently, the stream is too narrow to make the rod work, and the casts are so frequent that they become hard work pretty quickly. The best aid is a heavily overloaded rod for the short throws.

MUDDLER "THINGS"

The Muddler Minnow, originated by Don Gapen, has been eulogized for so long that any recital of its effectiveness is a waste of time. Suffice to say that, under various circumstances and in various streams, it has been fished to represent grasshoppers, dragonflies, stone flies, sculpins, and almost any living baitfish.

It has a burr head made of deer hair or very similar material, and the rest of it is simply a streamer, usually dull-colored, with wings, tail, some hackle, and a metallic body.

Although I was brought up on deer-hair bugs for black bass, the Muddler had caught a good many thousand big trout before I ever owned one. When I looked at the buoyant head, I naturally assumed it was to be fished dry, and that's the way I did it. I murdered the browns during a salmon-fly hatch, caught a lot of fish in grasshopper country, and carefully anointed my Muddlers with dry-fly dope. When I heard it was being used as a streamer, I assumed it was because the others lacked my consummate skill and simply couldn't fish dry flies. I still think it is most fun as a combination dry and wet, something very rare indeed.

Cast it over likely water, allow it to float dead on the surface for a moment, and then pull it under, and it will start out as a live grasshopper, and then become a minnow for a while. Let it drift a little before picking up at the end of the cast, and you have a drowned *something*. Fish take the Muddler at all these

The famous Muddler Minnow (left), the Spruce Fly, and the Spuddler—a combination of the two— all favorites in the West.

stages of the cast. Lately, it has been combined with a dark western streamer favorite, the Spruce Fly, and has come forth as the Spuddler. It's now tied in many colors.

Although larger ones are favored for late-fall casting in big rivers, the number 10 is a very good choice for all-around fishing. Put any Muddler on a sinking line and it becomes a very effective deep-going streamer. But I like its buoyancy, which will hold it somewhat above bottom as the heavy line sweeps it downstream.

LINES FOR STREAMERS

Where streamers are fished over shallow water, the floating line is most satisfactory. When they are worked in deep rivers for large trout, I suspect the sinking line is almost invariably the most productive. One of the strong points of the Muddler and its off-spring is their ability to stay a little above hang-up level on a sinking line.

When the Muddler and other big streamers first became popular on the big trout streams for fall fishing, they were held very near the surface, often making a trace of wake, even in the heaviest runs. Some of the strikes were splashing charges—it was not unusual to see a three-pound brown trout jump above your lure and come down on it violently.

Much as I love to fish streamers near the surface, where much of the action can be seen, I confess that the deeper presentations seem called for with some of the bigger fish when the water is big.

TEN

The
Salmons

THE ATLANTIC salmon is the most glamourous of any fly-rod fish, partly because of its romantic life history, partly because of its present scarcity, and partly because of its popularity with the noble, rich, and famous. Few Americans have the opportunity of casting flies for it, and its future lies in the balance in a paradoxical crisis. Beset by the ills of industrialization and human crowding, it has been the object of concentrated study, but as knowledge reached the point where the salmon might be helped, the same knowledge made it vulnerable to human greed.

It is hard to avoid getting maudlin about the salmon. The simple facts are that in the United States we nearly fished the salmon out, then destroyed most of its remaining streams by one means or another. As study of the fish advanced, commercial fishermen learned where they congregated at sea and decimated them with new and efficient machines and methods. Now the American salmon is being quarreled over off the European shore, where foreign fishermen are overharvesting fish that are born (and must spawn) in American streams. It is an international situation with no true parallel and no precedent.

The salmon was not always valued as highly as it is today. There was a time when indentured servants complained that they were fed little else. And, at one time, salmon were even used for fertilizer along much of the Atlantic coast, diminishing the salmon population to a large extent. It remained only for commercial fishing, pollution, and river-damming to wipe out what was left of the once-great Atlantic salmon population in U. S. waters.

Although it is possible virtually to wipe out a salmon run by commercial fishing at the mouth of a river, such fishing can be regulated, while a brood stock could be allowed to run the gauntlet of sports fishermen on the way to spawning areas upstream. Admittedly, many salmon rivers have been overfished at their mouths, but something much more deadly has developed. After being at sea for from one to several years, the salmon "stage" in certain ocean areas before turning homeward on their spawning runs. Thus, almost the entire mature population from a given American stream can be located in one spot, many miles from home, and virtually wiped out by modern fishing methods. That, at least, is the opinion of students of the migrations. One such staging area is located near Greenland. Salmon from other parts of the world have been mercilessly swept up by European fishermen. The Danes, with hardly any productive salmon rivers of their own, are blamed for the heaviest depredations. This has caused an international confrontation, with much talk, veiled threats—and little result. There is talk of boycotts and high-level diplomacy, but while the quarrel goes on, the salmon continue to suffer. Just how much will not be known for years. Suffice it to say that there has been an enormous increase in the Danish catch at a time when, according to the estimates of Western biologists, salmon supplies are very low. The leader in the fight to stop the Danish abuses is the Committee on the Atlantic Salmon Emergency, a group drawn from leading conservation organizations and made up of well-known sportsmen and conservationists.

Good salmon runs still exist on the Canadian coast, and anyone wanting to fish for salmon—and willing to spend some money —can do so in Canada. There is an earnest effort being made to

A British Columbia king salmon is landed more than 100 miles from the sea in waters more noted for steelhead. Such fish are nearing the end of their spawning run and lack the vigor of fish caught near salt water.

bring the salmon back to New England, but it will be a long time before that area becomes a significant sports fishery again—if ever. There is also some salmon fishing in the rivers of Maine, and a great deal on the shores of Quebec, Nova Scotia, and Newfoundland. The British Isles have Atlantic salmon, but many of the runs have ceased in European rivers. Once the salmon ran freely in the Mediterranean. Norway is famous for very large salmon on some wild and steep rivers.

Salmon water is often very expensive to lease, but some government-controlled waters are open to all. Newfoundland has more than a hundred open salmon rivers, and Iceland has much salmon fishing, although the fish are not large. Some of the best salmon fishing is to be found in undeveloped sections of Labrador. Fishing is not expensive in Newfoundland, but many of the rivers play host mainly to small fish.

The salmon is a fly-taking fish, so most salmon waters are restricted to fly fishing. I doubt that we can say fly fishing for Atlantic salmon approaches the more delicate forms of trout fishing where finesse is concerned, but no one can deny it is a complex sport. Here is a fish that may grow to great size, that takes small flies, that fights very hard—but isn't supposed to feed during its spawning run, the time when most fly fishing is done. A detractor may say there is no hatch to be matched, no feeding station, no feeding period, and no logical reason for a salmon to strike in the first place. He may say it is freakish fishing. But the salmon fisherman will counter that there is a great deal to learn about salmon migrations, that the fish is frustratingly unpredictable, and that the expert will outfish the novice by a wide margin.

Also on the plus side is the fact that the salmon can be taken with very light fly tackle if one has the skills and inclination. A salmon fly can be small enough to cast with the lightest of trout rods, and the leader can be as fragile as the angler wishes.

THE FISH

Atlantic salmon are called "alevins" when first hatched, "parr" as juveniles in fresh water, "smolts" as they begin their ocean lives, and "grilse" when they return after one year at sea. Spawned-out salmon that are returning to the ocean are called "kelts," or black salmon. These terms are also applied to Pacific salmon occasionally. Atlantic salmon can spawn more than once; Pacific salmon only once.

The steelhead is a close relative of the Atlantic salmon, and size of mature salmon varies greatly in the same way that steelhead size varies from river to river. For example, Iceland is noted for small salmon, while some Norway rivers are noted for very large ones.

Fresh-run salmon, just in from their life at sea, have the reputation of being the hardest fighters. After a long stay in fresh water they lose some of their fury, but not to the same extent that the dying Pacific salmon deteriorate. Grilse afford excellent sport and they vary greatly in size, generally weighing several pounds. The black salmon, or kelts, are legally fished in some rivers; in others they are protected. They are in fairly good condition and sporty fish in some areas; in others, they are in such poor shape that they are not worth fishing for and often die from predation.

THE TACKLE

Salmon rivers come in all sizes, much as the fish do, and the tackle varies considerably, but the trend is toward lighter equipment. Perhaps the typical American salmon rod would be an 8½-footer, taking an 8 or 9 line, and this comes very close to being our all-around fly rod. A weight-forward floating line is most popular, and the tapered leaders usually run down to about 10-pound test.

A peewee rod can cast most salmon flies, but you'll need some backing on the reel. Some of the users of ultralight fly rods still insist on big salmon reels with high-quality drags. In most rivers the expert plays a salmon lightly enough that it seldom moves to another pool. Despite its tremendous energies and high leaps, the salmon can be controlled by experienced anglers using very light stuff, providing there are no obstacles to foul line or leader.

On some of the wildest rivers a long rod is needed to keep line out of the water and thus allow the fly to drift naturally, when desired, without being yanked prematurely by the line.

Most salmon are caught on wet flies, and although the sizes vary greatly, they are small lures for so large a fish. Salmon flies are often ornate, and some of the traditional patterns employ wide varieties of exotic materials, making them very expensive items. Since, in most cases, these patterns represent no particular

Canoe is used for river travel by Newfoundland salmon fishermen, although the actual casting is done while wading. Guides use poles instead of paddles at low water.

insect, they are largely traditional, and a collection can include the most beautiful specimens of the fly-dressing art. Simpler ties, even ordinary bucktails and Muddlers, have proved efficient, and it seems now that the old complex patterns, many of them from Europe, are giving way before newer and cruder offerings. Some of the well-known complicated dressings have been simplified somewhat and sell at moderate prices in salmon country. It is almost shameful that they seem to do as well as the old standards.

Wet flies for salmon are generally rather lightly dressed. The lower and clearer the water, the smaller the fly and the lighter the dressing. Some of them are little more than a good-sized hook with a fly pattern tied to the eye end of the shank, and most of the hook completely devoid of any dressing. Whether to choose a single or a double hook seems to be a matter of personal preference, but doubles do go deeper in the stream.

When water is very low, the dry flies come into use, but they are little known, even now, on many salmon rivers. Most salmon dries are fluffy or bushy and they certainly seem to be simpler than the wets. This is probably because they are relatively new and haven't felt the influence of traditionalists. Salmon can be caught on very small trout flies, but usually the hook sizes are 10 or larger. The wet flies can run from very small trout sizes to some that would work very well for large tarpon.

The principle of playing salmon with light gear is to make the fish swim constantly, but experts are careful not to attempt overpowering pressure. Although the fish can jump more than ten feet up a waterfall, it is not equipped for long periods of extreme exertion. Therefore, users of light tackle prefer to maintain very light pressure while the fish is running and jumping. Then, when it sulks, they increase the tension. The fish takes off again and they give it a fairly free hand. If the fish has become accustomed to a pool, it may actually return to its original lie with the fly in its jaw. This should be followed by more persistent prodding, resulting in another wild dash around the area. The fish is an open-water resident and prefers to avoid—rather than try to overcome—any kind of obstacle.

Salmon have a small "wrist" ahead of their tails, and the salmon tailer is simply a device that can be extended with one hand and clamped about that wrist. Experts can tail salmon with their bare hands, although most of them prefer the landing assistance of net, gaff, or tailer. Salmon can also be beached, if the shoreline is suitable.

The ultimate strain on tackle comes when the fish is tired and being worked toward the fisherman. Unless very heavy fish are anticipated, a large, boat-type net is highly satisfactory. And since guides are required on much salmon water, the fisherman frequently leaves the netting to the guide, or to another fisherman. There may be some who would consider it taking an unfair advantage of the fish, but many salmon are netted a long way from the rod. I watched a pair of experts handle a fish in fast water, with the netter a full 30 yards below the fisherman. When the fish was pretty tired, and simply holding against current and leader, the netter scooped him up from downstream. If the fish appeared too green and likely to tangle things up the netter would simply scare him off. Then after several approaches he would decide the time was right and make his move.

THE METHODS

Most salmon are caught on wet flies, which are cast across current and allowed to swing down and around. I have watched highly successful salmon fishermen who never seemed to vary the presentation. Others will go to great effort in mending casts so that the fly goes down in a natural drift, at least part of the time, and is shown broadside to the fish. However, some of the best fishermen have never heard of these refinements, and although I rely strongly on such techniques, I find it hard to argue with success.

In Newfoundland I was guided by a highly successful fisherman who used a straight delivery of his fly, letting it swing around on the leader. He felt my line mending and carefully engineered natural drifts were the result of inept casting. He also used 20-pound tippet material and insisted that I do so. I'd change to something lighter when he wasn't looking, reasoning that, after all, these were a sort of trout, with a trout's caution. But salmon are seldom leader-shy.

If a fisherman has moderate casting ability and a few of the flies preferred locally, his next problem is to learn where the fish usually lie—and, more important, where the devil they are lying on a particular day. This is complicated by the fact that the fish are not in typical feeding spots. In theory, they are only resting

Casting a wet fly on a Newfoundland salmon river, one of more than 100 such streams on the island. Salmon often lie in very shallow water if current is satisfactory.

before continuing on upstream for their spawning chores, and the fact that they may hang around for weeks, or even months won't necessarily change their choice of holding area.

Salmon generally select their resting areas with regard to current speed, rather than for purposes of concealment. There are some preferred spots, occupied year after year, but the fish will sometimes change lies because of water levels or temperatures. For example, salmon that lie in the tails of pools may move forward, toward faster water, as the river goes down; and then appear nearer the lips of the pool when it rises. It's a matter of locating the exact current speed they prefer. If there is little or no current, they tend to move about, evidently seeking either other fish or water movement for comfort.

The "decoy theory" is an important one. It states that the fish will tend to group together in suitable lies, even when they arrive separately, generally seeking and keeping to individual positions. If mildly disturbed, they are likely to seek the same position in another formation of resting fish. Before moving upstream to other holds, the fish will become restless and change positions or tour their pools. This doesn't necessarily mean they are likely to strike, but it often does. Once they move on upstream, the abandoned lie may be vacant for days, and then be occupied again by a growing school of fish as new travelers move in from below.

Salmon lack many of the fears of resident trout and unless he cuts them off from deeper water, they will often permit a fisherman to wade very close, even in the shallows. If he gets too close, they may turn and drift back a little, only to return to their original positions when the waders are gone. Good-sized salmon sometimes choose very shallow spots—often slight depressions on a gravel bottom—and inexperienced fishermen are likely to be wading where they should be fishing. Told that there was a hole in what appeared to be a fairly level-bottomed pool, I waded in and then turned to my guide for further instruction as I worked out line. I was only twenty feet from the shore, but he sadly explained it was too late. I was already standing in the "hole."

Salmon, like steelhead, often rise after watching hundreds of casts. You might say this is creating a hatch, but since the fish aren't really feeding, it may be they simply rise from irritation or boredom. As with resident trout, it is frequently possible to get a strike by changing flies—size, pattern, or both. There is a theory of casting rhythm, which claims that the fish can be somewhat mesmerized by the rhythmic reappearance of the fly, finally taking if the fly returns at accurately spaced intervals.

Wet salmon flies, many of them tied from exotic materials, are frequently dressed on double hooks. Most of the newer patterns are simpler and less expensive.

Fish can sometimes be goaded into striking by methods that would ruin most trout fishing. Sometimes, for instance, anglers throw rocks into a pool to get the fish moving. In trying to photograph salmon in their lies, I have waded to within less than ten feet of them. The fish merely moved over and dropped downstream for a few feet to await my departure.

As with other gamefish, salmon will sometimes become receptive all at once. After casting dry flies for two hours over a cluster of grilse and salmon lying in plain view at low water, I raised four different fish in rapid succession. After that the activity was ended for the day.

Salmon are addicted to playful rises and splashing, sometimes causing the fisherman to think he has been too slow in setting the hook. But solid takes are likely to be deliberate and

225

unhurried. Salmon are not noted for the quick expulsion of a dry fly that can be so exasperating with small trout. When the fish are jumping about in a pool they are not necessarily ready to take flies. However, a jumping fish serves as a good marker of salmon lies, and you may get a strike in the area, whether it is from the jumper or not.

After a period at sea, during which he has fed on baitfish and crustaceans instead of insects, a salmon is out of practice in taking flies, and some of what seem to be just playful salmon antics are probably unintentional misses. Don't forget, a wet fly near the surface appears as a double image in many cases, the fly being reflected from the surface mirror when outside the fish's window of surface vision. Some of the strikes may be at the reflection rather than at the fly.

Apparently, salmon rise to the fly in many different ways, and there is considerable conclusion-jumping by casters who have watched them on only a few occasions. Undoubtedly, they are great followers of wets at times and frequently take flies while headed downstream. They also take "dangling" flies, which are simply held in the current, with neither drift nor retrieve.

At times, salmon seem oblivious to flies, leaders, and even sunken lines, and a leader dragged across a salmon's back will then produce only an irritated shifting of position. Most authorities believe that the more times a salmon has looked at a fly the less chance you have of catching him, but they've all raised fish after a long series of presentations. The assumption that an alarmed salmon is always going to dart away is wrong. Like many other species, a salmon may lie watching a fisherman for hours, evidently on guard and with no intention of taking anything, but unwilling to leave his position. Unfortunately, this characteristic makes it possible to snag, or "snatch," salmon if a fly drifts just right. The procedure is illegal, of course, but pretty hard to prove after a fisherman has his fish. A big double-hooked fly with light dressing can snag a fish. I once watched what appeared to be a successful fisherman who operated a long distance from any other angler, only to learn that he is regarded as a highly successful

*Most of the dry flies used for Atlantic salmon are bushy ties,
generally featuring hair instead of feathers. Wide use of the
dry fly is a recent development.*

snatcher. It works best (or worst) in warm, low, clear water
when fish are highly visible and often sluggish.

THE SALMON'S LIFE

Whether or not salmon take nourishment on their spawning
trips is the subject of much learned study, considerable misunderstanding, and occasional dignified arguments. It is known that the
fish's digestive system changes during this period and can't cope
with solid food. Many believe, however, that the salmon does
take insects, squeezes out the juices, and swallows enough to

acquire some food value—though certainly not enough to keep a big fish charging the fast water. He must draw on the resources he has accumulated from feeding at sea.

While traveling thousands of miles of the Atlantic, salmon feed mostly in the depths. Thus, there isn't much Atlantic salmon sports fishing, except during the annual spawning runs in the rivers.

During the spawning, the female salmon scrapes out a nest, lays the eggs (which are fertilized by the male alongside), and then covers them with gravel. A nest (also called a redd) may cover considerable area in a small stream, the eggs covered quite deeply with gravel, often more than a foot below the natural stream bed. The freshly hatched alevins will grow into parr, fully formed small fish that remain in fresh water for considerable time. Although the overall routine is the same in all salmon rivers, the elapsed time varies greatly. In some northern waters where growth is slow, the parr may stay as long as four years in fresh water before migrating to sea as smolts. In some rivers the period is only one or two years.

Before going to sea, the smolts spend some time at the edge of tidewater, usually leaving with high water in spring. They may spend only a year at sea and return as grilse, or they may return after two or more years, sometimes as very large fish. The size of salmon in various river systems varies widely. In some cases, the fish return mainly as grilse and are therefore quite small. In others, the returning fish are older but still not large, evidently because their ocean feeding areas were not highly fertile. In some rivers, the returning fish are very large, having spent a long while at sea in very fertile waters. The repeaters, those which have spawned more than once, will be large fish, and there are enough of them in most salmon rivers to complicate the entire picture.

Those facts don't help catch salmon on a fly, but knowledge of the river-climbing process will. The calendar is important in spring, summer, and fall salmon runs, but the fish go by water temperature and the amount of flow from their home rivers. They

Tom McNally, outdoor writer, displays an Atlantic salmon, a fish that has suffered from high-seas overharvest and habitat destruction. Credit: Johnson Reels Photo.

spend considerable time just offshore, and sometimes in tidewater, before beginning the final trip. When congregated at the river mouths, they are highly vulnerable to commercial fishing, but there's an important difference between this and the high-seas operation. Fish congregating at a river mouth are considered natives of that river and, as such, are protected by the same governmental laws that regulate the catch during the river run. The take can be adjusted so that a satisfactory rate of reproduction is assured. This is not always done, however, and the agencies in charge have only themselves to blame for the resulting decimation of their fish.

Latitude is not the only factor in the timing of salmon runs. A river that runs slowly through rolling country will be warmed quite early in the spring. One that drops steeply from mountain snows will stay cold until well into the summer, which means that two rivers very near each other may have runs at much different times.

During a drought, some salmon rivers will run hardly at all, and fish will wait at their mouths until there is sufficient current to activate the migrating urge. They'll also postpone their trip if the water is unusually high and cold. While staying in slow-moving estuaries, or just offshore, the fish will move a great deal. Evidently, motion is necessary to their comfort, so if the water doesn't move, they will. While the mature salmon wait on one side of the tide line, the smolts may stay on the other side, both waiting for suitable traveling conditions.

In some rivers, the best salmon fishing is very near the mouth, for fresh-run fish that have just left the salt. In other rivers, the run may first make its appearance miles upstream. The earlier runs are likely to move slowly, while late runs waste little time in getting to the spawning gravel. All the migrations include resting periods, however, and it is the salmon's favorite holding areas that become most lucrative when a stream is leased by private interests. Hundreds of salmon pools are named, and have been so thoroughly studied by the regulars that they can generally tell very quickly whether salmon are present. The most reliable holding areas are either below difficult passages of water, where the fish stop to gather strength before the assault, or immediately above steep water, where tired fish pause to regain their vigor. Although many salmon are caught in fast water, there are some rivers where fishermen express little hope of doing business at the very foot of a cataract. Their explanation is that the fish will be thinking of the task ahead, rather than of flies.

Atlantic salmon can leap and swim up falls that seem impossibly high. They gain part of their thrust from careful use of current at the base of these falls. When water hits the bottom, it recoils back upward, and the migrating fish comes out of the upward shove with added momentum. Fishery workers have endeavored to design waterfalls so the fish can get the most help possible.

It is in low, warm water that salmon fishing becomes most difficult, often when the run is at a temporary standstill awaiting new rains. Dry flies are most effective in low water, but only a small percentage of salmon fishermen use them. When salmon turn off during drought, the fishing can come almost to a complete halt and won't start again until there is new water, but sometimes only a few light showers will cool a river enough to renew activity.

The farther an Atlantic salmon proceeds toward its spawning area the more valuable it is to the species, for it has proved capable of surviving a long series of natural and human predations. One salmon near the head of the stream is worth a hundred, or possibly a thousand, smolts just beginning their ocean careers. The more miles it travels, the more likely it is to reproduce. I have never understood the practice of killing nearly all salmon caught by sports fishermen. Salmon anglers are among the leading conservationists, and many of them spend large sums in enhancing their sport. Yet they kill a great many salmon if they get the chance. I do not accept the argument that a hooked and landed salmon is likely to die—unless it is a spawned-out kelt, or black salmon. Black-salmon fishing is illegal or in disfavor on many waters, and rightly so, for these fish can stand little abuse in their enfeebled return to the sea.

LANDLOCKED SALMON

The landlocked salmon is to the Atlantic salmon what the rainbow is to the steelhead, although its range is much smaller. Maine is the best known home of landlocks, and they are caught on flies, most of which are trolled. There are times, when the surface temperatures are ideal, that landlocks will strike cast streamers or dry flies near the surface of lakes and adjoining streams. The landlocked has been planted in numerous lakes over much of New England, and the spawning migrations are abbreviated to fit the situation, eggs often being laid near inlets and outlets of the lakes.

Much of the trolling is done with fly rods, and streamers imitating the smelt are most popular. The Grey Ghost and Black Ghost are old and established patterns and are also favorites for smallmouth bass, which frequently share lakes with landlocked salmon.

The ouananiche is a Canadian branch of the landlocked tribe, living in Labrador, Newfoundland, and Quebec. Although evolution has taken slightly different directions with the landlocked fish, they're accepted as Atlantic salmon. Differences in color and shape are discounted by taxonomists.

PACIFIC SALMONS

The silver, or coho, salmon is the fly fisherman's most likely candidate among Pacific salmons. It takes flies offshore when feeding on the surface and it occasionally also takes them far up the rivers. Like the other Pacific salmons, however, the coho dies after spawning, its condition deteriorating as it goes inland.

Since its successful introduction to the Great Lakes, the coho has become one of the best known of game fish. It has been caught by fly fishermen in tributary streams while on spawning runs. However, the vast majority of coho are caught by deep trolling, or mooching with bait. I am afraid of general statements about fly fishing for coho, for I have found them behaving differently almost everywhere I have fished for them. I assume it is a difference in the stage of migration.

Pacific salmon reach the end of their journey in an Alaska creek where spawning fish mingle with the dead and dying. Unlike the Atlantic salmon, the Pacific travelers spawn once.

At times, a powerful arm and a long rod will reach feeding schools off the mouths of Pacific rivers, and these fish should be in peak condition. I have met with dismal failure in several Alaskan spots when the fish steadfastly refused to take flies, although they struck spoons, which were cast or trolled. The fish were easy to reach; they just wouldn't take any fly I could offer them. While trying to catch coho on flies, I have hooked chum, or dog, salmon;

humpbacked, or pink, salmon; and chinook, or king, salmon. Some of the most obstinate cohos were in a small Alaskan creek where they enthusiastically walloped streamers accompanied by a small spinner, but paid no attention to the flies alone. I am tempted to say that the inconsistency of their behavior is due to differences in various strains of fish. But I suspect it is really a matter of how nearly they have reached spawning condition (and hence, death).

Almost any Pacific salmon can be caught if you'll get the big streamer to them at the right time and depth. Fast-sinking lines have made it much easier, and lead-cored fly line has accounted for fresh-run chinooks in a specialized form of deep fishing. Since these fish die after spawning, their strikes are even more puzzling than the Atlantic salmon's, once they have passed tidewater. Like many steelhead fishermen, I have caught them in all stages of deterioration as they near the spawning grounds. Unfortunately, it is seldom possible to reach them with cast flies when they are offshore and in peak condition.

ELEVEN

Some
Occasionals

WITH THE fly fisherman planning steadily for his next trout or bass trip, a great deal of other fishing is missed. Some of it is narrowly seasonal, as in the case of shad. Some of it, as with pike, is nearly always available but is seldom tried, simply because the fisherman doesn't associate that fish with fly tackle.

NORTHERN PIKE

Although there is no reason in the world why a northern pike shouldn't take a streamer fly, or a popping bug, it is very difficult to convince most fishermen that they will do so. Trout traditionally take flies; northern pike traditionally take spoons or big plugs.

Many excellent fly fishermen have no intention of bothering pike with fly tackle. When it comes time to fish for pike, they put their fly rods away and get out something else. Actually, I believe pike go for streamers and bugs about as readily as black bass do, and I have seen times when the fly rod was definitely superior. I probably wouldn't care to make a career of fishing for pike, but it's a lot of fun now and then. I have seen times when pike would strike almost anything that moved, I have seen other times when I was unable to get a strike even though I knew I was fishing over pike on every cast.

The easiest pike to catch seem to be in wilderness lakes, and, in clear water, it is sometimes possible to hook almost every fish you see. I have been told by bush pilots that there are certain lakes where the pike will always strike—at any time of day. Generally, such fish are not extremely large, and I'm inclined to believe such waters are overpopulated and the fish always hungry. Although I can think of a couple of spots where I've never failed to catch pike of small and medium size on a streamer fly, I haven't fished those places long enough to say that they *always* feed, regardless of conditions. I have failed miserably on good pike waters when the fish were near the surface and willing to follow everything thrown at them. They simply wouldn't strike— whether at flies, plugs, spoons, or anything else.

I think big streamers and big bugs are best for pike, unless you're satisfied with the smallest fish. That means the rod and line should be capable of handling big wind-resistant stuff. A rod using a No. 8 or No. 9 line is close to minimum for best results, and an even heavier saltwater outfit would be better for the larger fish. I have not found that pike make particularly long runs, but they frequently go through weeds and other obstructions, so it's no place for light tippets. A shock tippet or a very short wire leader will avoid tooth trouble.

Someone once said that lures make no difference because "when they're hungry, they'll hit anything, and when they aren't, they'll take nothing." That's going a little too far, but I don't find that fly or bug design is particularly critical where northerns are concerned. I do think that the speed of the lure should be varied from day to day. I also believe that flash and glitter are helpful. The streamers I've liked best have had some Mylar strands among the bucktail and feathers. Big tarpon streamers work beautifully, but one or two small fish can wreck feathers, whereas hair might last a bit longer. A shiny hook helps too.

The pike is an ambusher and does much of its hunting while

lying still until the food comes near it. A surprisingly large pike can disappear in the shimmering reflections and shadows of a weed bed, the spotted pattern of the fish's side seeming to merge with dappled light from the surface. It not only lies at the edge of weed beds; it lies within the weeds themselves and its head is likely to be facing toward open water where baitfish may pass. If a passer-by happens to be another, smaller pike, the larger fish

Nothern pike like this one will take flies readily in northern back country. This one came from the Yukon.

has no aversion to cannibalism. Once a pike has caught another fish, it seems in no hurry to swallow it and often carries it for a time, crosswise in its jaws. This habit has led to the belief that the fish is deliberately cruel, but chances are the procedure is simply a matter of weakening the prey before positioning it for swallowing. Pike are noted for their insatiable hunger and have been described as digestive systems with teeth.

The pike is a cool-water fish, if not a cold-water fish. Ideal temperatures are somewhat below 65 degrees. In midsummer, near the southern part of its range, the fish is likely to go deep if deep water is available. In any event, these fish become quite sluggish in hot weather, so it's a poor time for fly fishing. You can work deep with a sinking line in lake fishing but it's very difficult. After you get the line down deep enough to reach the fish, you have only a little distance to work your streamer before it begins to climb back toward the surface. Then too, when warm-weather pike are found in somewhat shallower water, there is likely to be considerable vegetation. Working on pike with flies is mainly a cool-weather sport.

Many pike are found in fairly swift rivers, but the best fishing spots are likely to be in sloughs or eddies. In spring, they are often caught in fairly strong current below falls or other obstructions, and I suppose this is a matter of migratory tendencies. They do travel for considerable distances during the spawning season (shortly after the ice goes out). But whether in rivers or lakes, it seems the best pike fishing is found around weeds, either underwater or emergent. Lily pads shade many large pike.

I have been unable to ascertain time-of-day feeding periods for pike in general, but have heard reports of tests in which they fed in midmorning, rested during midday, fed again in midafternoon, and rested in late evening. I have also found fishing good in early morning and late evening and have known reliable guides who insisted upon twilight fishing. It must be a matter of the individual waters.

Many of the northern lakes, where pike are thick, have a band of rushes or other growth around their edges, but have a

*Author drags inflated boat across old beaver dam while
searching for northern-pike water near Alaskan Highway.*

fairly open area between the weed beds and the shore. On an early pike trip, I was trying to find a boat to rent when a local grade-schooler explained to me that the fish were watching both sides of the weed streak. He said I could catch just as many fish by casting from shore as I could from a boat at the other side of the weeds. He was right, but it developed that the larger pike were lying next to the deep water.

We once fished the perfect pike lake in the Yukon while trying to learn just which flies worked best. The lake was deep at one end where a tangle of fallen conifers had slid down an abrupt hillside. The shoreline carried heavy weed growth, most of it submergent, at the deep end, and extending out for 30 or 40 feet. The shallow end sloped up into a long slough, with a wandering creek that appeared to have no current at all at that time of year (early August). Best of all, the lake was a little difficult to reach. I dragged, pushed, and paddled my small inflated boat along the narrow creek, and finally slipped out into the lake itself. My wife hiked through the woods to meet me because the creek was so narrow and shallow we felt one person could negotiate it better than two. Anyway, here we were on what was supposed to be a good pike lake, and it was obvious it hadn't been heavily fished.

Our most successful streamers proved to be light in color, with tinsel or Mylar flash. The fish were plentiful enough to give a pretty good test, but not so thick and eager that they would take anything and everything. After catching a few pike on streamers, we tried spoons with a baitcasting rod. Our assessment was that the streamers were catching a few more small pike than were the spoons, but that the spoon-caught fish ran somewhat larger—a very common situation when flies are compared to bigger lures. However, the largest fish of all, I recall, was hooked on a feather streamer. These were not giant pike by any means and few of them would weigh more than seven or eight pounds. If they had been larger, we might not have made so good a showing with streamers. Popping bugs, it seemed, fell a little short of streamer performance.

As in other cases, the most productive method was to cast the fly parallel to the edge of a weed bed, thus showing it to any pike that happened to be lying with its head facing the edge of the cover. Many times we could get a second or third shot at a fish that missed, either deliberately or accidentally, on his first pass. Usually, the fish would simply lie near where the fly was picked up and would often strike hard when it came back, evidently taking no chances of letting it escape a second time.

Like the smaller, but equally toothy, Eastern chain pickerel, the pike sometimes choose a lure that is going quite fast. I have frequently hooked one when I was in the act of picking up and the fly was darting along the surface. Incidentally, the methods that work for pike also work for muskellunge.

Northern pike are residents of the most northern parts of the northern states and are plentiful in Canada and Alaska. They are good table fish, although the derogatory names of "jack" and "snake" have made them unpopular with many fishermen. They're also pretty bony.

The pike is one of the best known fish in antiquity, mainly because of its great size and vicious appearance. Any fish that eats young ducklings and wears a perpetually leering expression is a fertile subject for superstition. Hence, many of the European lake monsters were believed to be pike. It was also believed the pike was a sign of evil and that young fish hatched from sections of water weeds. Whenever anyone perpetrated a hoax in the form of a giant fish, the subject was generally a pike.

CHAIN PICKEREL

The chain pickerel looks like a northern pike and acts much like a northern pike, but is much smaller, tolerates warmer water, and has a more southerly range. It's best known in the Atlantic states, but you'll find pickerel in the South and as far west as Texas.

The pickerel takes streamers, worked fast along the surface of weedy areas, but I have found that a small spinner doubles the action on most days. The pickerel seems especially fond of a chattering, sputtering action on the surface, and the retrieve works best when considerably faster than that used for black bass. Although pickerel will take popping bugs and hair bugs (especially those fished like frogs and in shallow water), I am inclined to believe the spinner is the most reliable. Most of the pickerel I've caught on flies were taken while I was after bass.

Chain pickerel, lovers of thick grass, are frequently found in black-bass waters, and will take streamers and bugs, preferably worked at high speed.

On many weedy lakes the pickerel seem to live in colonies— not close enough together to be called schools. Sometimes they occupy the same general areas year after year even though these spots don't seem to differ at all from the rest of the lake in depth, bottom conformation, or vegetation.

Chain pickerel tolerate a wide range of water temperatures.

I've found them active when the water was warm enough for wet wading, as well as when there was ice around the edges. Pickerel are leaders in the ice-fishing take.

Redfin and grass pickerel are small relatives of the chain pickerel. All are good food if the bones can be managed.

SHAD

Nearly all the fly fishing for shad is in fresh, or very nearly fresh, water. They are anadromous fish, but the fly fishermen can't get at them when they're at sea, and I doubt if they would take flies then anyway. When offshore, they are very deep, at least part of the time. The American shad, *Alosa sapidissima,* appears in rivers of both the Atlantic and Pacific coasts, having spread rapidly after its introduction to the West. The hickory shad takes flies well, but is considerably smaller.

The freshwater invasion is for spawning purposes, beginning as early as late November in the St. Johns River of Florida, and reaching its height in late spring in New England. Biologists say that most of the southern fish die after spawning once, but that many of the northern fish return to spawn again. An occasional northern fish will weigh as much as eight pounds, but it seems the southern fish run smaller. A four-pounder from the St. Johns is a good fish.

Fly fishermen can usually locate shad hotspots by inquiry or by simply watching casters and trollers along the coastal rivers. Fly fishing for them in the South is a neglected sport, and the slow rivers often have concentrations of fish that have yet to be located by either trollers or casters. Until I tried it some years back, I had never seen a fly fisherman casting for shad on the St. Johns, although the trollers and spin casters were thick in the well-known stretches. Incidentally, the fly rod with monofilament line is an excellent trolling tool for small spoons and jigs, or "darts," since the long stick with soft tip works well with the shad's papery mouth. Before spinning gear became popular, the fly rod was used extensively for trolling.

The late Norton Webster, an excellent fly caster and fishing authority, is credited with starting sport fishing for shad on the St. Johns River, still one of the most productive shad fisheries of all. Webster usually trolled with a fly rod. The same system was used on the St. Johns by the late Joe Cather. He manufactured a tiny spoon that is one of the best shad lures, generally trolled in company with a small jig. Cather caught many schooling bass

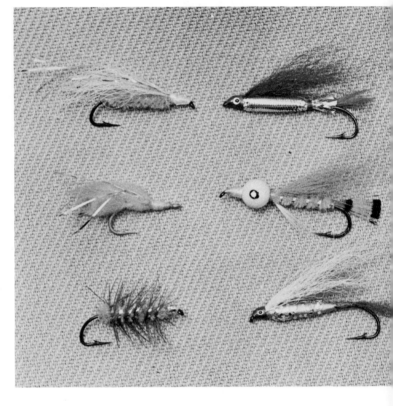

Some successful shad flies. Those on left are yarn and Mylar miniatures of West Coast steelhead flies. On right are flies tied especially for shad by Chester Cooper, South Hadley, Massachusetts.

with his little spoon by casting it on a fly rod, but he generally went to trolling when after shad. Both men used monofilament line for trolling.

When fast-sinking fly lines became available, I tried them on shad, finally locating a concentration of fish in the St. Johns' Puzzle Lake area, some distance from where the trolling boats would interfere with my experiments. I used the tiny Cather spoon in fly-rod size and threw it with a heavy fly rod. Although the water was slower than that usually fished with flies, I caught fish with a very slow retrieve, keeping the spoon very near the bottom and fishing from sod banks, or wading. A boat wasn't satisfactory because I had difficulty keeping the spoon deep enough from the higher position. I got tired of casting the spoon and gave it up after proving I could catch the fish by casting.

It was several years later that I began using flies, and Ray Donnersberger came along to help. I confess that he took over my experiment with a more scientific approach and more perseverance than I could muster. By checking the reported results of the trollers, we concluded that our method was just as productive as trolling. We were, however, less mobile and had difficulty staying with the fish concentrations which seemed to move almost continually over a mile of river. The best part of it was that we used real flies instead of the spoons.

The water we fished was around seven feet deep. We used short leaders with shooting heads, and cast upstream, letting the fly bump along the bottom as it drifted down, sometimes with a very slow, twisting retrieve. It was sandy bottom for the most part and our catch also included numerous clams, an occasional small crappie, and at least one eel.

Since the spoons and flashy little jigs were so successful for trollers, I at first thought a fly consisting only of Mylar strands would be perfect. But it just didn't work out. Ray tied up a handful of gaudy things, most of them steelhead patterns in reduced sizes, and after catching a few fish with a given fly, he'd retire it and try something else. The most successful ones were simple yarn flies with Mylar ribbing. Orange and fluorescent green were about as good as anything. Ours were no better than the established shad patterns used along the upper Atlantic coast and along the Pacific, but they seemed to be just as good. Using the same ties, a few other fly fishermen have caught St. Johns shad, but it is a neglected business.

I have gone into this at some length because it's one form of fishing in one particular area that is almost completely ignored. The best shad fishing on the St. Johns seems to be in the Sanford, Florida, area, and inquiry will get you to where the fish are running in any given year.

In deep water, shad take the fly with a gentle nudge, make fairly long runs, and usually jump freely. The shad mouth simply won't stand much rough treatment and the landing procedure is complicated by the fact that the fish continue to fight after they no longer have strength for runs or jumps. A great many shad are lost at the net, or while you're trying to get a handhold on a squirming, flopping target.

Shad do considerable rolling when near their spawning areas, but it takes a little experience to identify them positively. The roll is not as high as a tarpon's; veterans call it "washing." It is especially difficult to pick out when there are small gar in the area, as in the case in some southern rivers. It's a gentle splash and can't be called a head-and-tail rise. The fish merely surfaces and makes a firm tail-stroke or two as it goes back down. After you've seen several such disturbances, the chances are you're in business if you can get your fly to the bottom. There are a few places where shad will take dry flies, but it's a less reliable method.

Commercial fishing takes a great many shad and undoubtedly hurts the sports fishing, but there seems no likelihood of the shad becoming scarce at an early date. It's river netting that does most of the damage.

ROCKY MOUNTAIN WHITEFISH

Like a mudfish caught by a black-bass angler, the Rocky Mountain whitefish (*Prosopium williamsoni*) is a disappointment to any trout fisherman. It takes flies readily, especially dries, and can be caught in very cold weather when trout fishing is poor. Two-pound whitefish are quite common in many of the larger Rocky Mountain rivers, and almost every western fly caster has played a whitefish with care, only to learn it wasn't a brown trout after all.

For good reason, Joe Brooks once called the whitefish a

Rocky Mountain whitefish are an extra bonus for trout fishermen in many rivers of the West, sometimes weighing as much as four pounds.

"practice fish." Although it is sometimes easily fooled by dry flies, the small whitefish is harder to hook than any trout I've ever encountered, largely because of its suckerlike mouth. It also has a disturbing way of rising to the fly and then turning away as if it had taken, leaving a drowned fly and a small disturbance that I cannot tell from an honest strike. It has a fairly high dorsal fin and is often confused with the grayling.

The smaller whitefish frequently gather in schools, but the larger ones are less likely to do so. They take very small insects, most often in water of moderate speed, although they can be found in sloughs and lakes as well. They are especially active in the evening, and their dimpling rises cause many fishermen to search frantically through their boxes, only to be disgusted with a small whitefish after missing a dozen strikes. However, there are frequently trout among the whitefish.

The whitefish pulls hard immediately after being hooked and will flounder as it is being brought in, rolling over and over in the water. I consider it somewhat less powerful than any of the trouts, but where I have caught whitefish and grayling together, the whitefish seemed to be the stronger. It does not make clean jumps, although it will lunge across the surface. The large ones are much easier to hook than smaller fish, mainly because they can get the flies into their mouths more easily. I think many small whitefish are missed because they are unable to actually engulf the fly and it is snatched away while they are chewing at it.

Rocky Mountain whitefish make excellent eating and have been fished commercially. The only true complaint is that they often compete with trout for food.

TWELVE

The Smaller Ones

MOST OF US began our fishing careers with sunfish of one kind or another. Mine were green sunfish, which we called "black perch," and when I graduated from worms to a treasured Black Gnat, No. 10, I used a fly rod that had cost less than two dollars. I had a forty-cent fly reel, but I had never seen anyone cast a fly, and I used crochet thread for line. The six-inch snell on the Black Gnat was leader enough for my purpose; I guess it was a little pathetic. Unlike the self-satisfied urchin with willow pole and worms, I was trying to do something I didn't understand. But I caught a few green sunfish anyway.

It was some years later, after I'd learned baitcasting, that I got a real fly outfit and went back to the green perch. At first I flopped around with a luminous tandem spinner, wading up to my adam's apple in places I could have reached an easier way if I'd known how to cast, still catching green perch and an occasional small bass. Then I saw a man really casting a bass bug, and the spinners were put away. I got three bugs, one of them a small hair mouse, one of them of the old Callmac design, and one a cork and hair dragonfly. The hair mouse was death on green

249

perch and caught some bass, too; I was fly casting and things would never be the same after that.

THE EQUIPMENT

There are times when the very lightest of fly equipment is ideal for panfish. I have seen it so when the subjects were yellow perch along rocky shores, when they were bluegills along steep

White perch is a leading northern panfish, living in both fresh and salt water and sometimes competing for food with the smallmouth bass. Excellent table fish, they have been an East coast commercial favorite.

banks, or rock bass against Ozark bluffs. Even so, it's best to use a weight-forward line, for that will turn over the little bugs well, and there are few times when the most delicate presentation is necessary.

But when the big, rusty-headed bluegills are plopping in the pad pockets, or making little bulges around the pickerelweed, it's good to have a rod at least seven feet long, and eight may be better. Holding some line off the water is a help when there are obstacles between you and your fish, and although there are scoffers who say a longer cast is never necessary for panfish, I have often stretched my arm to get into a distant hole in the cover.

If I could use only one fly rod for all of these small fish, it would be about 7 or 7½ feet long and would take something like a 5 or 6 weight-forward line. That's enough stick to throw a full-sized bass bug in an emergency, and at the moment I can think of no panfishing I ever did when there were no bass around.

The reel can be anything that holds the line, as no warmouth perch or crappie is going to strip any gears. The leader should be tapered to something near five-pound test for most panfishing. Anything heavier is likely to interfere with the action of your flies and bugs. Also, there are times when the fish are a bit leader-shy. Most of the fishing is with floating lines, but there are occasions when a sinking one is a big help.

I guess I've caught more panfish on bass rods than on anythinge else. Some of the pleasantest fishing comes when the bass and panfish are working together. I have studied hook sizes a good deal to come up with something that would handle big bluegills and bass, too. It comes out about number 6. If you're dealing with white perch, it can be a 4, and big crappie would just as soon take a full-blown bass size.

THE BLUEGILL

The bluegill (*Lepomis machrochirus*) is the best known of the panfishes and is now found in all of the contiguous United States—except Maine, I believe. A fisheries man in Maine stoutly disclaimed the presence of bluegills there some years back, and I don't know if any have sneaked over the border since then or not. There are bluegills in southern Canada.

Bluegills will take almost any sort of small fly, streamer, or surface bug at times, but they seem to be especially touchy about the depth at which these are worked, leading to many sage observations that "you can always catch bluegills if you get down far enough" or that "nothing beats a floating rubber spider if you really want big bream." Such pronouncements are the results of sketchy experience. Sometimes bluegills are deep and sometimes they are on top—and sometimes they refuse to change their depth to strike anything. This persnickety business about depth has caused numerous fishing failures.

I can give you an excellent example of bluegill stubbornness, exhibited on a backwater of the Tuolumne River in California

Little popping bugs with rubber legs are hard for bluegills to resist, especially during evening feeding sprees.

some years ago. After an afternoon in which I had failed to catch any bass, I noticed some small wakes in a very shallow spot against the shore. As the sun set, I cast a small dry fly in there. The response was an immediate plopping strike and the short tugs of a bluegill. I caught several on consecutive casts, then made several casts with no result at all. It developed my fly was sinking, so I put on a fresh one and was back in business immediately, getting a strike on every throw. I doped it to sink and the striking stopped. The remarkable part of the situation was that the water was only six inches deep where the fly was landing. It had to float, and if it got a fraction of an inch below the surface it was ignored. Pattern wasn't important, but it had to stay on top. In other places at other times it's the other way around.

On the other hand: During bluegill spawning season I was fishing with Al Klemack, a fishing guide who has wide experience with trout, bass, and panfish, and who has tied up thousands of green nymphs for sale in tackle stores. It is much like a small woolly worm, short on the woolly part, and with a small tail. He told me this nymph was highly successful on big trout in spring holes during hot weather.

We were working an area where we were sure the bluegills were bedding. On two previous days I had done very well in similar waters, using small popping bugs with rubber legs. But on this day, the sun was hot, the surface was glassy, and my bugs went begging. At Al's suggestion I tried the nymph, and results were almost instantaneous. The slightly weighted nymph would sink about two feet before the big bluegills would latch on. These fish were averaging almost half a pound, and some went up to around ten ounces. It was hard for me to believe the fish wouldn't move up two feet for the poppers. It was a fairly steep shoreline with a fringe of weeds.

On a later day, this time cloudy and windy, I found the little green nymph a killer again, while rubber spiders and popping bugs had indifferent success. The logical move was to try other underwater stuff, but the green thing was the answer. Small black woolly worms and yellow woolly worms simply did not score. I don't say green is the answer even most of the time, but it certainly has its days. I confess that much of its success may have been due to its exact weighting, for depth is very important.

Small dry flies are a great deal of fun for bluegills and their relatives. They can, however, be a nuisance with very small fish that you may want to release, as tiny fish tend to swallow them in carefree fashion. If fishing is good, dry flies don't stay dry very long. Most bluegill water is quiet, so I twitch the dry flies. I also retrieve sunken flies and nymphs with slow twitches. I operate floating bugs about as I would fish for bass, but I move them more gently.

I am sure that rubber legs add greatly to a small popping bug's effectiveness for bluegills. The rubber spiders and bugs that float soggily on the surface film are among the most effective lures of all, but they don't seem to pick up as many occasional

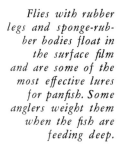

Flies with rubber legs and sponge-rubber bodies float in the surface film and are some of the most effective lures for panfish. Some anglers weight them when the fish are feeding deep.

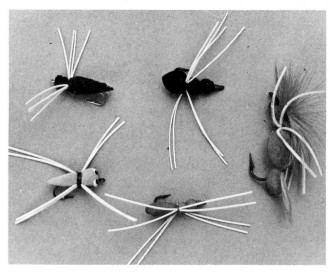

bass as the popping bugs do. A popping bug with a 4 or 6 hook will occasionally take good bass, either large or smallmouth. I've caught quite a few over two pounds, but I do not recall catching any as large as four.

The time of day is especially important with bluegills, and in most of the areas I've fished, their evening feeding begins somewhat later than that of bass. They often give themselves away with their plopping rises. Very small ones will often feed noisily among the roots of floating water plants, such as water hyacinths and duckweed. Although these little ones may not be what you're after, they indicate that surface feeding is starting and the bigger fish may be around, too.

It's no fast rule, but sunken lures generally do their best in bright daylight. At dusk, the bugs are frequently more productive and that's when sunken flies and nymphs sometimes produce nothing at all, the fish having turned completely to the surface. Some fishermen like to weight their rubber spiders or "bream killers" during the heat of the day.

In most bluegill waters, I have found that flies and bugs will take more fish than bait. But there are times when bait will beat you badly. Some of my most frustrating fishing was in the Okefenokee Swamp in Georgia, where bait fishermen caught buckets of "fliers," close relatives of the bluegill, and I couldn't produce. The flier, or "fly-perch," is a southern fish (*Centrarchus macropterus*).

Bluegills have a reputation for great strength for their size, and the typical fight is rapid circular swimming with the fish turned on its broad side. Although the fight is short, many a light leader has been snapped when a fisherman tried to horse his catch and concluded he'd hooked a big bass. Hold the tension for a short while and the fish will simply pop to the surface, but he must be hurried along if there is underwater cover. Other sunfish act much the same way.

Bluegills are so widespread that it's natural to assume their management is easy. Actually, the balance is very difficult to maintain, and many panfish waters are swarming with stunted fish that are much too plentiful for their own good. The combination of bluegills and black bass is excellent, if cover is just right, because the bass can keep the numbers down. Then you'll have some big bluegills and big bass, too. However, it's possible for the bluegills to take over, ruin the bass fishing, and crowd themselves into insignificance.

Bluegills have spawning habits similar to those of largemouth bass. Sometimes bluegill nests are found over large areas, and so close together that they almost overlap. The eggs are laid by the thousands in shallow depressions, sometimes in very shallow water. Where banks are steep, there may be bluegill nests within inches of the shoreline. They are fond of bass spawn, but this is a part of the natural balance in most cases. Farm ponds make ideal bluegill habitat, but the vegetation can become too thick. Also, fish managers are likely to be a little vague as to just what is going to happen after they're introduced.

THE CRAPPIES

Most crappies are caught on bait, and often from very deep water, especially in the impoundments. When they're very deep they're too far down for fly fishing, even with sinking lines. Some of the largest crappies I've caught have taken popping bugs, but small streamers are more reliable as they're not primarily surface feeders.

No panfish congregates more persistently than the crappies.

Canoe fishermen work shoreline pockets for panfish. Surface lures are almost essential in these surroundings.

They school up around brushpiles and weedbeds. A sinking line and a streamer will get them then, but I have found them selective about colors; the fish that take white streamers today may show a strong preference for yellow tomorrow. They are vulnerable to a jigging action, frequently taking the fly as it sinks. Short casts are best if they're in more than two feet of water, and an intermittent retrieve will make a heavy fly go up and down. If you care to cast spinners, they often increase the catch. Very light spinning tackle and small jigs will generally beat a fly fisherman, but the fly rod has its days, especially when crappie are along the shore in the shallows. During the spring spawning periods, I have seen crappie plentiful in a scant foot of water, although the actual spawning seemed to be occurring where it was considerably deeper.

The black crappie (*Pomoxis nigromaculatus*) is generally found in clear, weedy water. Although it was formerly an easterner, it has now been introduced over most of the country. The white crappie (*Pomoxis annularis*) is somewhat lighter in color, has six spines in its front dorsal, as against seven or eight for the black crappie, and is more tolerant of silty waters.

Crappie occasionally take large bass lures since they have large mouths. The strike is generally light, and they make definite efforts at reaching cover. They're usually easy to find during spawning season, but many fishermen say they "disappear" afterward. Although their hot-weather locations may be hard to find, they still tend to bunch up. I have found them at the mouths of small creeks in very hot weather, and at such times they sometimes take large popping bugs, evidently competing with bass for bait that works out of the creek.

ROCK BASS

Most of the rock bass I've caught have been in smallmouth rivers, mainly in the Ozarks of Arkansas and Missouri. They're called "goggle-eye" there and will come steaming off a gravel bar or out of jumbles of chunk rock to hit a bug or streamer. The mouth of the rock bass is considerably larger than that of the bluegill.

Like most of the other small sunfish, these become stunted through crowding and they run very small in some of the tiny, rocky creeks. I believe the largest ones are found in the North, and they are an important species in the Lake Erie area. I have never been able to catch the larger ones in great numbers, and nearly all that I have taken were less than 10 inches in length. A bluegill fisherman is at home with them.

OTHER SUNFISH

I am somewhat partial to the green sunfish, partly because I grew up with it, partly because I know that it offers some good fly fishing that is seldom touched. In the Midwest, I have found excellent bug fishing for this one in creeks that stopped flowing in early summer and became only mud-banked little ponds as the hot weather came on. A small hair bug worked well for both the sunfish and an occasional bass. Like the rock bass and the warmouth, the green sunfish (*Lepomis cyanellus*) has a large mouth, an extremely important feature since it allows use of bigger lures that may be attractive to bass.

The warmouth *(Chaenobryttus gulosus)* has a silhouette similar to the green sunfish and is capable of living in mudholes with catfish and grindle. It is a willing taker of flies and is as good to eat as any other sunfish when it comes from suitable water.

Other sunnies, such as the longear sunfish, the pumpkinseed, the redbreast, and the stumpknocker, are good fly takers, too, but I have a bass fisherman's prejudice against their small mouths. The shellcracker is a big southern sunfish that prefers snails to feathers.

WHITE PERCH

The white perch (*Roccus americanus*) is a member of the sea bass family (unlike the black basses, which are members of the sunfish family). It's both a salt and freshwater fish, but in fresh water it tends to become overcrowded. Fishing combats the propagation rate. In some areas, the white perch is a competitor of the smallmouth bass and eats bass eggs and fry. It is an Atlantic coastal resident.

White perch take dry flies, especially in the evening, but most of the ones I've caught have been taken while I was fishing with streamers or poppers for smallmouth bass. The most I've ever caught were in the Belgrade Lakes of Maine, where I found them in very shallow water in early June. One congregation of

Basslike mouth enables the warmouth to take large flies and bugs intended for black bass. It thrives in warm water of weedy ponds.

them was in a shallow bay that shelved up, with a gravel bottom and large chunks of granite. Many of the fish were moving around very near the surface, some of them on top of flat boulders. I first cast to the slow wakes, believing they were bass, but it developed all of them represented hungry perch and I could catch all I wanted on small streamers or bugs. On that particular lake, I found the bass were in somewhat deeper water, for the most part, with the perch working at the very edges.

White perch have considerable commercial value and are an important part of the catch in the Chesapeake Bay area. They have habits similar to the striped bass and ascend rivers to spawn. Some of the best fishing is in brackish ponds. White perch are taken by fly fishermen working Currituck Sound for bass. This is an exceptionally fine food fish with a good-sized mouth for a fly.

YELLOW PERCH

Yellow perch (*Perca flavescens*) are not noted as fly fish but they are among the leading panfish of the northern part of the United States. I have read that they will not take dry flies, and perhaps they won't very often, but they will occasionally take a popping bug. Perhaps it's a matter of what part of the country you're fishing.

Generally, yellow perch run somewhat deeper than the fly fisherman works. They bite freely in cold weather and make up much of the ice-fishing catch. They're important as a forage fish for bass, pike, and walleyes. I won't put them in the top bracket of fly fish, although small streamers and wet flies have caught many of them.

THIRTEEN

Brackish Water

BETWEEN FRESH and salt water lies an area offering the greatest variety of fly fishing; an area unexploited by fly fishermen, though heavily covered by other fishing methods.

The brackish belt is an indistinct line, changing with tide and rainfall. It has its migratory visitors from deep sea water, visiting for spawning purposes or to take advantage of seasonal food supplies, and it also has temporary residents from the rivers. Salmon and sea-run trout may spend time there, acclimating gradually to fresher or saltier water. Black bass may be pushed into brackish water when inland habitat is reduced by dry weather. They may even spend their entire lives there if the salinity is satisfactory.

SNOOK

There are other brackish water fishes of special interest to fly fishermen. A few of them are capable of living at the ocean's edge through a wide range of conditions, and it is difficult to set down a preferred salinity for some of them. The snook is one of these, often found hale and hearty a hundred miles upstream in a freshwater spring, and at other times appearing as a surprise catch from a reef far offshore.

The mangrove demands brackish water, and evidently the snook's preferences are similar, for the two go together. There are many snook in Central America, but most visiting fly fishermen are there for other fish. Although the snook, or robalo, migrates about the Gulf of Mexico, nearly all snook fly fishing is done along the southern coast of Florida. They are not regular visitors north of Florida, having small tolerance for cold.

The first snook I caught were in open inlets where they performed as strong enough fish without breaking much tackle. It is in the tidal creeks and against snaggy mangrove banks that a snook becomes an antagonist to defy all logic and planning.

My first back-country snook took my yellow and white popper against a buttonwood stump, ten miles from the sea, then scooted behind the dangling mangrove roots and around a bend in the shoreline. When he was followed by boat and miraculously landed, he weighed only five pounds. I had expected him to go at least twenty.

Because the snook is usually manhandled with heavy tackle, many fishermen do not consider it a fly fish. They may have the idea that all fly tackle is gossamer, and have not heard of big fish on the long rod. Early in my snook-fishing career, I was mentioning some of my exploits in a tackle shop, perhaps a little too loudly, when a browser stepped from behind a rod stand and looked me in the eye.

"Nobody," said he, "can catch a snook on a fly rod." So saying, he walked out, leaving me sputtering.

I have pretty well settled on a rod taking an 8 to a 10 line. I then overload it one weight, using a 9 line on a number 8 rod. I use a fairly slow action and this makes it easy to cast short distances that would not be comfortable with a stiffer stick. I generally use an 8½-footer, but some snook fishermen prefer a shorter rod for firing under shoreline branches. There is also an argument for stiff rods that throw very small loops. This works, but entails more labor.

The snook, or robalo, sometimes rivals the tarpon in head shaking during jumps, but is less of an aerialist. It's runs for cover break fly tackle.

Snook fishing involves violent runs, but they are usually short and I have seldom needed much backing. Nearly all snook fishermen employ a shock tippet, which should be about 10 inches long. Generally 25-pound monofilament is enough, but if the fish are large, 50-pound is safer. Wire is good, but easily kinked.

Snook do not have cutting teeth, but their mouths are highly abrasive. On their gill covers they have very sharp plates, for which I can see no purpose, but which can slice a careless hand or cut a leader. Then, in the roof of his mouth the snook has another small, sharp blade, installed crosswise and retractable. I assume it aids in holding baitfish. For years I didn't know it was there and couldn't explain the tiny cuts I kept getting on my thumb when I cleaned snook.

Tales of the snook cutting, or "popping," commercial nets verge on folklore and superstition. I don't see how he can manage it, but I have heard the stories from reliable men and I believe them. The fish is not especially dangerous to handle—just un-usual. You can hold him with your fingers *under* the gill covers. The blades are on the outside and lie nearly flat.

In years of fishing streamers and popping bugs alongside surface and underwater plugs, I have concluded the fly rod will take more snook and the plugging rod will take larger ones. I began my snook fishing with very large tarpon streamers, then went to smaller bucktails and feathers because they seemed to take just as many fish. Recent experience has changed my mind to some extent, especially where the fish run to good size, and I have gone back to the outsized streamers for at least part of my fishing.

On a recent shoreline-casting expedition, a friend with noisy surface plugs had six solid strikes from good fish while I drew only one halfhearted swipe at a popping bug, and nothing on small streamers. I put on a big, white feather streamer, fished it slowly back over the same water and got four good fish. The largest snook, an eleven-pounder, scooped the streamer off the bottom while I fussed with a minor line tangle. All four of the fish were hooked in the gills after they had tried to expel the fly.

Most saltwater fish go for fairly rapid fly-stripping, but there are days when they want the fly "soaked," as Ray Donners-berger says.

Snook fishing may be crude compared to the dry-fly fishing for trout, but it has its complexities. The most common strike of the resident snook begins back in the shoreline cover. He comes out for the fly, takes it in a turn, and is already aimed back at his starting point. On the occasions when he takes very deliberately, however, he may be towed toward the boat before he becomes truly alarmed, and he will then be at a disadvantage in turning. It is when he drives with the leader over his shoulder, and has plenty of momentum going, that he pulls unbelievably hard. I have long said that the hardest snook to stop weighs something like seven pounds. A bigger fish is less likely to drive far back into the mangrove roots because there is simply no room for him back there.

There are numerous landing schemes, any of which may work, but all of which are more likely to fail. The only sure approach may lie in black magic or astrology, but there are several plans worth a try. If you get him moving away from cover, let him go for a while before using heavy pressure. If he is heading for home, bear down on him. Some say that you can stop him

Good rig for fishing inshore waters. Boat has spare motor in case of a breakdown and for close maneuvering, and is sculled by man in stern.

by slacking off completely when he heads for the shoreline. It has happened, but such a method can end in a monumental mess. If he's going to make the roots anyway, you can stick your rod tip far underwater and sometimes keep the line and leader from hanging up; then work him out as he tires. This latter method offers some comic relief, whether it gets the fish or not. An oarsman or motor operator who instantly heads for the open is a help.

One snook-fishing associate of mine says it's helpful if everyone present chants, "Hold him out!" He says it is also good if everyone points toward the bushes, in case the beleaguered fisherman forgets the object of the game. I consider this frivolous.

Of course you might use 80-pound leader. One friend says the snook would break it anyway, but I doubt it.

There are conflicting opinions about shoreline fishing from a boat. Bob Ramsay, a fine Florida fly fisherman, much prefers to fish streamers behind a noisy lure, whether plug or bug. His theory is that the fish are aroused by a noisy lure and begin to move, and will then take the streamer when it comes along. This plan has worked many times, especially on snook, although it is only one more method to try.

A fly fisherman who becomes too set in his ways, especially in salt water, will lose much of the good fishing. Fish preferences can be completely inexplicable and can change within hours, or even minutes. The complexity of their response is even greater when it is considered that none of the saltwater flies are true imitations in the sense that a freshwater nymph or mayfly is imitated.

The back-country snook appeals for several reasons, not the least of which is its homeland of twisting roots and dense mangroves—a setting that seems almost unreal, and can be depressing to some. But it is a fly-taking fish and its fight is unusual, causing utter frustration at times and hilarity at others. Many a fine salmon or bass fisherman becomes a quivering victim of broken leaders.

There are snook the year round along the southern Florida coast. During the winter months, most of the fishing is in the back country, often many miles from open beaches, and the fish caught there are dark olive in color from a life in water stained by vegetation. The "back country" is a skein of rivers, creeks, and bays, lined by mangroves that may be as tall as 70 feet. Much of Florida's best snook fishing is in Everglades National Park.

Fishing improves in the offshore islands when weather warms; the run of big, silvery, outside snook occurs in late spring and early summer. At least part of the spawning occurs in the island passes, and small snook—about a foot long—can be caught by the dozens by fly fishermen near the heads of the tidal rivers. But there is some mystery about the six-inch and smaller fish. Biologists have found them in a few inches of inshore water on occasion. I have tried to catch very small snook, using trout-sized streamers, and once caught a single little fish, about six inches long, in a barrow pit open to salt water. That was the only one.

The big fish that come into the passes to spawn probably work inshore progressively as the water warms, appearing at Florida's southern tip first, and farther up the coast later on. With cold weather they disappear again, evidently to offshore reefs. Until recently, it was believed the same fish simply toured the coast, working northward as the weather warmed.

Most snook fishermen operate only when the big outside fish are in, trolling, casting big plugs and jigs, and using live bait. The fly fisherman can fish the outer island edges just as he does the inside creeks and bays. Occasionally, he can catch snook in the surf. Most of the best fishing is found when the tide is moving briskly, whether in or out. Dead low tide is seldom good because the cover that the fly man casts to is frequently out of the water then.

A point with swirling current is good, the fish tending to lie just out of the fast water, protected from the tidal shove by small bars or tree roots. It is the same kind of feeding station chosen by smallmouth bass or cutthroat trout, a spot found instinctively by river and creek fishermen, no matter where they learned their trade. Although the fish here run larger than in the back country, the angler has a somewhat better chance once the fish is hooked. This is because the "outside" snook may be a migrant and lack intimate knowledge of the available hideouts. There are some areas where the only cover is oyster bars, and some of the largest fish are taken under such circumstances. A rising tide, barely breaking over an oyster bar, makes a feeding station for many kinds of inshore fish, a situation recognized instantly by weakfisherman, striper expert, or channel bass veteran.

Roadside ditches that connect with salt water often contain snook, especially if they are affected by tidal rise and fall. Most famous of all is the Tamiami Trail canal which follows the high-way across southern Florida. One side is against the sawgrass, and the caster stands on the highway side to work fish against the opposite bank. Snook can be caught by blind casting, but the best fishing comes when fish are visibly taking bait on the sawgrass side. This usually occurs on a falling tide that carries minnows out from sawgrass creeks.

Generally using small streamers, the fisherman tries to get as close to the sawgrass as possible and, at the same time, avoid hooking passing automobiles with his backcast. Probably many a tourist has arrived home in Ohio or New Jersey to find a streamer fly attached to the grill or bumper of his car—a mystery he can never solve.

Like many other kinds of saltwater fly fishing, these canal operators appear deceptively crude and simple. But though almost anyone who can get a streamer into the water will catch an occasional fish, the expert will catch many times more than the beginner. I learned one of the more subtle lessons many years ago from Rocky Weinstein, who fished the ditches for years.

There was a midday rally of snook on the Tamiami Trail (U.S. 41) between Ochopee and Marco, and one of those rare times when the ditch is full of bubbles, the sawgrass shakes with explosive strikes, and even the speeding motorists gawk at the splashes. I had fished hard all morning, but the fish had ignored my efforts, except for one undersize "snooklet" who had somehow gotten mixed up.

I came upon Rocky Weinstein, vigorously hooking and playing snook, and asked him what I was doing wrong.

"Oh," said Rocky, "the snook are driving that small bait clear into the sawgrass and pinning it in there. When they pop, they're facing that side of the canal. You have to throw clear up into the grass and bring the fly out fast."

As he explained, he cast his little white fly up into the grass, yanked it out, and hooked a snook. It was a special fly with a small hook that would cut through the grass blades without breaking a 10-pound leader. My heavier hook would hang me up.

I borrowed one of the little white calftail flies and began catching snook. Well and good.

I was back on the job early the next day, and the snook were popping away—and ignoring all of the little white calftail flies tied on the thin wire hooks. Frustrated and sheepish, I found Rocky again, and again he was catching snook.

"Whatsamatter, man?" Rocky wanted to know. "Can't you see they're facing this way today? Throw the fly a couple of feet from the edge and let it sink slow."

I did, and a snook grabbed it. It was a subtle change, but the bait was moving along the canal rather than hiding in the grass. The small sinking fly evidently represented a crippled minnow.

A snook, one of the top gamefish of mangrove waters, is landed by Milt Culp. Mangrove roots in background make ideal cover for snook and necessitate careful casting and a firm hand once the fish is hooked.

If you must move fast, ditch fishing is a grim test of tackle, regardless of the fish sought. The rods are subjected to violent whipping and all sorts of hangups. There are destructive things to be hit by the backcast. The line is likely to be trampled in the sand, mud, and grass, then yanked loose when the fisherman flounders along the shore, trying to keep some line in the air while heading for a striking fish. It is hardly the tranquil joy of a limestone trout stream, but it is fly fishing, and the same fisherman can be ecstatic over both.

There was one season when a small Muddler Minnow, natural bucktail color, did best on striking fish. It would go down two or three feet, I'd detect a slight twitch of the leader, and hook a snook. My theory is that the fish had finished striking, was sinking toward the bottom, and scooped up something he thought he damaged on the surface.

Dawn is the most likely time for canal fishing, and the ideal combination is a falling tide at sunup, a busy time in the Everglades. Along one shallow canal run-in, I have seen a dozen wading birds, a raccoon, an otter, and an alligator—within a 20-foot stretch of sawgrass and mud—while the minnows showered, and the snook popped with a sound like gigantic champagne corks. The cork simile is a worn description but is certainly hard to improve.

Canal migrations occur most consistently in early spring, and I have seen hundreds of fish going resolutely upstream in schools in early March. Occasionally such traveling fish can be caught on streamers, but they're usually more interested in getting wherever they're going. Evidently, they separate after getting several miles from the sea. Many of the larger fish have remoras, which drop off in fresh water, and some fishermen believe that is why the fish are there. But many of the fish have no sign of remoras.

Not all snook take to the canals, of course. "Cruiser" snook are large fish that move so close to the surface they push a bow wave. They are best known in canals, but sometimes travel the same way in bays and rivers, shoving along the very edge of mangrove shores. The trick is to cast well ahead because the fish is preceding his bow wave by considerable distance. I have caught cruisers, but my percentage is very low. Most of them are easily put down as they are in a position to see the fly line, and possibly the fisherman.

In describing snook streamers, we run into the usual nameless void where saltwater flies are concerned. The big tarpon flies are well known, usually on 4/0 hooks. I have leaned toward white as the basic color, but yellow is used almost as much. White can be seen for a considerable distance underwater, while a sound reason for yellow is hard to come by as there is little snook food of that color. Most snook streamers are tied on 2/0 and 3/0 hooks. Where fish are small and plentiful, bucktail is much more durable than feathers, and double-tied bucktails will give greater length.

Sportsmen have long tried to achieve legislation that would help the snook population. In Florida, the snook has been made a gamefish, with a legal limit of four fish of more than 18 inches in length. Unfortunately, there are some species of snook that never get 18 inches long and are, therefore, never harvested. The legislation, passed with great effort years ago, was primarily aimed at commerical fishing for snook. It's now generally believed the size limit does no good, and may in fact, be harmful, since small snook are released, even when badly damaged by multihooked lures. But once having achieved at least some sort of protective law, the conservationists are content to let well enough alone.

Although all of my fishing friends consider snook one of the very finest of saltwater fish for eating, I have read repeatedly that they are poor food, and they have been called "soap fish" and other derogatory things. I don't know what the chefs do to them, but I hope their reputation for being inferior food can be retained. Less fishing pressure.

It will be overdrainage, coastal pollution, and destruction of shorelines that will eventually stop snook fishing, if the biologists' educated guesses are correct.

RED DRUM

The red drum (also called channel bass or "spot tail") comes as a target of opportunity for many fly casters, although few specifically go forth after it. The best known fly fishing for "redfish" is on the grassy flats of the Florida Keys, where they are generally sighted before the cast is made. Even then, the fish may be taken for something else, unless the caster is a veteran.

Thinking about bonefish and talking about bonefish, Ted Smallwood and I slid down Florida's west coast from the Everglades in an outboard boat. We began poling a grassy flat in a dead calm, a Keys bridge barely visible to the south, and the flat seemingly endless, merging into a hazy horizon. It was drought time; Everglades fires made a gray haze, and an occasional scrap of ash dropped into our boat.

We saw no tailing fish, but found a clump of gentle bulges and swirls over the blotchy bottom and stalked them cautiously. Ted's pink-shrimp bonefish fly was taken in bonefish style, and the run began with what seemed satisfactory bonefish speed. It continued for some 50 yards, and stopped in a deep hole where the fish resorted to grumpy jerks and what felt like bottom rooting, which it was. I poled toward the deep hole, but Ted had worked out his six-pound redfish before I got there.

There were still a few signs of water movement, and we caught several more fish, using the pink shrimp. After two fish had been caught, the school scattered a little and the individuals lay quiet on the grassy bottom. That's typical channel-bass procedure, although there are other times when a school will move away as a unit. Even while sulking, the redfish were willing to take a fly, but it was hard to see them before a cast. Each fish that we hooked ran for the deep hole. Evidently they had been operating there for some time.

In deeper water, the redfish is noted for his dogging tactics, but like most fish that are hooked in very shallow water, he will make quick runs on the flats.

This particular spot is not the place to catch the giants. For years, the largest redfish have come from the lower Atlantic

Small redfish, or "puppy drum," are good fly takers at times. This one was caught on a bucktail by Fred Terwilleger. Such fish are sometimes caught by sight-casting on clear flats.

coast, generally having been targets of surf-casting rigs, and very few fly fishermen even try for them. In 1967, Ree Ellis recorded a 38-pound, 12-ounce fish from Chesapeake Bay, Virginia, on a fly. For the most part, fly-caught fish are classified as "puppy drum," and a 15-pounder is a big one. Widespread use of sinking fly lines may produce some new techniques for the bigger fish.

Redfish will strike streamer flies or popping bugs, and once you locate a concentration of small fish, they often continue to take as long as there are any left. Basically a bottom feeder, the red drum has an "inferior" mouth (one located on the underside of the head), and he must do some maneuvering to make an accurate surface strike. Many chances are missed because the fisherman tries to set the hook too quickly, while the fish is still gumming around over the fly or bug, trying his best to get it.

273

I've caught redfish repeatedly by casting back to the scene of a missed strike. The victim hit even harder the second time, evidently disgusted at bungling the first chance.

The primary diet of the red drum consists of crustaceans and mollusks, although they will take baitfish as well, especially mullet. Tidal currents washing over oyster bars or sand banks make excellent feeding spots for them, and they sometimes cause enough surface disturbance to be located from considerable distance. They seem remarkably nearsighted, hence a slowly worked lure is best. They sometimes tail on shallow flats, and aren't always easily flushed. The best policy is to put the fly as close as possible to the fish. Although they school, I have never seen them breaking the surface in large numbers.

Generally speaking, the smaller fish are found in bays and estuaries, and the really large ones work the surf. I have caught small drum where the water was fresh enough to drink and they may live in such a spot for a considerable time.

Bucktail streamers with plenty of white or yellow will work well, and many drum are caught on small flies used for bonefish. I've had trouble hooking them on really large feather streamers. As near as I can tell, this is because their mode of attack, with that downstairs mouth, makes them prefer to suck in a fly. Their startling crashes at a popping bug are caused partly by the entire head coming out of the water as the mouth descends on the target. But even when the fish turns on his side and takes shark-style, he can produce a drowning-horse commotion. If you yank the bug away from him, he wanders forlornly about, wondering where it went.

There are year-round red drum residents in many southern areas, and the biggest fish seem to come inshore in early fall along the southern part of the range. For the most part, the Gulf of Mexico fish are smaller than those on the Atlantic side—they're found all around the Gulf Coast and are a mainstay of the fishing on Texas beaches. Frankly, they are not usually considered a fly fish.

Spawning information on red drum is skimpy.

WEAKFISH

Grass beds, warm water, and no direct sunlight is the best formula for big spotted sea trout on the fly. There is some confusion about the name of the fish, some calling it a "spotted weakfish," and others classifying the common weakfish as something quite different, insisting the spotted species is no weakfish at all. (The term "weakfish" incidentally, evidently refers to its papery mouth.) In any event, the spotted trout, or speckled trout, gets most of the fly caster's attention.

The take is dramatic, especially on a popping bug, and the run can be fast and strong in shallow water. When the water is deep, the fish seem to have no particular destination in mind and are likely to devote their energy to simple tugs and bottom rooting. Thick grass is what makes the landing operation difficult, and even on an otherwise open flat, a heavy trout can end up in the center of a swirled mess of weedy wrappings. I will not say the sea trout is one of the hardest of fighters, but a five-pounder on a shallow flat is no sure thing. His typical program is a boiling or banging strike, a fast run toward deeper water, and then a dive into the submerged shrubbery when rod pressure stems the rush. Having caught many smaller trout in more open water, my first grass-flat view of a big speck underway with a fly in his mouth was quite disturbing. He escaped.

The biggest weakfish are found on the Atlantic coast of Florida, mainly in the estuaries and along the tidal inland waterway. Cocoa, Florida, is the center of the best of it. In chilly weather, most of them are taken from deep holes on bait, or on bottom-bumping artificials. It can be done with a fast-sinking line and a streamer fly, but that is not the most entertaining method for the fly man.

I was dredging a deep coastal canal for some holed-up bluefish, using a fast-sinking shooting head and a Mylar-trimmed streamer, when something big came off a sloping sand edge, churned the water, and went on down with my fly. I announced to my friends that it was a big bluefish, subsequently changed that identification to channel bass, and then landed an eight-pound spotted trout that never got more than 50 feet from the boat. It was fairly chilly water, but a sunny day, and I assume' the fish had come up out of the deeper hole to sun himself on the sand bank. I'd normally have preferred warmer water for fly-fishing trout, as the surface temperature was less than 70 degrees and he should have been way down deep. But it was the old story of the shallows warming first when the sun shines and the current is slight. That was near St. Augustine, Florida.

Most of the spotted-trout fishermen I go with have a preference for sticky-hot, predawn beginnings—when the mosquitoes buzz in clouds around the dock lights. In the afternoons of those summer days, we usually leave early to avoid the inevitable thunderstorms.

The preferred method is to take a boat to a good spot, then disembark and wade wet, feeling cautiously with your canvas shoes along bottoms that are frequently muddy and may have stingrays. We give special casting attention to the grassy edges of mud or sand bars and the steep dropoffs along the spoil banks. Streamers are worked briskly with foot-long strips, using a floating line, and poppers are yanked pretty hard. Extremely long casts are unnecessary, but ultralight tackle is inconvenient since the bugs and streamers are likely to be fairly large. We watch for working gulls and pelicans, give attention to wading egrets and herons, and look for the quick swirls and occasional pops that mean sea trout feeding on shrimp or baitfish. Strangely, trout feeding on natural foods seldom make as much commotion as when taking artificials.

I am inclined to feel that trout are fairly dumb. But they're extremely particular about what they're dumb about, and their choice of streamers or bugs seem to be without rhyme or reason. The white bucktail that gets them today won't work tomorrow. And yesterday's successful popping bug goes begging today—same tide, weather, and location.

Of course, there's much of this in all kinds of fishing, but I consider the spotted sea trout the champion in irrational behavior, especially on the grassy flats of the central Florida coast. They have even given nervous tics to several flytiers I know. Fly fishermen often beat the pluggers and bait fishermen, only to get their comeuppance the following day. If you want to catch quantities of these fish consistently, use all methods—but the fly rod is by far the most pleasant way. The speck is a fly fish.

Across Florida the fish seem to be more plentiful, but run much smaller. Whereas a five-pounder receives little notice between St. Augustine and Palm Beach, it is a geewhiz fish across the peninsula. But the fish are hard to figure, even in the deep, spring-fed Crystal River on the west coast, where they come during cold weather. Ray Donnersberger, he of fly-tieing persistence and tireless arm, has carried on a remorseless assault on these fish for some time. He uses a fast-sinking line and streamer fly, and anchors his skiff in brisk current.

Ray's campaign is especially interesting because he's generally anchored within chatting distance of friends fishing for bait. Usually they beat him, from what I've observed, but there are days when the trout prefer feathers to shrimp. His fishing method is a slowly worked streamer very near the bottom.

The deep fly fishing is for stubborn purists. The flats fishing, whether along the Gulf Coast, in the Florida Keys, or along the Atlantic coast, can be the choice of any angler who wants to catch fish, for there are some days when the fly rod will beat everything else.

The common weakfish is similar in silhouette to the spotted weakfish, but the spots on its back and upper sides are more irregular, simply darker shadings of their usual bronze or silver color. The spotted sea trout has round, black spots, sharply defined along the back, sides, and tail.

They take similar baits and lures, but the common weakfish prefers a sandier bottom, instead of mud. It likes the surf, and does not seem to venture so far into the coastal streams, evidently desiring more salt. I find few fly fishermen that specialize in the common weakfish. Sometimes the common weak is found in a deep inlet, only half a mile from shallow flats covered by specks, with very little overlap.

The common weakfish lives as far north as New England, while the spotted trout seldom appears north of New York. The spotted trout is a favorite around the entire Gulf Coast, as well as far up many brackish rivers. They spawn in spring and the eggs are discharged into fairly deep water. The common weakfish spawn in spring and summer, about the mouths of estuaries.

There are two lesser species of weakfish, the silver trout and the sand trout. Neither of them approaches the size of the common weakfish and spotted trout, either of which may weigh as much as 15 pounds. Both of the larger species tend to school, although very large individuals are generally alone.

Although the yellow-mouthed speck has some long grasping teeth, best described as fangs, they are not dangerous to handle and are not particularly hard on leaders. A 20-pound shock tippet might be advisable if the fishing is fast, as there is some abrasion. I use 2/0 streamers and bugs most of the time.

Although I have watched a crowd of jetty fishermen pulling weakfish from a small area for an hour or longer, the fish of the flats are inclined to be nervous and won't tolerate much boat-banging before they shove off. Generally speaking, the deeper the water, the less timorous the fish. With a careful approach, however, large fish can sometimes be sighted on the bottom within casting range.

Restaurants charge well for saltwater trout. They're just ordinary fish for my palate—but then, I love snook, and others call that a "soap fish."

TARPON

Consider the range of fly fishing for tarpon. When you're lucky enough to find them, baby tarpon of a pound or two can be touchy customers on a trout rod with number 6 streamers. Those fish may be found in barrow pits or housing-development ditches. At the other extreme, the fly-rod record for tarpon is more than 150 pounds. Although most of the big ones are caught on ocean flats, there are times when the 100-pounders come into coastal creeks and canals.

Since tarpon flesh is not on the gourmet list, there has been little study of the big herring. It was only recently determined that their eggs are laid at sea and that the fish goes through several stages before it looks like a miniature adult. The original larva is unrecognizable as a fish, let alone a tarpon. I have never seen a fully formed tarpon of less than 10 inches and I don't know where they live. I have caught tarpon only a foot long when there were swarms of them around my little fly. But I have fished

Tiny tarpon, dwarfed by fly tackle intended for much larger fish, is of a size seldom caught. Movements of tarpon are too erratic to establish a pattern.

the exact same areas for several years in succession without so much as seeing one of those juveniles.

Although they appear farther north in summer time, tarpon migrations are poorly documented. Tarpon must do a lot of traveling, for they have been sighted far out to sea, traveling steadily in great schools of big fish of 100 pounds or more. When season and weather are right, they may arrive in the Florida Keys in mobile schools, and are often very large. There are also resident tarpon (fish that stay the year round) in many areas of south Florida. Most of the fish that appear in the northern Gulf of Mexico and in the Atlantic, north of the Florida-Georgia border, are warm-weather transients. Tarpon, on the whole, are widely distributed on the Central American coast of the Atlantic, but despite the long existence of the Panama Canal there is no record of their being established on the Pacific side.

The silver king has elementary lungs, and some of his rolls are for the purpose of gathering air. However, the more he exercises, the oftener he comes to the surface, though it is doubtful just how long he could remain underwater if he kept quiet. Tests on confined tarpon show that they will die after a few hours if they don't reach the air, but the fish might well burn up extra oxygen under the stress of restraint, and it may not be a true gauge of the wild fish.

I have fished in some areas where fish rolled constantly, although not seeming to feed. There are a few areas where they hardly ever surface, even though considerable numbers can be seen on the bottom in shallow water. The sometimes quoted rule that rolling fish will not strike is false, although it is easy to draw that conclusion after casting a few thousand times at rollers which ignore your fly.

What makes the tarpon especially interesting to the fly fisherman is the fact that he continues to be a fly taker—sometimes preferring streamers to any other lure—even after becoming quite large. There are other very heavy species taken by fly casting, but most of them are hooked in very specialized fishing, sometimes through the use of teasers or chum, nearly always with seagoing boats. The tarpon angler needs no more equipment than is required for black bass.

If a tarpon weighs more than 20 pounds, his fight is so spectacular that most beginners despair after the first unnerving jump. I have seen a skilled caster shocked into immobility the first time a 100-pound tarpon rolled within easy casting distance. But the tarpon is built for flies; he is a leaper instead of a sprinter, and

Stu Apte lip-gaffs a tarpon for the author. Not large enough to be a contest fish, this one is to be released. Note butt extension on rod used for heavy fishing.

he is often found in shallow water where he can be played out with skill—and a little luck. The truly deep-water tarpon is something else, and fly tackle does not apply well when the bottom is more than ten feet down.

The most effective fly for large tarpon is the big feather streamer, often with as many as eight long hackle feathers. The whole unit is more than six inches long, the hook is probably a 4/0, and the colors are usually white and red, or yellow and red, sometimes spiced with a few strips of Mylar. The same thing, on a reduced scale, is good for smaller fish, and bucktails are fine when fish weigh twenty pounds or less.

The ideal popping-bug action for tarpon is a more or less steady gurgle, with the bug moving almost constantly, not too easy a trick with fly tackle. You'll get strikes with more hesitant action, but the gurgle seems best. It's hard to hook a big fish with the bug. For one thing, he tends to push it away with his bow wave and then lose it in the froth of his strike. I think the explanation is that any living thing that made as much noise as a popping bug would be much heavier and wouldn't move from the strike as the cork or balsa bug does.

From somewhere came the idea that the tarpon is a lightning striker, probably because all violent things appear to occur swiftly. He may splash loudly and leave an enormous boil, but he comes slowly, generally taking in a slow turn. Because of the commotion attendant upon his approach, many anglers repeatedly take the fly away from him. The problem is compounded by the fact that you nearly always see things happening before the fly is taken, especially if the fish are big. If there is a rule for hooking tarpon, it is to be sure the slack is up, wait until you feel a solid tug, and then pull his head off!

The smaller fish come a bit quicker, it's true, but a drowsy ladyfish or runty jack crevalle can give a baby tarpon a head start toward the lure and swallow it before he gets there. I have seen ladyfish and tiny tarpon feeding together in clear water, and the tarpon simply took what was left.

The first instruction I received for hooking baby tarpon was to strike when I saw a flash. My instructor told me that human reactions just wouldn't work fast enough to do it otherwise. I once watched two casters working over what seemed to be an endless supply of 15-inch tarpon. One of them was a longtime rainbow-trout fisherman, and the other had never used a fly rod outside salt water. Each had a strike on every cast; the trout fisherman caught none and his friend caught 26 while I watched. The trout man simply beat the tarpon to the strike every time. Too bad the water wasn't muddy so he couldn't see them on the way.

I guess there is some sleight-of-hand to it, at that. Most beginners have hooking trouble; then suddenly begin to produce without knowing what has changed in their operation.

Tarpon have hard mouths, but there are some excellent places to sink a hook in the tongue or in the corners of the jaw. Quite a few are caught in the gills when they have tried to expel a fly after taking it deeply. The best way is to hook the tarpon as he turns, after his strike. If he's a big fish, the trouble with getting him in the gills is that he may then have his abrasive mouth against the leader, above your shock tippet, on so deep a take.

In casting to rolling tarpon, you must decide which is the front end quickly and get the fly well ahead of him. He may be moving in that direction, or he may be just settling back to where he came from. You assume he's moving. It takes judgment to cut off traveling fish, such as those often sighted in clear waters of the Florida Keys and similar locations, and the tendency is to cast too far back.

But the technique is simple compared to the emotional dither of fishing to the "loafers." These are found lying up in shallow water, and are often seen as greenish-gray shapes, distorted by surface ripple and sometimes by cloudy water. A bit of boat noise can spook them, and they may rush off in a balloon of mud when a fly line throws a moving streak of shadow. Why a 100-pound fish flees from a few grains of fly line is difficult to understand when he need fear nothing short of a ten-foot shark in his normal existence. Certainly he's long past the point of being snatched up by ospreys and pelicans. Of course, there are some days when you can virtually comb his back with fly and leader, but it doesn't happen often. Occasionally, a fish that's not too scared will take a fly, even after being mildly spooked by the fisherman. He takes it as he leaves.

The tarpon feeds from top to bottom and roots crabs from the mud or sand. His undershot jaw slopes upward from his belly line. At rest, he often lies with the jaw parallel to the bottom, probably against it, and with his tail somewhat elevated. If a

Catching small tarpon in a roadside canal. Some such ditches have carefully mowed edges where a caster can walk with dry feet and comfort.

tarpon sleeps, I guess that's how he does it. I have found loafers in that position much less wary than those lying with their bellies parallel to the bottom. The fly should come pretty close to the nose of a "tilted" fish. Sometimes, large tarpon lie silent, with the tips of their fins showing above the surface, but I wouldn't know whether they do this in rough water as I've been able to see it only when the surface was calm.

Along with this near-surface drifting, there is some sort of phenomenon that sends a set of tiny wrinkles to the surface, as if the fish had shivered. Ted Smallwood, the Everglades guide, first mentioned it to me. I'd seen the little surface shiver before, but it hadn't made an impression. Sometimes, it is the only mark of a fish that doesn't show his fins. Once you know you're in occupied water, cast to all bubbles if possible.

There are certain areas where fish of various sizes roll daily and never seem to strike anything. We can only assume that they feed at a time when no one fishes for them, or that they move elsewhere for their feeding. There are other spots where rolling fish almost invariably mean action, probably because they have chosen those locations to feed.

I've seen dramatic proof of the feeding-spot theory. One year, two of us fished tarpon regularly at the mouth of a creek that emptied into a tidal river. They would come up the river on the rising tide and were plainly visible, rolling briskly, as they rounded a bend. They struck readily at the mouth of the creek, but it was a difficult place to play them. We decided to intercept them in the bend, then come back to the creek when all of the fish had cleared. But they would not strike on the bend. Only when they had reached the creek mouth were they ready for business. We tried intercepting them only 50 yards away, but without result.

On another occasion, we located some very small fish, of about five pounds, that were coming out of a narrow creek on a falling tide. They would roll repeatedly as they came, but would not strike until they reached a certain distance from the creek mouth. When that point was reached—about 15 feet from the mouth—nearly every fish would take. Give him the fly five feet from the mouth, and nothing happened. That went on for an hour.

It is the spectacular jumps that give the tarpon much of its reputation. The first leaps come swiftly, with the fish writhing in the air and rattling gill covers loudly. This aerial twisting is so rapid, especially with the smaller fish, that only a high-speed photograph really shows what happens. At times during the first jumps the body is so bent that the head and "neck" seem to be at a right angle to the rest of the body, in a sharp bend, and fish occasionally kill themselves this way. They also jump into trees, against pilings, and occasionally into boats. The latter isn't common but can happen when a lot of pressure is put against a green fish. Even a small tarpon can cause considerable damage inside a boat, as they are tremendously powerful and hard to get hold of. A big, green fish in a boat is a serious hazard, and I know of one that wrecked a light wooden skiff by simply beating it apart. The sections of the skiff floated away, the tarpon swam off, and the fisherman waded ashore, glad it hadn't happened in deep water.

But despite the explosive beginning, a tarpon fight slows down rather quickly. The later jumps can usually be predicted by the fish's actions, and the later runs are not particularly swift. A tarpon that comes up slowly and takes air during a fight is showing signs of tiring, but it may still be a long while before he's done. Even when he turns on his side, a clumsy gaffing attempt may start the brawl all over again, the fish calling on some reserve that would have never been used if the gaff had struck properly. But most tarpon are released, unharmed, by fly fishermen, only trophy fish being brought to the dock.

In most cases, a big tarpon could escape a fly rod by simply swimming away to sea, or up a coastal river, while he is still fresh, but that isn't often the tarpon's way. He jumps instead of running, and that gives the angler his chance. The really long, stubborn runs generally come after the edge has been taken off the fish. The occasional big fish that greyhounds in aimed leaps toward the horizon usually makes his escape, generally with some tackle attached.

In shallow waters, resident tarpon can actually be herded with an idling motor. I have seen rolling fish that wouldn't strike at first, but would take flies after being gently pushed into a deep hole. This practice should be employed only by someone who knows his fish well and is completely familiar with the bottom. Loafing fish can sometimes be aroused by a boat engine, and

Mangroves and palmettos line banks of a brackish-water canal, typical habitat of small tarpon.

sometimes they begin striking flies they wouldn't have touched before the commotion. It is the same principle that causes some Atlantic salmon fishermen to throw rocks in a pool. Persistent motor noise, however, will cause the fish to leave a shallow bay, often for good.

Tarpon dislike wind in most areas. Reasonably calm water is usually essential for success, although a slight ripple may aid in stalking. Boat noise that drive the fish away today may have little effect tomorrow.

Because of its specialized breathing apparatus, the tarpon can live in stagnant mudholes that would kill most gamefish. They are sometimes caught in fresh water, far from the sea, and their coloration often indicates they have been there for a long while. So far, there has been no conclusive proof that they reproduce in fresh water.

So far, there seems to be no danger to the world's supply of tarpon, but the fishing has deteriorated in many areas because of heavy boat traffic and fishing pressure. In the latter case, it is not the number of fish caught that has an effect, but a matter of the fish being tormented by anglers until they move out. These factors have little bearing on deep-water tarpon, but those aren't the ones the fly fisherman is after.

LADYFISH

Ladyfish are found in many of the tarpon waters, though strays get as far north as New England, and they generally move in sizable schools. They're excellent fly-takers, but are too often caught on heavy tackle intended for bigger fish. The nature of the lady's fight is pretty well illustrated by what happened when I caught my very first one. When hooked, it jumped into the boat on its own. When it was released, it jumped back into the boat again. It was a colorful beginning, but that particular stunt hasn't been repeated for me since.

A three-pound ladyfish is a big one. They live in many of the warm-water oceans, are especially active at night, and often get far up the coastal rivers. It is said they reach ten pounds in some parts of the world, but I can't recall having seen one over about five pounds. Most of them are much smaller. Their strike is really fast, their jumps are high and wide, often pinwheeling, and they can whirl and twist unbelievably underwater. They take shrimp and almost any small baitfish, and will strike either streamer flies or popping bugs.

When you're into a school of ladyfish and can't hook them, you're usually retrieving too slowly. I have sometimes caught them only by starting a pickup with my rod tip, since I couldn't strip line fast enough by hand. You often have to change fly sizes to fit the fish, but they have large mouths and a number 1 hook is generally small enough.

Because the strike is so swift, I believe there's a misconception about what happens. Some fly fishermen believe the fly is taken and expelled before the hook can be set. That may happen occasionally, but I think most of the flashes and swirls are false strikes, with the fish failing to touch the fly at all. I also believe many of the strikes are nips at the feathers, or hair, with the fly never enclosed by the fish's mouth at all. They are great followers; several will often gang up on a fly, making a churning commotion worthy of a single large fish and causing all sorts of fisherman fumbling.

Ladyfish sometimes are informers, revealing schools of bait that are being followed by larger fish. Two of us once found an especially large school working in a narrow pass and we stopped to fish them from a skiff. After catching several ladyfish of about a pound each, we hooked a snook and, a few minutes later, caught a small tarpon, both of which seemed to come from beneath the ladies. The larger fish were either scooping up the bait battered by the wild ladyfish rushes, or were feeding on the ladyfish themselves. Probably both. The school stayed right there for five days, and we kept coming back for a mixed bag, while the numerous passersby apparently decided we were real ladyfish nuts. No one else fished them, as far as I know.

Discussions of fighting qualities are largely academic because there are so many ways of a fish escaping, but I believe the ladyfish is the wildest-jumping fish I have ever caught on a fly. I believe that the jack crevalle and its many relatives are the most powerful.

There is some question of the identification of ladyfish and we must resort to the Latin name, *Elops sauris.* They go by a host of local names, including "chiro" and "ten-pounder."

They have very abrasive mouths and will wreck a small tippet quickly. If the fish run large, a shock tippet is recommended, although it may hamper the action of flies used for the smaller specimens.

This is a much-maligned species, detested by heavy-tackle users because they will wreck natural baits intended for bigger fish, and will tangle wire leaders beyond all usefulness. Ladyfish are used as bait, both as whole fish and as cut strips and chunks. They're tasty, but are so filled with bones that they seldom get to the table.

STRIPED BASS

The striped bass on a fly is a sometime thing. Even some very fine and ardent fly fishermen have given up on them, for the striper is a different fish in different locations, and the first problem is finding him at the time and place where he'll take a fly. There are certain areas, stiff with stripers, where the fly simply does not seem to work.

Probably the best known fishing for stripers is in the surf, a tough place for a fly rod most of the time. Most fly fish are caught in inland bays or creeks, or from fairly large boats close to inlets and river mouths. Fly fishing for stripers is a growing thing, but it has been done for many years. It has been only recently that the bigger fish, in the 30-pound class, have been coming in, and that's probably a matter of tackle. The early fly fishermen for stripers usually used small flies, and in this case the small fly seems to mean small fish. Until the past few years, very few casters had the equipment to throw big streamers and bugs for good distances under tough saltwater conditions. From what I have heard of very early fly fishing for stripers, I would guess it was first done with Atlantic salmon gear. Perhaps some refinements of black-bass tackle would have gotten bigger fish.

My first striped-bass fishing was in San Francisco Bay, a long time ago, and the people with whom I went considered flies only for the smallest fish. The fly rod stayed in the case until little stripers showed up, then heavier gear was put away. Now the San Francisco Bay people catch bigger fish on fly tackle and use more appropriate flies and bugs. As in the case of tarpon, I doubt if any fly-rod lure can ever be too big for bull bass.

Most striper fishing requires powerful rods and heavy lines, all the better for delivering a big, wind-resistant lure, and anybody who fishes in surf will want a nine-foot stick before he's through. The honest-to-goodness surf is a hard way for the fly fisherman to go, but things are simpler in the bays and creeks. Most good striper fishing is done in moving water, but some of the best fishing is found where the angler can walk along sod banks or use a light boat, in fairly calm water.

On New Jersey's Barnegat Bay, Pete McLain gave me a demonstration of striper spotting from an outboard boat. He was running fast over an early morning calm, in shallow water with patches of bottom vegetation. I was sitting in the bow, sleepily digesting my predawn breakfast, when Pete suddenly cut the engine and announced we were into the fish.

Since the fish appeared to me only as urgent swirls, I assumed the game was lost, but Pete began poling in the direction the fish had flushed. Either they had stopped, or we had found a new bunch, for we started fishing when a few shadows moved over the bottom, some three feet down, and had strikes almost immediately. A ten-pound striper can deliver a startling blast at a popping bug, especially in the hazy quiet of early morning. The strike is no less dramatic if he has stirred some ominous swirls beneath the target before charging.

Pete McLain, of Toms River, New Jersey, catches a striped bass on Barnegat Bay. Like many other coastal waters, Barnegat has both resident and transient stripers. Fly fishing is best in spring and fall.

Popping bugs used for stripers are usually most effective when popped loudly. Generally they are worked with considerable pause between jerks, and a long, hard pull will take some bugs under and leave an attractive trail of bubbles. This is the same method used for freshwater bass, but the pops for stripers are usually louder. It is much like snook fishing, with less continuous manipulation than is recommended for tarpon. Like other salt-water poppers, these are built for a long silhouette—a long cork or balsa body, with a tail of hair or nylon. I see no need for rubber legs or other frills for anything that is to be worked so energetically. Besides, they would make the big thing that much harder to cast. I don't think color is important either.

The streamers are mostly nameless but effective contraptions, changed by each individual tier. Double-tied bucktails of the "blonde" type are very good, adding to the overall length by virtue of two ties, and enhanced by a little tinsel or Mylar. Popular colors are white, yellow, red, and combinations of the three. There is one that merits special mention, the Harold Gibbs Striper. It is one saltwater pattern that has retained its name through many years. The original Gibbs flies are smaller than most of the striper numbers used nowadays.

Striped bass are hard strikers and make fairly long runs, jumping occasionally. Feeding fish will swim powerfully through high-breaking surf. At least in the smaller sizes, the striper also has a very quick strike, proven by casting flies to them under controlled conditions in a hatchery pool. The take is similar to that of a freshwater smallmouth.

Only fishermen with local experience are likely to make accurate forecasts of striper activities. Around most river systems with stripers, there are both resident and migratory populations, each with movement routes of its own.

Striper history has been strange. In the late nineteenth century, the bass clubs along the New England coasts were strongholds of the business tycoons of the day. Then, between 1900 and 1936, the fish practically disappeared from the coast. Since 1936,

Atlantic striped-bass fishing has gained in popularity. The Pacific coast fishery got its start in 1879 with the introduction of New Jersey stripers into San Francisco Bay. From there they spread over the coast.

The future may prove to be as strange as the past, for there has been a rash of introductions to fresh water. Hatchery fish thrive and prosper in many fresh lakes, although they do not reproduce in most of them. The Santee-Cooper impoundments in South Carolina, however, are a different story. Their upstream spawning areas were not destroyed when their saltwater migrations were blocked, and stripers have reproduced and lived with no recourse to the sea. The exact relationship of stripers to fresh or salt water has been puzzling. The striped bass, powerful though he is in the water, has proven much more delicate than, say, the freshwater bass, when handled by fisheries workers.

Fly fishermen must wait to learn how their sport will be affected by new introductions and management techniques.

FOURTEEN

Flies on the Flats

FISH CHANGE when they approach shallow water, for they are very near to the land and a thousand enemies, real or imaginary. Saltwater fish, once they are found in inches of clear water, take on a new and different appeal, for now the game is hunting as well as fishing, stalking as well as presentation, and fish reactions are violent, and magnified by the surroundings.

Weakfish are commonly sought over the shallows, but are not often seen as individuals before the cast because they are usually found in rather cloudy water, and against bottoms not conducive to sight-fishing. The same is generally true of the striped bass, although many bay fish are seen as schools. To most American fly rodders, flats fishing means the tropical and subtropical marl bottoms of the Caribbean, the Florida Keys, the shallows of Central America, and sometimes Bermuda. The bonefish heads the list of flats quarry. It has all the qualifications of an ideal shallow-water subject, being unpredictable, sometimes extremely wild, and usually powerful enough to take considerable line from any outfit that will induce a strike.

There are many other fish frequently taken on the flats with flies, including small sharks, red drum or channel bass, mutton snapper and mangrove snapper, tarpon, and barracuda. The top prize is the permit (a variety of pompano), which has been caught only by a handful of fly casters, even after years of careful and studious fishing. Some of the fly fishermen who have caught a number of permit in shallow water insist that its appeal is largely due to the fact that it is not truly a fly fish and much prefers live crabs or weighted jigs. It is a postgraduate fish, and I know of no successful permit fishermen who have not had successful careers with bonefish.

Nearly all fish—of any variety—caught on shallow flats by sight-fishing are only temporary visitors there, coming and going with the tides, and this makes them especially wary, for they are not at home. Virtually all of them spend much of their time in deeper water, but move to the flats to feed. Some of the best flats are completely out of water at low tide. A fisherman can successfully fish all day on the flats if he moves a great deal and has studied his area carefully for the exact depths and conditions most likely to produce whatever he is after. The best guides know the fish's routine—sometimes so well that the word "schedule" is more appropriate.

There are basic things about procedure and equipment that are accepted automatically by veterans, but must be learned from the beginning by any fly fisherman who expects to catch flats fish on his own. Use of a guide, to begin with, can be an excellent shortcut, and possibly an economy in the long run.

THE BOATS

Most flats fishing requires the use of a boat, even though you may actually hook the fish while wading. It's a matter of needing transportation to and from the fish. Fish that can be waded to from a highway are getting scarcer, due to fishing pressure, and the wader who has no boat is generally restricted to a short period of fishing when tide conditions are right in one small area.

The ideal flats boat for the fly fisherman would be about 16 feet long, fairly slender, low-sided, and with a flat bottom that's preferably carried well up to the bow for stability. There are very few cases in which one man can both pole and fish, and the ideal arrangement requires a poler who does no fishing at all. The length I specified keeps the poler pretty well out of the way.

The catch is that the ideal bonefish skiff is a very poor craft for crossing rough water. If you know of a flat that can be reached through sheltered water, cherish it, for the boat required to cross a choppy channel in high wind is a long way from being ideal once you see the bonefish tails. For this reason, unless he uses two boats—one to reach the fishing grounds and another for the actual fishing—the professional guide has an awesome handicap, fraught with hernias, pulled ligaments, and a great deal of sweat. Not all of his customers are fly fishermen. Not all of them can keep their balance in a light skiff under the pole. Some of his fishing may be in deep water, and he may have to go through whitecaps on the way to his chosen flats. But the sight of the perfect bonefish skiff at the dock beside sturdier boats causes tourist fishermen to recoil in terror.

The guide usually has a fast outboard boat, generally made of fiber glass, and probably with a fairly deep V-shaped bottom for soft riding. This boat won't pole easily, and will drag on a truly shallow bottom, but the guide is stuck with it. Most guides pole from the bow and shove the boat backward. The fly caster sits in the stern, faced by one or more tipped-up outboard motors the size of an apartment building, and other casting obstacles that may include anything from a fathometer to a deep-sea fighting chair. The beginner gets roughly one-third of his casts out of the boat, and many bonefish and tarpon owe their survival to such casting obstacles. I am not complaining about this situation; if I had to do general shallow-water and reef guiding, I'd probably have exactly the same type rig. As mentioned earlier, I sincerely believe the plastic garbage can for your shooting line is the best solution, despite the wondering looks you get at the dock and the ill-concealed embarrassment of your guide.

The big outboard boat is more easily poled from the bow

because the poler can operate on either side with only a minor shift in position. He can turn easily, and if he hurries to head off moving fish, he can get his passengers back into the bow, lifting most of the stern out of the water. There is very little drag from the bow if it is a V-type. Also, being in the bow, the poler is usually higher than the fisherman and can spot fish more easily. Most guides are better than their clients at fish-sighting.

Spotted weakfish or "speckled trout" prefer grassy flats and are among the most unpredictable of fly fish, changing preferences from day to day. They are often found in inland waterways as well as just offshore and in estuaries.

Although professional guides are likely to have 16-foot fiber-glass pushpoles, an occasional flats fisherman can get by very nicely with a 14-footer made from 1½-inch round stock he can get at most lumberyards. A triangular piece of wood screwed to the side of the pole can make a satisfactory "foot" for soft going. The ideal pole has one sharpened metal end for staking out the boat when movement is undesirable, and a foot on the other end.

The duckbill foot, which opens and closes with the poling motion, works well, but used roughly, metal can make grating sounds on a rock bottom causing the entire population of a flat to change locations.

Most good polers do their shoving with the pole worked against the hip. This helps them keep their balance and gives them good steerage. Probably the toughest part is learning to keep your pole out of the way of the caster. If you want to be a specialist, you can carry two poles in the boat, a shorter one for extremely shallow water. The waving pole is generally the highest part of the entire rig, and I think it is often the first thing sighted by suspicious fish. Tarpon fishing generally requires a long pole, as the water may be several feet deep.

When you have the ideal bonefish skiff, you can pole well from the stern and give the fisherman a better shot at the fish by having a simple poling platform about even with the gunwale. I go into this in some detail because the stalking is an essential part of flats fishing and too often ignored until the fish is staring at the fisherman.

Quiet is extremely important. A gentle grating of the push-pole on bottom or gunwale will often scare bonefish, permit, or tarpon. Small waves make a great deal of noise against the sides of many boats, and I am sure this often scares fish, although it is not an unusual sound to them. Some fishermen are extremely critical of aluminum boats because of the sounds of lapping water. I believe this depends upon the design of the boat, the weight of the aluminum, and how heavily the boat is loaded. I have caught many bonefish from aluminum boats but I think wood or glass is quieter. Many of the tri-hull and cathedral hull designs add to wave-lapping noises. Stomping about the boat, dropping rods and tackle boxes, and falling over anchors also scares fish. My wife occasionally falls overboard while poling and I consider this extremely bad form.

There is generally enough tide or wind to keep the boat moving, and most experts plan to float the flats so that little pole work is necessary. Where water is deep enough, an electric motor can be used without undue fuss.

The business of voices and fish's hearing has been the cause of loud arguments. If fish hearing is similar to that of humans, as some researchers claim, talking would make no difference to the fish some distance down. Yet within three or four inches of the surface fish can hear loud voices quite plainly, I believe. Experiments on both mullet and bonefish seem to prove this.

THE LOOKING

Seeing fish in the water is mainly a matter of perception, rather than visual acuity. Practice is most important, but there are some fishermen who just naturally do it better than others, practice or not. I am not very good at spotting fish in the water, having aging and mediocre vision, but I can see them better than people with better eyes. As in hunting for big game, much of the battle is in learning what to watch for. It is difficult to avoid looking for picture-book views of fish, whereas you're more likely to see vague shadows, indistinct movements, and unidentified parts of fish. With a poler and a fisherman operating together, it seems best for the poler to watch the more distant areas so that he can warn the caster in time for a cast if fish appear. I think the fisherman should confine his inspection to the area within a long cast of the boat, unless fish are already in view. Many fish are flushed after the boat has approached within a few feet of them. They were unseen because everyone was watching the extreme limit of the visibility, and the fish sneaked in without being sighted.

Polarized eyeglasses are of so much help that it is rare to find a flats fisherman who doesn't use them. These glasses polarize the light rays so that most reflections are eliminated and the eye can look *through* water rather than at it, a process that is partly mental. For those not using prescription eyeglasses, large wraparound polarizing glasses are best, as sunrays from the side can be distracting. Prescription eyeglass wearers can use every light clampons, which are completely efficient, except that most prescription

A tired bonefish turns on its side as fisherman prepares to land it. Fish came to this shallow flat during high tide from deeper water in background.

glasses have no wraparound feature. Prescription shooting glasses can be made with polarizing lenses, but they are quite expensive and many opticians would rather not go to the bother of getting them. The necessity for wraparound or very large glasses depends considerably upon your head construction. If your eyes are deep-set, much of the side glare is eliminated.

The main thing is to be sure that dark glasses are truly polarized. Other glasses will dull the glare but won't break through surface reflections for you. Polarized eyeglasses are a great help in bright sun anywhere, and are very good to have about any kind of fishing.

The standard method for calling out sighted fish is to give their direction as if the boat were heading at twelve o'clock. A little to the right would be one o'clock, and a right angle to the beam on the left would be nine o'clock. If the poler is operating from the bow, the stern of the boat would be pointed at twelve o'clock. This is more efficient than it sounds, and many a fish is caught by a caster who has never seen it but is casting from directions given by someone else.

The best visibility is on sunny days, between about ten in the morning and two o'clock in the afternoon, and flats fishermen are careful students of tides, hoping to coordinate the proper tide with proper light. You can catch fish on cloudy days, but the visibility is limited.

There are, of course, all sorts of bottom to be watched. Fish generally appear conspicuously dark over a white marl bottom, and when there's a choice, they prefer to move over grass and across areas where the view is broken by vegetation. I fished one flat where bonefish tended to move in a certain direction each day and in doing so, were forced to cross a band of nearly white bottom between grassy areas. It was very difficult to fish them while they were in the white-bottomed area, but we tried watching from a distance and found we could discern the wriggly dark shadows from more than 100 yards. Knowing exactly where they were coming from, we had little trouble spotting the fish as they moved into casting range.

Tailing fish, usually bonefish or permit, can be seen at any time of day, although sunlight is helpful in picking up reflections from wet tails and fins. Experience will teach you to diagnose distant wakes, even when fins are not seen, and some watchers can name the maker of only a tiny water movement. The best I have seen was a Cuban who would take off his polarized glasses when clouds covered the sun and point out bonefish movements when I saw nothing. He was accurately identifying only minute movements of the water, which was almost a foot deep.

THE CASTING

The problem in flats fishing is to make a throw to a visible target without excessive false casting. The line is a floater, and the fly is frequently an awkward one. In the case of tarpon, it is large and wind-resistant, and in the case of bonefish, it may be weighted.

False casting wastes time and gives the fish a frightening view of whipping line and waving rod tip. So the lines used for most flats fishing are weight-forward, with short heads that will permit an easy cast of 60 feet, preferably with only one backcast. There are numerous ways of doing this, but the main problem is how to handle the head and leader before the cast is actually made. One way is to coil the leader very carefully and hold the fly in the fingers, then coil the head in larger loops and hold the whole works in one hand. Some fishermen hold the fly in their fingers and coil the head and leader on the deck. That way it can be picked up with a single rod motion, often a forward gesture, with the line then thrown into a single backcast before the fishing cast. If you're careful, the thing won't tangle, but it is very easy to get an overhand or wind knot in your leader, and attention to these details can save the day.

Rods used for most such fishing should be slow—I'd prefer nothing shorter than 8½ feet. I'd choose a rod that bends well down into the handle, as it is very forgiving about the amount of line picked up and will get off a respectable cast even if the backcast is less than perfect. Rod requirements must be compromised for tarpon fishing because of the extra beef needed for playing heavy fish.

There are times when distance is necessary, but it is a mistake to throw too far if there is likelihood of getting nearer, especially when fish are moving. If you throw a ninety-foot cast, it will be impossible to pick up again until after considerable line has been stripped in, and there's no telling what the fish will be doing during that time. If the fish is within more reasonable range, he can be bombarded with a series of casts and shown the fly in several different ways.

Flats fish will be traveling, feeding actively in a small area, or just resting. The most common error is to underestimate the

Milt Culp plays a baby tarpon in a mosquito-control ditch on the east coast of Florida. Small boat is used since banks are brushy and water too deep for wading.

lead necessary for a fish moving at right angles, or nearly right angles, to the cast. The ideal cast would go well ahead of, and across, the course of the fish. Thus, the fly would not be close enough to spook the target, but could be moving right past his nose as he continues. Note, too, that if he becomes spooked from the caster, but hasn't truly flushed, he is almost certain to turn away, probably right toward the fly. A large percentage of the fish caught on flies have seen boat, caster, or rod, and are mildly disturbed. They intend to leave the area, but are willing to stop and scoop up something they think is food. This is especially true of bonefish.

If I saw a bonefish lying still, but making no move to feed, I would try to throw the fly a couple of feet ahead of him, close enough to give him a good view, but not close enough to startle him. If he were tailing, or visibly grubbing on the bottom, I would plan a series of casts, working gradually nearer to him, finally throwing right where I thought his nose was. This strategy seems to work as well as any. If it were a channel bass, I'd throw much closer to him as they seem to be short on vision and aren't as spooky as bonefish. I'd throw pretty close to snappers.

It is in very shallow water that your shots must be especially accurate because you're likely to hang on the bottom on the first try if nobody takes. There is a great deal of difference between fishing in a foot of water and fishing in six inches of it. Flies that work best in very shallow water sink slowly and can be worked a little above the bottom, even when the retrieve is very slow. Many of these are nearly weedless, tied with fairly bushy hackle and light hooks. The design is somewhat similar to a dry fly. When the water is two feet deep, a weighted fly is needed to get down to where the fish are traveling. The worst trouble with the weighted fly is the spat it makes when it hits the water, a sound that is occasionally actually helpful in attracting fish, but sometimes causes them to abandon the area in swirls of mud and boiling wakes. The second worst spat of a weighted fly is when it hits your neck.

A bonefish on a flat is a bottom feeder and doesn't habitually look upward for food. I have seen them take a fly at the surface, but it is unusual and generally the result of competition when several fish are moving in a school.

Thus, when you cast at a moving fish in very thin water, you gauge your cast and retrieve so that the fly can be moving slightly, right at the bottom, as the fish nears it. If you have cast farther than necessary and the fly is a fast sinker, you may have to strip it very rapidly for a few feet to keep it off the bottom and away from a hangup. These problems don't occur much with tarpon or barracuda since they're usually in water deep enough to give you retrieving room.

THE FLIES

Most bonefish flies are designed to imitate shrimp or crabs, so the favorites involve pink, blue, brown, and gray. Hardly any of them can be called streamers, and although a bonefish might take a small fish, that's a small part of its diet in most estimates. Fly size varies greatly to match the fish.

The perfect bonefish presentation would be a small creature that appears to leap off the bottom, move for a short distance, and return to the bottom again, seemingly in order to hide. This is typical of the short flights of little crabs and small, shrimplike crustaceans. Most fishermen prefer to work their flies in short hops along the bottom, allowing them to sink, or nearly sink, after each brief expedition. Once the fly has been sighted by the fish, it may well be allowed to sink to the bottom because the bonefish is well equipped for scooping it up. It should be moved only very slightly once it has sunk, they say. Nevertheless, a fish that has examined a sunken fly in plain sight of the fisherman is likely to show renewed interest when it darts away from him. Bonefish are great followers, as are permit, and will trail a slowly moving fly for a considerable distance. Since they are known to feed largely by smell, I am sure they are trying to get a sniff of the unfamiliar subject.

This fly-following business can be unfortunate, for once a fish has trailed your fly almost to the rod tip, it has undoubtedly seen you or your boat. When a fish has followed to within 20 feet of the caster, I think he's wise to pick up and cast again, for sometimes the new cast will get immediate action. If there are other fish (bonefish often move in schools), he should try for a new customer, preferably farther away. The other alternative, if the fish follows and does not take, is to retrieve the fly rapidly. Sometimes it works.

Ordinarily, a fish that is tailing and actually grubbing on the

Bonefish flies are tied to represent the little creatures flushed from the bottom by feeding fish. The deeper the water, the heavier the fly. Weedless model at lower left is for grassy bottoms.

bottom is not particularly spooky. When they're sighted from a boat, I think it's best, in most cases, to get out and wade. Such a fish is so absorbed in the wondrous things he is rooting out of the bottom that he may pay no attention to a fly that alights some distance away. That same fly would be noted instantly by a moving fish or "cruiser." A busy tailer may also have stirred up mud that obscures much of his vision.

I once waded to within 50 feet of two tailing bonefish—big ones—and cast a pink shrimp between them. One of the fish took

off with a splash and violent wake, churning mud. The other
paused momentarily in his operations then went right back to his
rooting, apparently having no faith in his jumpy friend's judgment. I cast to the second fish, and the fly landed within a foot of
his nose, but drew no attention. After doing this a dozen times,
I actually laid the leader across his back, and he simply moved
aside and continued rooting. In the meantime, I had waded so
close that I resembled a man whipping a mule, and for lack of
anything better to do, I made a froth around him to see just what
it would take to drive him away. Then he suddenly began to
follow my shrimp as I stripped it slowly. When he didn't take,
I stripped faster. The fly was within ten feet of the rod tip, the
leader nearing the guides, when the fish struck like a hungry bass
and smoked across the flat, while I frantically tried to get him on
the reel. It was more luck than management when I did so, for
there was line festooned all over the place. Keep trying. You
never can tell.

In sight-fishing, we tend to become obsessed with casting,
rather than fishing. Many times a cast ignored by the target fish
is taken by a completely different individual, especially when fish
are moving. It is not unusual for a school of bonefish to stop and
mill uncertainly about a boat, their orderly travel disrupted by the
casting and the strange floating obstacles. If one passes your fly,
you may be able to leave it on the bottom and wait for another
prospect, in the meantime keeping the rod tip down and pretend-
ing you are a mangrove bush. The results may sometimes be a bit
silly, and after a few fish have been caught, bonefishing can
be pretty funny.

There was the time that Buddy Nordmann, a beginning
bonefisherman at that time, had spent a frustrating day of good
casting at big, cruising bones, without so much as a follow. On
the preceding afternoon he had caught a good fish, but now he
was completely discouraged, as anyone is likely to get when he
can see fish refusing the best he has to offer. It is less painful to
be unable to see such refusals. At any rate, several bonefish were
approaching the boat, well spread out in a feeding formation,

and Buddy made two perfect presentations to one fish. After the second was made, the fish flushed and then streaked off toward deep water.

"I just can't do it," Buddy said, and he flicked his backcast well behind him and let it fall on the water. I was poling the boat and I sighted a burly shadow coming in the general direction of Buddy's fly, so I told him to leave it there. When the bone was within two feet, I told him to twitch it. The bonefish took unhesitatingly. I then told Buddy to set the hook, as he hadn't sighted the fish from his position. He landed the fish.

"Muds" can be caused by anything from whip rays to nurse sharks, but many of them mark the bottom ruminations of bonefish or permit. A mud can be a baseball-sized puff on an otherwise clear bottom, or it can be acres of cloudy water, with bonefish rooting like a drove of peccaries. When approaching muds, you should note the direction of the tide or wind, for many a fisherman flails fruitlessly at a milky patch that has long since drifted away from the fish that made it. But if the fish are still in a big mud, about all you can do is to comb it with casts. Preferably, start at the edge and then go deeper into the cloudy area so you won't line a fish and flush the whole school. Although I've caught bonefish by blind casting into muds, I have had some unfortunate experiences, actually leading them out into the open where they could be thoroughly scared. I once cast into a 20-foot mud while wading, and as I worked my fly out of it, I found that six big bonefish were close behind it. In fact, they were jostling each other in their effort to keep all noses within three inches of my twitching, hopping little fly. I retrieved and retrieved, until the nine-foot leader bumped into the tip-top. There I stood, still as possible, with a nine-foot fly rod and six big bonefish nine feet from my vibrating knees. I wiggled the fly, and they displayed interest, but there was nothing more I could do. So when they became bored, I watched them swim away.

Fish in thin water sometimes act strangely about boats and waders, and I believe it is a matter of incomplete vision. At some distance away they can see nothing but the boat's bottom, but by that time they're listening and looking pretty carefully.

THE BONEFISH

The bonefish (*Albula vulpes*) is found over most of the tropical seas. It has a reputation as a shallow-water fish, but that's largely because it is generally fished for in shallow water. It may be that many bonefish spend much time in deep water. About the Hawaiian Islands, for example, they are fished at considerable depth.

When the flats get a little chilly, the bonefish simply don't appear. Something around 70 degrees is generally accepted as the lowest temperature they will take without going to deep water. The bonefish is largely a mystery, but it is known that it first appears as a flattened, wormlike larva, which changes into a tiny bonefish after *reducing* in size.

Rules that "bonefish feed only at high water," or "only on the run-in," are wrong. The bonefish may be fishable on any flat with shallow enough water, but it's true that a rising tide is a good time. This is largely because the routes of the fish can be figured, and fishermen can work on them as they come in from deeper water, often along small swash channels that show green at the edge of a shimmering flat. Often there are routes between open water and inland flats where bonefish travel at rising and falling tide. The spots can be learned by fishermen who work them regularly. Generally, such a tidal migration consist of individual fish and small schools, but I have watched thousands of fish move through a small pass in the Bahamas, crowding so close together that they actually pushed each other above the surface occasionally. On some days such fish would take eagerly, while on other days they refused everything we showed them.

Well equipped for grubbing crustaceans and mollusks, the bonefish has a piglike snout, tough enough for persistent rooting, and powerful crushers in the back of his throat. I have not found that they reject a fly quickly once it is taken. The fly's hook may feel to the fish like the shell of a crustacean.

Releasing a bonefish at low tide. None of this bottom is more than six inches deep, and that in the background is completely out of water. Grass on bottom hides small crustaceans that make up much of the bonefish's food.

A bonefish interested in a lure generally gives a few quick motions of its tail. The strike seldom comes fast, generally just a matter of the fly stopping. When the hook is set, the fish invariably heads for deep water if it is not confused about directions. There may be a pause between the first dart and the first long run while it decides on its course. This sometimes turns into a series of short rushes if the boat or wader seem to cut him off from deeper water. Then the run come at high speed. I believe a hooked bonefish can make twenty miles an hour, and that's very conservative. I have heard some dazed fishermen guess it's nearer seventy, but I think much of the illusion of greater speed comes from the shallow water, the sizzling line, the cloud of mud, and the seething wake. At any rate, when the fish leaves, you have a problem if your line is lying all over the boat or water. If you have any good way of getting line to go through the guides without tangling, now is the time to bring it forth.

Bonefishermen usually use a light drag, partly because they like to see the fish run, and partly because a moderate drag will save breakoffs with big fish. A leader of at least nine feet is good for bonefish, and an eight-pound tippet is a good average choice.

The fly reel will need considerable backing. A bonefish's performance is fairly predictable once it is hooked, and a four- or five-pound fish generally takes about 100 yards of line on its first run, then stops to root on the bottom, or simply pauses. The first run is usually straight toward deeper water. The second run, starting in a few seconds, is nearly always in the same direction, but much shorter. Then, after some very short runs, the fish usually starts circling, swinging in a wide curve. It seldom runs back toward the boat, but once it is stopped from its deepwater course, subsequent running is less purposeful. When the circling starts, there is great danger of hangups in bottom vegetation of any kind. Where I have fished bonefish, the chief hazard has often been the sea fan, which grows to very near the surface. Most hooked fish try to root the fly out on the bottom at one time or another, so the rod tip is held high to minimize line drag and avoid obstacles.

The length of the initial run depends mostly on the size of the fish. Some very large ones, only slightly impeded by the light drag, will take everything unless you tighten up as the backing dwindles. Anything more than about six pounds is considered to be a big fish.

Small bonefish are not plentiful around the Florida Keys or Biscayne Bay, and there are many flats where the average will be more than four pounds. I have caught very small ones in the Bahamas, and at the Isle of Pines before politics interfered with fishing in Cuban waters. There are small fish to be had along the Central American coast. Many excellent bonefish spots are almost completely unknown, simply because boats, guides, lodging, and transportation aren't present.

I don't enjoy it as much as the other method, but it is frequently possible to catch bonefish by chumming in channels leading from deep water to the flats. Any chum will usually do, and the Bahama guides frequently use conch or crabs. Once they have a number of fish working, they let up a little on the seafood and you present your fly.

Bonefish, like permit, are prone to follow big rays or sharks,

*Typical bonefish of the Florida Keys, weighing about six
pounds. Average sizes vary greatly with area fished. Bonefish
are found in most of the warm seas of the world, and range
in both deep and shallow water.*

evidently looking for the stirred-up bottom food. For that matter,
they frequently follow a wading fisherman for the same reason.

One of the best locations for bonefishing is where wide flats
pinch down to narrow shelves, generally where points of land run
near to deep water. The fish often establish a pattern of moving
along the coast, and are concentrated in the narrow section.

There are times when bonefishing is very easy, but many fly
fishermen have spent weeks of casting without a single fish. The

bones near to civilization may not appear wild, but they learn to be very difficult. The big ones tend to appear as singles or in pairs. School fish are usually small- or medium-sized.

Bonefish are good to eat and are treasured by some islanders but are very bony. Most sportsmen release all but the trophies.

THE BARRACUDA

Barracuda are generally considered somewhere between gamefish and trash, and are found about most saltwater flats in warm seas. Big ones will strike in a chum line. Most of those caught on flies are small, although a big streamer or popping bug will get heavy ones.

Where I have fished for them, it is generally difficult to keep a streamer moving fast enough, and those who troll for them say that a speed of almost 10 miles an hour will give best results. After wearing out my patience on barracuda that follow with interest but won't take, I have trolled through shoals of loafing fish and caught them until my arms ached.

Barracuda will travel across shallow flats, but seldom in the scant film of water that appeals to bonefish. The larger ones can be found resting in the deeper spots adjoining the flats proper. Shallow reefs covered by several feet of water and within a few yards of the flats are good places for them. Some very large ones have been landed without shock tippets, but heavy monofilament, or a bit of leader wire, is necessary if you want to land them consistently, for they have some of the most efficient teeth in the ocean. There is nothing wrong with their fighting qualities; the 'cuda is capable of good runs and high jumps. On some occasions I have cast blind into tidal rips on rocky points and had my streamer followed by half a dozen large fish, ominous shadows that cause a wader to take an involuntary step backward. They have considerable curiosity about wading fishermen. The big ones that lie in plain sight and watch you fish are generally difficult to fool with a fly. Long casts, generally striking some distance from the target fish, will get the most action.

The great barracuda (*Sphyraena barracuda*) is the best

Barracuda of the Bahamas, willing to take streamers or bugs but often insistent upon a fast retrieve. Tippets must resist some of the most efficient teeth in the fly-fishing business.

known and will get as large as 100 pounds. The much smaller Pacific barracuda, which has similar habits, is found extensively along the southern coast of California and the Mexican coast. There are several other small species that the average angler can't distinguish from the "great" one. The great barracuda is frequently poisonous to some degree, seldom fatally, but is eaten by many natives of warm-water areas.

Generally speaking, the deeper the water you find them in, the larger the barracuda run. The most consistent fly fishing for small ones is along mangrove shorelines, and I have done especially well where small creeks feed into flats. The saltwater creeks, considerably deeper than the flats, can become crowded with barracuda at low tide. Then, as the water rises, the barracuda will scatter over the flat. Small streamers with Mylar spicing are especially attractive, but I have caught very few of the smallest fish on popping bugs. Generally, I just use whatever I have been throwing at the bonefish, but work the flies much faster.

SNAPPER

Mangrove, or gray snapper (*Lutjanus griseus*), are excellent fly fish and have a silhouette similar to freshwater black bass. Along the flats, they are most frequently caught very close to the mangrove roots, generally on small, bright flies. They have a preference for grassy areas (especially turtle grass), which are fertile feeding spots for most flats residents.

Fishermen who have caught snappers only along the inshore shallows will argue that the fish never gets very large. They will swear that a five-pounder is a trophy, and will insist that the truly big ones, caught from offshore reefs, are another fish entirely. But the big gray snappers from deep water are the same species, even though their color may be quite different, sometimes appearing reddish instead of gray or olive. Many biologists insist that the gray snapper is the most intelligent of all sports fish, and it is true that a school of fish may swarm after a fly, but when one is hooked the rest suddenly become reticent.

Although I have caught a few on surface bugs, I have done better with short streamers, usually white bucktail with tinsel or Mylar, tied on a 1/0 hook. I know some specialists who have caught snappers consistently with these same flies, but my success has been very spotty. My best days have come as surprises, usually when I took a brief period off from some other kind of fishing. Most days which I conscientiously dedicated to snapper catching were miserable failures, even though I returned to the scenes of earlier triumphs.

"Blue holes," deep caverns occasionally found adjacent to the flats, sometimes fill up with mangrove snappers—and other varieties of snapper, too. In some of the Caribbean islands, these holes resemble freshwater springs in appearance, although they are responsive to tidal movements in some cases. A cautious approach to the holes, which may be only a few feet across, is likely to get one or two strikes from mangrove snappers, but that's about all.

It is unusual to find a school of mangrove snappers on an open flat, far from shoreline cover, but the very best snapper fishing I have had was in a shallow inlet of Abaco Island in the Bahamas. Accompanied by a local guide, we had planned to wade the little channel, some 50 yards across. We were hoping to meet bonefish that were leaving mangrove bays for deeper water on a falling tide. The water was coming out fast—only about a foot deep when we arrived—and the guide announced the bonefish would be coming out when it got down to six inches. I noticed

Mangrove, or gray snappers, are believed by many to be the most intelligent of saltwater fish. These small ones were caught on imitation shrimp, flies that were originally tied for bonefish.

some little depressions in the bottom, only a foot or two across, and only four or five inches deeper than the rest of the bottom, and idly cast my pink shrimp fly at one. A mangrove snapper grabbed it immediately, and I found each little depression had one or two fish ready to strike. By the time I had cleaned out all of the depressions within sight, the water was going at trout-stream speed and was only ankle deep, except in the little depressions. The fish weighed a little less than a pound, but they effectively diverted me from any other activity. As I scooped up my last snapper, I turned to see the guide landing a good bonefish on his spinning rod.

"The bonefish have now all gone, sir," he explained sadly. And we climbed back into the skiff for a long, rough-water journey back to the hotel.

Thus I learned that fishing concentration is fine, but it's nice to keep your eye on the original project. Unless you'd rather have snapper—which are much better to eat.

The mutton snapper (*Lutjanus analis*) runs big, but is sometimes found on shallow flats, generally identified in the distance by its reddish tail. This one is not consistently taken on flies. He is a hard runner and occasionally breaks fly tackle.

THE PERMIT

Only a few permit have been taken on flies—they show a strange aversion to hair or feathers—but they are an irresistible challenge to some fine fly fishermen. Having caught almost everything else, they are looking for new and tougher worlds to conquer. At risk of losing what reputation I have, I confess I have never caught a permit on a fly. I've thrown to many, have had them follow and turn away, and I have scared whole schools of them out of the country. When someone talks of permit on the fly, I try to change the subject since my inquiries about flies and and methods haven't produced much.

Except where permit are chummed up over deeper water, the procedure is about the same as that used for bonefishing. Bob Montgomery, a Key West guide, recommends a brown fly that looks a little like the small crabs which permit take readily. Woody Sexton, who has caught some permit, say he hasn't decided on any specific pattern. Other permit catchers, like Dr. A. M. McCarthy and Joe Brooks, get bright-eyed over the subject, but cheerfully tell me that it takes a lot of casts.

SHARKS

Most of the small sharks found on the flats will take flies or popping bugs, and they are long, hard runners under such circumstances—if they don't cut your leader. They tend to be quite shy of movements nearby, although they will come very close to a boat or wader if you can keep things quiet.

Sharks rely strongly on their sense of smell, and the fly must be very close for them to see it. The ideal situation with a sinking fly is to cast so that it can be retrieved close to the fish's nose. A shark will often swim toward a fly immediately after it strikes the water, but will be unable to find it when he reaches the scene unless it moves precisely into his area of vision. If you take up shark fishing seriously, a little bit of wire as a tippet will make things easier.

Small blacktips, shovelnose sharks, and lemon sharks are good fly and popping-bug takers. The nurse shark is a sluggish customer and I have never had one take a fly.

FLATS TARPON

Fly fishing for big tarpon on the flats is simple, but not easy. They're generally found in water considerably deeper than ideal bonefish territory, and most of the big flats tarpon are not residents there. They come in on high tides and then leave by channels where a staked-out boat will give good shots at passing fish. Guides who specialize in tarpon fishing know their routes, and a beginner needs plenty of luck to find the fish.

The flies are the same big streamers used for tarpon elsewhere. There are some big resident fish that are seen repeatedly on certain flats, but these are hard customers to attract, apparently more wary than moving fish that are in strange territory.

Nearly all of the near-record tarpon are taken from clear and shallow water where the fisherman casts only after sighting fish. The fly fisherman has the advantage of working over shallow water (generally less than ten feet) that encourages jumping and gives him a chance to tire the fish quickly. Some of these fish are landed in short order by experts who can apply the limit of pressure at the right time, and many 100-pound fish are taken in less than half an hour.

Critical of my long-term operations, Stu Apte once promised to land a 50-pound tarpon in less than five minutes, using a heavy flyrod with 12-pound-test leader and heavy shock tippet. We found the fish, and he did it. The answer was relentless pressure when the fish was in the water, and quick reactions when he was in the air. Relaxed tension was necessary to avoid a breakoff. Since then, I have whipped such fish pretty quickly, although I still think five minutes is pretty quick.

On the flats, as elsewhere, the streamer is retrieved in foot-long pulls. The favored colors are white, red-and-white, yellow, and combinations of these, although some good fishermen swear by barred gray feathers. As elsewhere, the popping bug is not very popular for really large tarpon. It will get strikes but the hooking procedure is very difficult, the tarpon pushing the bug away with his wake.

After he has the fish taking, the beginning flats fisherman must resist the temptation to strike too soon, and should wait until the fish closes its mouth and turns. Often he can see the black spot of the fish's open mouth, even when the rest of his quarry is just an indistinct area of water-blurred green and silver.

FIFTEEN

Offshore Depths

OFFSHORE FLY fishing is probably the quickest way to becoming a famous fly fisherman, but it is not a place for all fly fishermen. Not that it is necessarily more difficult, but it is different, and not all fly anglers care for the coarse tackle and some of the roundabout methods of blue water. A fisherman who insists upon raising his own fish, without help of teaser, chum, or trolling baits, will have a hard time offshore.

There are times when offshore fish can be found in sufficient numbers that they can be cast to from a drifting boat, with no teaser or chum. At other times, deepwater species just wander a bit too far out of their usual habitat to be reached from shore, jetty, or small skiff. But the serious offshore fly fisherman often builds his sport into a big operation climaxing a long trip with the presentation of feathers or hair, endless trolling of teasers or skipping baits, and possibly the introduction of large quantities of chum. Compared to his preparations, a fully bedecked dry-fly angler pursues a simple sport.

This is not to belittle the skills and perseverance needed to land deepwater fish on fly tackle, for it can be a very demanding

Both hands are required when a big fish takes off against heavy tackle, and the boatman must be ready to follow if necessary. Shallow seas are best for the fly fisherman.

sport. If any fisherman wants to set world records, the offshore fly rod is the tool to use, but he must have time, equipment, and sometimes considerable money. The surface of deepwater fly fishing has barely been scratched, and the lighter leaders have been used very little—a check of the records will show great gaps. So if you have the time, the equipment, and the enthusiasm, you can score.

A superb fly fisherman could pursue his deadly art for a lifetime and never catch a record, or near-record, brown trout or black bass. For most, breaking records is incidental to the day-to-day pleasures of fishing. Those who hunt deepwater records are a very small group, however skilled, and a man with a big boat, a big rod, and a record book at hand, could probably be a winner in a few months of work. He's a pioneer in an almost lonely business.

Many of the fish sought for records offshore are seldom suited to fly casting. The prospect of combing the continental shelf for billfish is a pretty dreary thought to anyone who has trolled for a few hundred miles without seeing even one. Most billfish are caught after being brought near the boat by trolling lures or teasers. The exceptions are fish who are found balling bait and thus easily approachable, or those found lying on the surface in calm water. The latter has happened frequently off Central America.

Both sailfish and marlin will take streamers, but it is in the nature of a stunt in most cases. The word "stunt" connotes exhibitionism, but I don't intend it to be derogatory. I have the utmost admiration for those who persistently follow the giants and occasionally win.

There are some medium-sized offshore fish that take flies with enthusiasm, such as bonita, dolphin, and cobia. Offshore stripers sometimes take flies, but most of the fishing for them is from surf or jetty, or in brackish bays and rivers, and the same goes for bluefish. Mackerel can be taken sometimes, and amberjack can be chummed to a fly. Perhaps the best fly taker of all is the dolphin.

THE DOLPHIN

Warm weather is best for dolphin and there is a period in early summer when they are caught by the thousands off Cape Hatteras, on the North Carolina coast. That water is not noted for glassy calms, but we had a good, smooth day there, on the *Early Bird* with Captain Emery Dillon and his mate, Bill Bazemore. The trip illustrates successful dolphin fishing with a fly.

Dolphin hang about floating debris in deep water and a 30-pound bull may come from beneath a floating board hardly large enough to shade a flying fish. Lines of seaweed or grass are the principal targets, and if they are near a tide line or current change, so much the better.

Dillon gave me some shots at floating stuff as we went out, but my streamers attracted nothing, so Joel Arrington and I put up the fly rods and we trolled strip bait and feathers. We'd gone several miles and were skirting the edge of a floating weed line when a small dolphin cracked one of the baits. We could see darting shadows and flashes of yellow and blue about him as he fought the hook. It was a school of busy fish, bright fish that chased the other trolling lures and leaped playfully in the wake. The skipper cut the engines, and the mate reeled a five-pound fish to the stern on the heavy trolling tackle. Twenty or thirty dolphin of about the same size slid smoothly beneath the surface, attracted by the contortions of the unwilling "Judas fish."

I cast a big white bucktail to the school and several fish tipped up, eyeing it uncertainly; then rushed it and turned away at the last instant, as I set the hook at what was really nothing but a splash. When I had untangled my backcast from an outrigger, I got the bucktail back to the school and one fish came up and took it deliberately, turning downward through the clear water as I set the hook. He thrashed briefly, three feet down, and then streaked off in a short run, ending it with two clean leaps. A brief sounding, and Bazemore grabbed the leader to swing the fish aboard.

It was one of those days when the supply of small dolphin seemed endless. They cruised about the stern, flashing at the chum that Bazemore gave them, and they took our streamers with such democratic nonchalance that I went to popping bugs, which were received with impartial chugs. When we finally tired of playing the frantically jumping youngsters, we simply cruised off and left them. They ran between four and five pounds, and only one larger fish showed during the orgy. It took Arrington's fly, but the hook came out.

It is apt to be feast or famine in dolphin fishing. There are days when they will take only occasionally, and possibly not at all. I believe a good-sized, flashy streamer is the best bet, but popping bugs are effective, too. There are some occasions when a sinking line would help, and many days when it's an advantage to sink the streamer quickly for only a couple of feet. A heavy hook and sparse dressing will accomplish that.

On that particular trip we were using heavy saltwater rods and reels, capable of handling 100-pound fish, which unduly handicapped the small dolphin, but that's a problem in most offshore fishing. Knowing the possibility of meeting something really big, most of us tend to be overgunned for 90 percent of the fish we catch. The solution is to carry two complete outfits for each fisherman, but the next thought is that you really need two big rods, in case the dolphin are 30-pounders and something breaks. Then comes the idea that you should have a spare light rod, too, and the cockpit begins to look like a tackle store.

Joel Arrington plays a wildly leaping dolphin off Cape Hatteras where they are especially plentiful in warm months.

Dolphin have abrasive mouths and are a little hard on leaders, but they don't require extra-heavy shock tippets, at least in the smaller sizes. If you can get into really big dolphin (they've been caught over 50 pounds on fly tackle), you'll need big-game gear, from reel to shock tippet.

Some fishermen say the dolphin is the best fighter of all, and I won't argue because it not only swims fast and jumps high, but it turns sidewise against the leader's pull when sounding and is often very tough to work up. I don't know about the real giants, but the small dolphin vary greatly in their fighting qualities. On one occasion, when I was nonchalantly trying to make a small dolphin jump for photographs, it zipped off across the surface and my broken leader snapped back into a very red face. I have caught a fish or two that seemed to give up almost immediately. So there are some big differences.

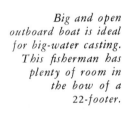

Big and open outboard boat is ideal for big-water casting. This fisherman has plenty of room in the bow of a 22-footer.

Bull dolphin have almost vertical foreheads, and the cows have sloping heads. The bulls can throw a geyser of water when rushing across the surface after a bait. Dolphin colors are spectacular and change so rapidly that they are sometimes called the most beautiful gamefish in the sea. They thrash violently when boated, and a big bull can take the place apart if handled awkwardly.

COBIA

Cobia are largely migratory, and their progress along some coasts is easily forecast. But like most traveling saltwater fish, they have some areas where they stay for long periods, and in some of the warmer seas they are permanent residents. They are caught in so many ways and in so many locations that cobia fishermen often don't understand each other.

Probably the surest way of catching cobia is to use chum over a wreck, or near an offshore structure. It is also possible to catch them by sight-fishing near shore during a migration, preferably using a boat with flying bridge or "cobia tower." As nearly as I can learn, the most reliable migration is along the eastern coast of the Gulf of Mexico, in the neighborhood of Panama City and Destin, Florida. That run comes close to shore and many of the fish can be caught from piers, but few fishing piers are suitable for fly rods—unless you want to charter the entire structure for a day or two. The run begins about April 1 and generally ends some time in May, after which the fish seem to spread out in the upper Gulf. There are fish which spend the summer near shore, off Louisiana, Alabama, and Mississippi, but once the northward run slacks off, it would be pretty tough for fly fishermen—except where the fish can be chummed.

The migration up the Atlantic coast occurs in late spring, but it is a ragged movement and it seems the fish are not resolute in their travel. They're often plentiful off the Carolinas in early summer but, again, there's not much chance for fly fishing except by chumming.

I am leading up to what I claim is the most sporting method of catching cobia on a fly (or any other way). The method has glamour, bruises, seamanship, casting challenge, and not a little foolishness. I'm not sure if it is dangerous or not, for marine authorities disagree. Anyway, here it is:

You do this when there are manta rays close to the shore. Cobia, which are a little like dolphin in that they like to hang around obstructions, tend to swim under the rays, a little behind them, and sometimes on top of them. I do not know if this is to gather food stunned by the ray, to enjoy the ray's shade, or simply to maintain a point of reference. Anyway, there are likely to be cobia around the rays, and a ray is likely to weigh a couple of tons.

The idea is to approach the ray with a boat (preferably a small one that maneuvers well) and cast your fly at the cobia in attendance. The possible danger comes from the ray's habit of leaping high into the air at intervals and coming down like a falling department store. Obviously, it would be a sticky wicket if your boat happened to be under such a jumper. I don't think there's any likelihood of a deliberate attack, but a careless ray doing his aerial somersaults (they actually turn over in the air) could conceivably blanket your entire boat. However, I've never heard of such a holocaust.

Investing a few bucks to rent a light plane is a good idea, for surfaced rays are easily seen from the air. They usually come inshore during the heat of the day and move off in the evening.

Milt Culp took me cobia fishing near Daytona Beach, Florida, using a 16-foot boat. The drill was to sight a ray jumping and

Ray Donnersberger with a cobia caught from beneath an offshore manta ray. Cobia swing very close to shore at times, but are also hooked well out to sea.

rush to the scene before the thing could travel enough to lose you. In a healthy chop this is a bruising business. You are trying to hold on to a fly rod, the boat, and a coiled line, while attempting to see the immense dark shadow that means a manta just under the waves. If you see no rays jumping, you simply run slowly along the coast and look for shadows. When you find one, you pull alongside, cut the motor, and cast to him, unless you actually see some cobia, in which case you try to get the fly ahead of a particular fish.

Both Ray Donnersberger and I have caught cobia this way, both of us with Milt Culp yelling instructions. The fish haven't run very large and could be handled well on a saltwater fly outfit. Hooked fish will try to follow their ray, will sometimes jump, and end up digging for bottom.

In my experience, plugs will catch more fish and sometimes cobia hit them on the surface, but there are some refinements of the fly fishing that I want to try next time. I believe you need either a fast-sinking fly, probably on a sinking line, or a loud popping bug. The streamer worked within a foot or so of the surface gets a lot of follows, but many fish turn away when they see the boat. The fast-sinking fly could be approached by the fish without causing him to direct his attention upward after coming out from beneath his buddy. The bug would force him to look nearly straight up. We'll try it some more and let you know.

CHUM LINE

With deliberate and plentiful chumming, the fly man can catch many fish he'd never show his fly to otherwise. Amberjack, usually considered deep operators, can be brought to the surface in a frenzy of feeding if the proper chum is distributed, and they often follow a hooked fish into fly-casting range and depth.

Chumming is usually done where fish are concentrated for other reasons, as over underwater obstacles. However, as in the case of the dolphin mentioned earlier, fish can often be started working with trolling rigs, and then held with chum. Many large offshore fish are caught on fly tackle while an attractor or a Judas

A dolphin jumps against the leader on a quiet sea offshore. Once attracted by chum or baits, a school of dolphin can often be held for considerable time to make casting convenient.

fish is held on a heavy trolling outfit. A combination of a hooked fish, a gallon of ground-up chum, and a drifting boat can get some species into a frenzy, eager to take almost anything that moves. This will happen over water so deep that the chum line could not be shown to the fish unless they were brought to the surface. But when a hooked fish is brought up, other fish follow it and can be kept up for some time, possibly to be joined by their friends.

If you're "contest fishing" with a fly rod, engines must be out of gear to make a catch eligible for most fly competitions. The idea is that fishing from a powered boat can easily be turned into trolling, and a fly rod would be about as efficient as anything else if you used it for that. "Fly fishing" is usually interpreted as casting to fish.

Few charter-boat operators have had much experience with fly casters, and most of them would much rather troll. They have several reasons, but their chief objection to light tackle is that it simply doesn't bring in enough fish. Even if the fish aren't to be sold, it's good for business to throw a lot of seafood on the dock each evening for prospective clients to look at. Most tourists looking for a charter boat don't care how the fish were caught and take a dim view of an empty fish box, even if the customers have spent the day casting flies. But a fly rod or two is poor competition for four big trolling baits and a pair of teasers, so some skippers don't want to charter to light-tackle fans at all.

It is highly unsatisfactory for a single fly fisherman to operate on the same boat with dedicated trollers, so if a charter boat is used, the fly fishermen had better charter specifically for that purpose. Your best bet is to look for a charterman who uses a big, open boat, inboard or outboard, but usually the latter, and who specializes in light tackle. Such operators are available in many ports and easily found through inquiry. Heavy-tackle skippers will often help you locate them. The cost is somewhat less than that of big cruisers, but bookings may be a little harder to arrange because the open boats are scarcer.

BREAKS OF THE GAME

Some of the best fly fishing in the ocean comes as a lucky break, often when a fish is found in a place he doesn't belong. Bluefish, usually considered traveling residents of big water, will sometimes come into salt canals and spend months in the same location. Several years ago, we caught blues in a housing development canal where they evidently spent an entire winter. We used streamers and sinking lines.

Bonito and their tuna relatives are excellent fly fish—when the fly can be presented to them. They are sometimes hooked when they follow trolling baits or teasers, but even the bonito sometimes appears in strange places where the fly fisherman can get an easy shot. I know of one inland harbor where bonito frequently school in hot weather to strike schools of bait within a long cast from shore. They are willing to take flies there, and when fished from a boat, the school can be followed to some extent. Any skiff will do, and a hooked bonito is a very severe test of a fly-fishing reel.

SOME EQUIPMENT

The offshore saltwater rod that is ready for anything is usually 8½ to 9 feet long and takes from a 9 to an 11 line. It has a large-capacity reel which should have a good drag, but will get by without it if the fisherman has learned to finger line or spool. The rod should have an extension butt, unless the fisherman is engaged in a contest where it isn't allowed. The butt can be pushed into the fisherman's stomach and still allow him to wind his reel without spooling his shirt. A second cork handle, part way up the rod, is helpful, not so much for hanging on, but because it makes it easy for the fisherman to take the same handhold each time and administer a pressure he's familiar with.

The backing should be a material that tests well over the leader's strength, and should have limited stretch. Dacron is a favorite material, but it is weak in knots and must be attached to the line with a loop, or other special connection.

The leader need not be long for most offshore fishing, as such fish are seldom leader-shy. The typical leader consists of several feet of heavy butt—around 30-pound test, a short section of the "legal tippet," and a section of shock tippet—generally less than a foot—of any material the fisherman chooses. The "legal tippet" is 15-pound test, 10-pound test, or 6-pound test in the various classes recognized by the Salt Water Fly Rodders of America, but most fishermen who are not specifically competing in a tippet class will use 12-pound or 15-pound test. The legal tippet must be at least a foot long, and some fishermen are careful to have it no longer. Others argue that a longer tippet will have more stretch and thus take up more shock while playing the fish.

The shock tippet may be any size as long as it's less than a foot (according to most tournament rules), and it is often 60- to 100-pound monofilament. Wire isn't used a great deal but works better for some fish, such as the barracuda. Attaching the shock tippet to the legal tippet involves a touchy bit of splicing and there are some ingenious methods, as shown in chapter 17. Leader material is generally carefully stretched before it is tied, in order to assure as stable a knot as possible. This is not ideal from a

Some efficient saltwater patterns. From top: Silver Outcast (variation of Silver Doctor); a double-tied Blonde; an eyed Multiwing; and Lefty's Deceiver, a tie featuring Mylar strands.

casting standpoint, but the flies are usually large enough to turn over satisfactorily, and the fewer knots and other connections the better. An extremely long leader is highly undesirable because the leader-line knot might have to enter the guides under dangerously heavy pressure as a fish nears the gaff.

We have talked little of contest fishing elsewhere in this book, but it is such an important part of offshore angling that it deserved some explanation here.

SIXTEEN

Playing Fish

ALMOST ANY fish must be played for a few seconds. Even a cane pole fisherman "plays" a four-inch bluegill before he swings it to the bank. It takes only an instant to overcome the resistance of such a fish, but it does take that instant, and an all-out jerk as soon as the bobber goes under will probably break something. The cane poler probably wouldn't admit to "playing" his fish, but he does.

At the other extreme are the long, drawn-out efforts at landing very large fish that overmatch the tackle used. Such affairs may last for hours, with time for extensive strategy. Most fish playing comes somewhere between these extremes.

Although I love the plaudits of the multitude as much as any other fly fisherman, I must admit that for any fish short of twenty or thirty pounds the fly rod is one of the most efficient, if not the most efficient, landing tool around. Beef up the stick and install a special reel, and the fly rod will stay in there, up past a hundred pounds for some species.

The fly rod, because of its length and pliability, is very forgiving of fish lunges and fisherman mistakes. That's why the very short fly rod can be a more difficult landing tool than the long one—there's less margin for fisherman error.

Playing a fish is extremely simple once a very few basics are learned, and a few hours of practice can make a man an expert at it. But casual fishermen and nonfishermen are much more impressed by the fact that a prominent angler has been able to boat a sailfish with a wandlike rod of three or four ounces, than by the method he used to hook the fish in the first place. Master fly-presentation may take years to perfect, but it is the "landing" that counts. Most uninformed observers don't care whether he cast a hundred feet with a Black Ghost streamer, or stillfished with a pilchard. We are stuck with this public attitude, so if you want to be a famous fisherman, catch a 200-pound fish on a fly rod. You will automatically be considered twice as good an angler as anyone who has caught a 100-pound fish, and four times as good as somebody who caught a 50-pound fish. If you catch a three-pound trout on a 6X tippet with a number 22 fly in a weedy stream after years of trying, you won't get much glory, and may even get a snicker from the calloused public. If all of this bothers you, maybe you shouldn't be a fly fisherman.

But you must learn to hook and land the fish, or your other skills won't pay off. And, in order to do so, you may need to be reminded of some facts, reduced to figures. The first thing to learn is what the tackle will stand, best discovered by tying your leader to a fence and experimenting a little. Many fly fishermen who will go to the ends of the earth for exotic fish, and will spend thousands of dollars on tackle and superb flies, have no intention of being found in backyards, with their leaders tied to fence posts. They prefer to do all of their practicing on the fish, and most of them have no idea whether they're pulling three pounds or eleven.

Let's use the scales a little. Take a nine-foot fly rod in one hand and hold it parallel to a fence after you've tied the leader to a post. Then, without moving your feet, bend your wrist and arm to see how much you can pull on the leader. With a fairly stiff glass rod that takes a number 10 line, I can pull about $1\frac{3}{4}$

pounds without some important fudges that I shall explain in the following paragraphs.

I use the fence because it seems more like a fishing situation to be pulling fairly horizontal to the ground. The stunt is more usually performed by fastening the rod tip to a weight on the ground, or floor, and having the tester lift straight up. The scales will show about the same as the fence test, as long as the tip is fastened almost directly to the weight. If there is some line or leader to manipulate with, the "fisherman" can do all sorts of things. He can, of course, change the situation by pulling toward himself, instead of at right angles to the floor or fence, but we're doing this to learn instead of proving how strong you are.

So now we get to some of the points to be learned. If the rod is longer, the fisherman has less leverage and can't pull as hard on the fish. If it is shorter, he increases his leverage, providing the rod stiffness is about the same. However, in practical fishing, when the rod bends sharply it gives the same effect as a shorter, stiffer rod. The fisherman gains leverage as it bends, so he puts more pressure on the leader, with the same power applied to the handle. However, he can't hold that rod out there with one hand for very long and apply more than a pound of pressure, so he increases his power in one or more ways. He points the tip more toward the fish, in a modification of "giving him the butt," so that the fish pulls more on the reel than on the tip. He puts the rod butt against his body and pries with his hand, possibly with the hand considerably above the rod handle. He holds on with both hands, in a pitchfork posture, while the fish is running. All of these systems can put on more pressure and can rest a fisherman during a long fight. At the same time, sliding your hand up the rod a few inches while the butt is rested against your body (or against your other hand) can multiply your leverage greatly. Tipping the rod tip toward the fish does the same thing if the fisherman pulls instead of pries, and a heavy leader can go from gentle tension to a break when the inexperienced fisherman thinks he's changed his position only a little.

Very few readers will bother with it, but a few minutes with the leader tied to a post will make these facts very obvious. It is much easier than learning the hard way—with a record fish going over the horizon.

Before the happy business of subduing the fish, the hook must be set, and the motion is best described as a quick lift of the tip. In other efforts, there may be little difference between a "quick lift" and a "jerk," but there is when a fly rod is involved.

Bracing the rod against the body is standard procedure in playing fish that will take a long while to land. Fish should be played "from the reel" rather than with the line hand.

The catch is that when a fly rod is jerked quickly and hard, the tip bends toward the fish before it starts moving the other way. This means that instead of taking up slack instantly, the tip actually gives the fish more slack momentarily. Then, as the fisherman's strike is continued, the tip springs back, tightening the line and going with the fisherman's yank, placing a heavy strain on the leader. Not only is it easy to break light tippets this way, but the angler's too sudden strike actually gives a fast fish more time to discard the fly than if the move had been a sharp lift.

The physics of this business is nothing earthshaking. Just hold a rod a few inches above and horizontal to a table, and jerk upward. The tip will flick down and hit the table before following the motion of the rest of the rod. Now, of course, many of us get a little jerk into our lift and the rod tip may dip a little before coming up, but experienced fishermen learn to keep it to a minimum, and the "quick lift" or "quick sweep" is very different from the jerk.

Some finished trout fishermen have developed a delicate strike in which they actually thrust their rod tip toward the trout as it takes. The fish is hooked on the rebound of the tip, which springs away as the rest of the rod goes forward. It is an unnatural move, best described as a "jerk in reverse." If one's reflexes are properly conditioned for this maneuver, it is probably the quickest strike of all.

Quick striking is necessary with some dry-fly fishing and with most bug fishing. In either case, it is not so much because the fish are so fast, but because the slack line must be gathered before the hook will penetrate. Since most dry flies are fished with at least some slack, and often with a great deal, striking should be prompt. I find that small trout are much quicker than large ones, both in the strike and in their ejection of an unwanted fly. Even so, it may be that more fish are missed by striking too soon than too late. It is very difficult to wait for a fish that you see coming, or to resist striking when your bug is bouncing on a bubbling swirl, even though a fish is only making an investigatory pass. A manipulated bug usually has some slack.

Most flies are best fished with the rod tip pointing very nearly at them. This should minimize the reverse whip of the rod, which is so troublesome when the tip is high. It is also best to avoid the tendency to overwork the tip in manipulating bugs or streamers. Most good fishermen use their line hand a great deal. The tendency to overwork the tip frequently causes the beginner to find himself with his rod sticking back over his shoulder, unprepared to set a hook or make a pickup for a new cast.

Sharp trout hooks are usually set with very gentle pressure. A combination of tough jaws and large barbs makes it a different story with some species, and anglers often set the hook repeatedly after the fish is moving.

With any fish that is capable of taking line, it is best to get him "on the reel" as soon as possible. If you have 50 feet of line looped in the water or around your feet, this becomes a terrifying business. Every bonefisherman has experienced the chilling sensation of coils of line whipping about his legs and whizzing through the guides, and most have experienced the sudden chug as a tangle catches in the guide and the leader parts. All he can do to avoid this is to strip his line carefully and be sure not to have more loose line than he really needs. He should stretch it occasionally to make sure it does not form tight coils.

Fishermen with three hands have a distinct advantage if a freshly hooked fish decides to run toward the rod. The line should be kept as nearly taut as possible, and most of us can strip faster with our line hands than we can recover with the reel. When loose line is recovered and on the reel, the fisherman can go about the business of playing his fish—one hand for the rod and one for the reel.

Once a fish is solidly hooked, the problems of slack line are greatly exaggerated by many instructors, especially where flies are concerned. If the fish is moving briskly, the big fly line dragging through the water will keep a little tension on the hook. Jumping fish can throw the hook, of course, but they have much less chance with flies than with heavy lures.

When a fish is running fast and "hits the reel" after taking out the excess running line, there is bound to be some amount of jerk, and if the fisherman plans to play the fish against a drag, it may be considerable. His reel may have cost more than a suit of clothes, and it may have a drag that runs smoothly and endlessly at high speed, but if it starts hard, he's had it. It may have a two-pound drag and a six-pound starting weight. Care and lubrication

Playing a big brown trout from the reel. Note that fisherman has given slack line as fish jumps.

are necessary to keep most drags starting smoothly. I am so jumpy about what will happen when a fish hits the drag that I sometimes try to have the line paying out when the fish gets to it. In other words, when I see my loose line is all but gone, I grab the line very near the reel spool and get the thing turning so that the fish's start will be smooth. If I kept careful score I might conclude that I've done more harm than good through the years, but the pathetic effort makes me feel better.

When a fish is running with loose line, I like to pay it out through my fingers, either the ones on the cork handle or those of my line hand. It's natural to apply a little pressure, but I have burned my fingers on some fast fish by holding too hard.

There are individual problems with individual fish, but it's generally a matter of the water they're found in. Large brown trout are tough customers because they're often hooked on light fly tackle and because they are especially good at hunting cover.

In a big, fast river, you feel a heavy pull and then a quick run that usually slopes up-current at an angle. Fish live with their heads upstream, and that's the way they usually go, at least until they're tired. Brown trout are not noted for jumping as much as rainbows, but individual fish have different ideas. Since most river fish are in reasonably shallow water and there's a great deal of broken surface, it's hard to tell exactly when a fish is about to jump as you may not see the leader coming up. Therefore, very few trout fishermen do anything special during a jump except just hang on. Ideally, a jumping fish should be given slack.

If you fish a dry fly, it's likely you will hook your fish a little upstream and he may keep going that way until he's tired, possibly never getting below you. But this upstream business is no rule; many big streamer-hooked fish never get above the fisherman. I know of one spot on the Yellowstone where I nearly always fish streamers, and I've caught quite a number of three-pound fish there. None has ever gone above me, simply because there is very fast water at the head of the pool and the fish stay out of it. It's an easy place to land a fish because there's nothing much for him to hide behind and the main current is bordered by a wide swath of slow water that's right below me as I cast across and down. Within thirty seconds, a three-pound brown trout has generally quit facing the heaviest current, and has swung almost directly below me, where he doesn't run; he just tugs.

The head-shaking yanks, so characteristic of large trout on rocky bottoms, are easily analyzed once you've watched it a few times. The fish first runs fast, finds he can't run away from the hook, then noses down behind a boulder near the bottom and shakes his head. It's a time to apply heavy pressure and make him fight the current, for he may root as well as tug. Pull him out and he'll find another rock. More slow tugging. The chances are he'll end up hanging directly below you, too tired to run but holding his position. Soon he'll flounder on the surface, which is generally the beginning of the end unless he tangles the leader and breaks it with his body. If you can wade to him, you should have him. But if terrain or bottom keeps you from doing that, you will need to put terrible pressure on your tackle to skid him upstream in heavy water.

Sometimes he gives out completely and hangs on the surface like a stuffed fish with his mouth open. Unless you can get to him or swing him to the shore, all you can do in this case is pump the rod and try to tow him. Trying to net or grab big fish directly below you in fast water is very humorous to anyone who may be watching. To the poor soul with the fish, it is an unanticipated crisis, for he has already done what was supposed to be the hard part. Perhaps the best thing is to try to get him upstream, with the leader snubbed up tightly, and then swing him against your waders or attempt to net him from below, tail first. None of this is picture-book procedure. If another fisherman can wade in below the fish and net him for you, it's much simpler. Worst of all, the fish may come to renewed life when he sees your shaking hand or net.

Beaching a trout is simpler. If you can swing him into two or three inches of water, he'll be on his side and can be scooped ashore, picked up, or netted. Beaching is not difficult, but becomes a work of art with an accomplished practitioner. If the bank slopes gradually enough and the fish can be headed up to it, the chances are that it will beach itself, as its tail continues to work even after it's lost control of its direction. Fish are not very strong in reverse.

I have seen some good steelhead anglers who kicked their fish ashore for the last few inches. Most of them use their hands, or one hand and one foot. Before they do that, of course, the fish is generally in such shallow water that it cannot swim upright. Then, even if the leader is accidentally snapped, the fisherman could probably get his fish by discarding his rod and making an all-out, though undignified, attack.

I watched Forrest Powell, one of the better-known steelheaders, land a 20-pounder in amazingly short order at the head of a pool. Water coming into the pool was very heavy and quite fast, completely unwadable. As soon as the fish was hooked, it smashed into the haystacks of current and jumped several times, driving upstream with the leader over its shoulder. Powell held fairly tightly but didn't pull the fish out of the rapids, satisfied

to let it burn energy in booming leaps. When the jumping was over, he simply guided the confused victim ashore, and it almost drove to dry land. He scooped it a little, and that was that. Elapsed time—less than five minutes. There's a sequel to the story, for I hooked a fish of almost exactly the same size from exactly the same spot, and my fish also elected to make the long, low plunges against the heavy current just above where I stood. If my flustered arithmetic was correct, I believe there were seven jumps, after which my fish slipped back with the current, but refused to come ashore. Perhaps I didn't apply quite enough pressure, but anyway, I found my tired fish swimming across river, in slower water, then going downstream, alternately making short runs and twisting against the leader. There was nothing to do but go along, and I made one of those sloshing, stumbling, wader-tearing runs, crawling over streamside logs and through brush, and wading where I could. A long while later, I finally grabbed my fish by the gills, lucky it hadn't gone over another rapids where I couldn't follow it at all. It must have taken half an hour. Twenty pounds of fish is a rodful in fast water, even if it's capable of only feeble flopping.

It is an expert's game, but many fish are beached while still fairly lively. The main thing is to know what the tackle will stand, and this isn't to be confused with overanxious forcing of a green fish. When in doubt, take your time.

Whenever possible, it's good to plan a downstream route, just in case. Many a big fish is lost because the angler has no way of following it down without drowning himself. I know of one fine lady angler who tangled with a big steelhead when, as luck would have it, a man with a power saw was watching. She followed the fish along the brushy and wooded bank with the power saw howling out a path for her. Such a procedure is not always practicable, combination lumberjack-gillies being expensive.

On a very few occasions I have been the hero of fish battles. I once hooked a very big steelhead at the tail of a pool, just above a rapids that would have meant the end of the line—or at least the leader. I was wading in deep water and the fish ran in a circle about me and then went far upstream. When it tired, I managed to steer it into a cove of quiet water and a friend grabbed it. Another friend had been standing guard at the brink of the downstream rapids, hoping to scare the fish away if it seemed about to go over. For once, I did things right, and was rewarded by the comment of a bystander who said the fish must have been sick.

Nothing defeats a fish so quickly as hard pulling from above, so once a big fish begins to tire, boat anglers are wise to get fairly close to it and keep lifting. The fish is poorly adapted to swimming downward against a pull, and a very big one can be hoisted with comparatively little strain as he loses his drive. In fact, there are some cases in which a fairly good fish can be stopped immediately by upward lifting.

I once fished with an extremely powerful man who knew a great deal about tackle strength. As he prepared to make a cast, he saw a big snook alongside the boat. It was within inches of the surface, and had apparently come up from a tangle of sunken logs to see what was going on. My friend simply flopped a streamer at the fish's nose, no more than a rod's length away. The snook grabbed it, and knowing the fish would break off if allowed to run at all, my cohort simply held the snook's head at the surface with both hands on the rod. The rod creaked and my friend sweated, but he never let the fish get its head turned downward. After a couple of minutes, the fish stopped struggling and was hauled aboard. It weighed fourteen pounds, but the mathematics of the situation is logical: My friend, using both hands on the light rod, probably lifted four or five pounds, too much for the snook to turn against, with its head on the surface. The pressure was straight up, and the rod was ruined. It was a freak situation, but it demonstrates the inefficiency of a fish fighting an upward pull.

Really heavy fish that insist on dogging the bottom and can't be lifted straight up are especially tough for fly fishermen. Big trout that can't be moved from behind a boulder within a few minutes may be able to stick there indefinitely. I suspect that they sometimes get their noses against the rocks in such a way that the fisherman is pulling against the stone as well as the fish.

Dr. Andrew Jordan, of Choteau, Montana, once hooked what would have been a new fly record for steelhead in the Kispiox River, British Columbia. There is little doubt the fish could have gone more than 40 pounds, as several experienced steelheaders had glimpses of it. The fish just dogged it behind boulders, in a fairly fast pool, and the affair lasted for six hours and fifty-five minutes. During that time, several men threw rocks at the monster to move it and give Jordan a chance to wear it down. The leader finally wore out. Did he really apply all the pressure the tackle would stand? I don't know, but Jordan has caught a lot of big steelhead and I'll go with his judgment. I do know that I once broke off a steelhead that never moved twenty feet from

Submerging the rod tip is one way of getting line and leader under the mangrove roots while playing a cover-hunting snook.

where I hooked him, although I hauled on him for some time. Maybe I got too anxious.

Talking of 20-pound to 40-pound trout is heady stuff, but a two-pound fish can be just as tough to handle under the right circumstances. Weedy spring creeks and limestone streams find the fisherman using a minimum of tippet and very small flies, with the fish continually within a few feet of vegetation. Sometimes, even here, the current is a major factor. There are no rules, only probabilities.

When a trout is hooked very close to vegetation, it seldom dives in immediately. At first it seems to be most concerned with moving away from what has attacked it, and it may go straight to open water. Then, as it begins to tire, it is likely to dive into weeds. Slacking the pressure as it approaches thick stuff may cause it to turn back to the open. But if it is possible to get the rod tip over it, or nearly over it, it is surprising how large a fish can often be kept at the surface. Then it can sometimes be slid over vegetation so thick that the fish can be picked up or netted. Brown trout are noted for their affinity for thick cover, and are more efficient at getting into it than are other species in most waters. However, on very weedy streams where other species live in the same waters, they act almost the same as the others—rainbows, cutthroats, and brook trout digging in almost as well as the specialists.

I have never objected to fishing for largemouth bass in thick cover, and have caught many of them when only a few inches of water covered growth that might run down for several feet. Most good-sized bass will dive downward almost immediately; I've landed many of them that hadn't run five feet from where they were hooked, digging them out of a bushel of eelgrass, elodea, or coontail moss. Such a procedure ruins the fun for those fishermen who insist on fish that run and jump, but although that part of the game is omitted, it is fun to get the strikes, even if the fish must be excavated afterward.

There is a gimmick about weed fishing, though. If the fish decides to run in the fisherman's direction, he can thread his way through the open places. It is wise to give him his head without forcing too much, as it's quite possible to drag him into weeds he wouldn't enter on his own. If you can get close to him, the up-ward pull should decide things promptly. Long casts make weed fishing tougher. There have been a few times when I've been

Milt Culp lands a tired snook by hand, a risky business unless the fish is completely played out.

wading in weedy water, have managed to move up to a hooked fish, and gotten the rod tip almost over him before he decided to dive into something, and have then followed him, with the rod tip high, until he came up on his side.

No fish can put out maximum effort for long, and only a fish that overpowers the tackle can last more than a very few minutes. By that I mean that any fish that can't take line at will can be whipped very quickly if he's kept in the open. Unaided by current or cover, a five-pound fish of any kind should be landed within five minutes on a five-pound leader.

It is a puzzling thing that anglers polished in other respects will wield a net as if it were a tennis racket or fly swatter. Netting fish is not always easy, but there's little doubt about how it should be done, and haste or sudden movements simply have no place in it. Netting should be a rather undramatic collection of a fish, not a new ball game with new hazards. Learning to net fish should take about fifteen seconds, but many fishermen don't grasp it in that many years.

The net should be submerged before the fish is brought to it, and unless current prevents it, the fish should be netted headfirst. The ideal situation is to bring the fish to the surface over the submerged net, and then to slack off just as the net comes up gently. In heavy current, the netting is sometimes done from the rear, but there is always a chance of the fish lunging away when the net touches him from behind. If his head goes through the hoop first, there's nothing much he can do except swim on in, or flop uselessly. Many trout fishermen never use nets, pulling big fish against their waders, or beaching them. In fact, going without a net is a sign of expertise in some quarters. However, netting them while they're being unhooked is usually easier on fish that are to be released. Atlantic salmon are often tailed, as the salmon's "wrist" makes a good handle. Black bass can be landed by the lower jaw, and such a grip immobilizes them. Take hold gently.

There is an effective method of landing big fish while wading if there are two fishermen, or an angler and a guide. After a fish is tired, it can be approached from the rear and lifted gently, with both hands under its belly. Nobody is going to carry it back to camp like that, but it can be shoveled to shore.

Very large tarpon are a special problem, and the lone fisherman is in trouble when landing time comes. A big tarpon that is to be released can be lip-gaffed, generally with the gaff going into the mouth and then out through the lower jaw. One that is to be killed is often gaffed in the jaw or head from outside. Other experts say that gaffing the fish in the side or belly kills it quickly, and can be done without causing violent reactions.

The toggle gaff can be used alone or in conjunction with a conventional hook. It is simply a section of rope with a loop in one end and a wooden pin, a foot or more long, at the other. The pin is shoved through the mouth and gills and stuck through the loop. It's an effective way of securing a fish that has been gaffed with a hook, and is sometimes used alone when the fish is to be released.

Once a large tarpon is too tired to run or jump and is ready for landing, fly tackle can be put to tremendous strain, as the fish must be led to the gaff. Usually it continues slow movement and must be towed around the boat by the leader until in exactly the right position. This requires two hands on the rod, and the stick must be tough. Rods built especially for this have heavy walls.

Any big fish is likely to come to life again after a clumsy netting or gaffing attempt. This is especially true of tarpon, which are frequently landed before they really call on all of their reserves. A tarpon that is on its side, and apparently completely done, may start the fight all over again if startled.

Individual fish perform differently, of course, but many a whopper has been landed before it began to fight. Generally, attempts at this sort of thing are miserable failures, but if the fish can be led quietly and the net is ready, it may be practicable. It's not wise to attempt it with a species you're unfamiliar with. Sleepy fish sometimes explode when they see something is drastically wrong.

Fishing for steelhead on a stream that also had numerous spawning salmon, my wife starred in a classic booboo, with me in

A big tarpon is a worthy foe and requires quick rod manipulation when it jumps at close quarters. Fisherman bows quickly to avoid strain on tackle.

a supporting role. Unaware that really large steelhead are frequently slow starters, she hooked a heavy fish that swam slowly about like a drugged carp, and we both decided it was a nearly spent salmon. She wanted to get back to fishing, so she pumped very hard until she had reeled the thing almost to within a rod's length, unable to see it in the murky water, and with her drag tight. Then the program changed, and I can still see that big steelhead high in the air, ten feet from her, its bright red stripe dulled by flying water. Even through that holocaust, I believe I heard the leader snap.

Although they may do all of their fly manipulating with the rod tip pointed at the fish, most big-fish anglers prefer to keep the tip high during the fight. This is partly in order to utilize the maximum spring of the rod, and partly because a high-held line is safe from obstructions in the water. The high tip is especially important in bonefishing on very shallow flats; the fish goes at high speed and there may be anything from rocks to sea fans to catch the line.

With most large fish in open water, the rule is to apply very light pressure as long as the fish is expending energy. It is only when the action slows down that the drag is tightened or the finger pressure is applied.

Some of the best heavy-duty fly reels have smooth drags that can be tightened while the fish runs. However, many large fish have been landed with no drag at all, the fisherman using his fingers to maintain the desired tension. If he practices the method, and has a durable reel, he can get by with no drag at all, using a light click to prevent overrun when the reel is unattended. Running the line directly through the fingers may work for short runs, but will burn if a run is long and fast. With a little practice, a finger can be applied to the line on the spool, but the best arrangement is the reel with space for fingering the outside of the spool. This works on some free-spool reels. Some other units have the handle inset so that the finger can be used on the edge of the spool, making an effective drag—instantly effective, if you wish. This, of course, ties up both hands as long as there is tension on the spool.

All fly rods have a built-in potential for drag adjustment— the angle at which it is held to the fish. Line friction through the guides greatly increases drag, and when the tip is lowered toward the fish, the drag is automatically and instantly lightened. A sudden surge of the fish tends to aid in this adjustment, as the tip is yanked down more quickly than the angler could move it. Fishermen unused to powerful fish often fail to consider the effect of rod guides on drag tension. Most of them adjust reel drags by pulling the line directly from the spool. They don't know whether the drag is one pound or five, but as long as nothing breaks, they're satisfied. Well, set the drag at two pounds on a straight pull, and then raise the rod tip with the handle pointed straight up. The tension is roughly doubled with most rods. With a medium-action, 8½-footer I tested, it comes out exactly doubled. So that's four pounds of effective drag, enough to cause big trouble if there's a hard jerk, even with an eight-pound tippet. As the fish leaves and the line becomes shallow on the spoon, tension is quickly doubled again—to eight pounds. If the reel doesn't start smoothly—well, the catastrophic possibilities are endless. So the light drag setting is best to begin with. Later on, when the fish slows down, more pressure may work.

Stu Apte "bows" to a tarpon as it jumps, a standard procedure to save wear and tear on tackle. Heavy tension immediately following a leap shortens the battle.

When a fish jumps, most fishermen stare and hope for the best, but there are some things to do if the fish is important. "Bowing" to a jumping fish is the standard procedure. You simply thrust the rod straight at him; and some experienced big-fish anglers actually step toward the fish if footing permits. The idea is to give a little slack to keep the fish from falling against a taut line. With smaller fish on strong leaders, the bowing is less important but can help avoid a sudden jerk that may cause a pullout.

There is one objection to giving slack on a jump—the fact that a shaking fish has a better chance of throwing the hook. But this is considered important in fly fishing, as the lure is quite light. The problem is magnified with plugs. If you want to hold a small fish down, the rod tip can be shoved underwater.

With most fish, a jump represents an explosion of energy that takes a lot out of his fight. Most fly fishermen prefer jumping fish to do plenty of it. Aside from the fun of the thing, the jump helps wear down the fish. There is another rather complex thing that usually happens; immediately after a leap, or series of leaps, the fish is frequently sluggish, evidently gathering energy for another effort. If you put on pressure immediately after a leap, it seems to take a lot of starch out of the fish.

In trying to see what would happen, I used some unrecommended tactics on some medium-sized tarpon. One fish, estimated at 65 pounds, had been on for only a few seconds, and had made his second leap when I really leaned on him with a 12-pound leader. To my amazement, the fish stopped, and I actually pulled him over backward in seven feet of water. You could see him turn back in slow motion as if completely hypnotized by the leader's authority. For a few seconds, it appeared I was going to be able to tow him in, but he came back to life and broke me off in a completely normal surge. Of course, I was overdoing it. But it's a good lesson.

Playing fish is simple, but the technique should be learned before the fish is hooked.

SEVENTEEN

Flies
and Knots

THERE ARE fly collectors who do not fish, and there are excellent fly fishermen who cannot name a dozen patterns. Wherever you fish, you need a basic selection of flies, whether you work it out for yourself or get help from someone else. In new waters, experience will be a slow teacher, so you'd better seek advice.

Every trout-fishing locality has special favorites, but there are many patterns that are used almost everywhere trout are fished. The same is true of other kinds of fly angling. To show what I mean by a "basic" selection I am going to list the flies considered necessary by Chester Marion, a top fly fisherman who operates mainly on trout in Montana and the Yellowstone Park area. Although this is definitely a western selection, I picked Marion deliberately because he is highly productive but consistently uses what I consider a minimum of patterns. He fishes from the time snow goes out until the line freezes in fall.

Marion uses the Royal Wulff, in sizes 12 and 14. This fly imitates nothing in particular, but is highly visible and serves well in broken water. Then he chooses three other patterns for similar surfaces—the Goofus and a winged variant, in sizes 12 and 14, and an imitation hopper, number 10. All of these dry flies are in the same category.

Then come his small flies, primarily for imitation of mayflies that hatch on spring creeks with only slightly ruffled surfaces—sometimes almost a flat calm. He uses them in sizes 14 and 16, and they are the Light Cahill, the Quill Gordon, and the Light Hendrickson. With these, he feels he can come close enough to almost any hatch of small mayflies. They are used on 5X tippets, or smaller.

His selection of small nymphs is simple; just olive, tan, brown, and black mayfly models, in sizes 12, 14, and 16.

For his big streamers, to be used mainly in the fall on big rivers, he leans toward the Muddlers, Spuddlers, and the Spruce Fly. All of these are large, and if they imitate anything in particular it is the bullhead or sculpin.

For his reservoir and natural-lake fishing, he often goes to a weighted Woolly Worm or a big Montana Nymph.

He would be quick to say there may be other flies just as good. He has used an enormous variety, but comes back to his local basics. My point is that if you went to Marion's neighborhood, you could count on catching fish with just these patterns. I do not say there would be no times when something special could save the day. The smallest flies listed are 16s, but of course Marion has used 18s and 20s. He just doesn't consider them necessary in his basic box. His few selected flies cover a wide range of conditions.

There are fishermen in any trout community who are quite capable of giving you similar lists. As I said earlier, no matter how many flies you have in your vest, it's wise to supplement them with some local favorites.

When it comes to bass fishing, I've found the same streamers and bugs will work throughout the country. In salt water, there's not much difference in big bugs and streamers around the coasts. When you get into bonefishing, there are local favorites, generally with good reason. I've found that local fly choices are usually best in steelheading. Atlantic salmon patterns are fairly standard, although size is highly important.

MAKE YOUR OWN?

Fly tieing can be a hobby in itself, and many trout fishermen consider it as important as the fishing. Saltwater anglers and black-bass fishermen can tie their big lures with a minimum of training. Economy becomes very important here, especially in salt water, where good fishing means quickly destroyed streamers.

There are excellent manuals on fly tieing, so I'm certainly not going into the instructions themselves, but there is some good general advice from professional tiers and instructors.

For one thing, time is saved by learning sound basic procedures. Louise Monical, one of the best commercial tiers (Dan Bailey's Fly Shop), has trained dozens of professionals and starts them with the basic mechanics. For one full day she has each beginner work entirely on knots. "If it isn't fastened, you don't have a fly," she explains.

Then she teaches the method of making a simple hackle fly. She believes in specialization for commercial tiers, and usually decides the type of flies each worker is best qualified for. The fishermen who dresses only his own flies cannot afford the luxury of specialization, but probably has more fun anyway with the variety he produces. Most professionals keep a finished fly on the bench before them, even after long experience. It's a built-in method of quality control, and without it they sometimes end up with an offbeat creation that may catch fish but that has lost its original identity.

If a tier can learn some standard trout patterns, he should have no trouble with the coarser work for black bass and salt water. If he's sure he'll never cast for trout, he can begin with the big stuff, but trout flies are the ideal foundation for proficiency.

As in other fields, the advanced amateur may come up with the most beautiful work of all since he is not concerned with quantity and can work as slowly as he likes. Some of the finest fly tiers will readily admit they couldn't make a living at it, simply because they go very slowly and are meticulous about details that cannot go into mass production. There are custom tiers who work alone for a small clientele, and a few such experts are found in most trout and salmon areas. Some of their work is almost too pretty to use and is sought by collectors.

Largemouth black bass, favorite game fish of North America, are available for fly anglers during any month of the year somewhere in the United States.

Fly-tieing equipment is not expensive. In addition to the components, the tier needs a vise, a bobbin, scissors, hackle pliers, some lacquer, possibly a whip-finishing tool, tweezers, and wax. He might as well get good tools to begin with, and will do well to get the whole works from a concern that sells materials especially for fly tieing. He should start with real fly-tieing thread, available both round and flat. Later, he may want to substitute some exotic hair, or feathers, but to begin with he'll do well to get the best catalogued makings. Even after casting thousands of flies, a fisherman may be a poor judge of what they're dressed with, and things won't come out right with second-rate materials. The beginner needs high-grade feathers and hair even more than the expert, and he shouldn't skimp. Mrs. Virginia Buzick, a California dealer in fly-tieing materials, is not being immodest when she says she can select good feathers blindfolded, and there is no fury like that of a good fly tier who has been handed poor feathers. Merton Parks once angrily announced he must have been sent the sweepings from under somebody's tieing bench. Such discernment is beyond most of us, so if you're just starting, trust an expert.

Some of the essential materials would include brown and white bucktail (ordinary deer hair is used for many flies), tinsel and/or Mylar, some grizzly hackle (neck feathers), yellow floss, large neck feathers, peacock herl, muskrat hair (highly popular for nymphs), mallard breast, squirrel hair, polar-bear hair, marabou (finely textured feathers for streamers)—and you can go on from there.

Of course you can substitute in many fly patterns, and that's how some "new" flies are originated, but it is nice to keep them pretty standard so your friends will know what you're talking about. Some of the popular names are pretty fancy, but they're a lot better than no name at all. Have you ever tried to describe a fly by telephone?

We used to tie up an effective weakfish streamer from "Pogo hair." Pogo was a neighbor's dog, of unusual color and ancestry, and it was fun to see a fisherman's face when you told him how well Pogo hair worked. But the joke was on us when Pogo died and the whitish, brindle-ish, yellowish hair was no longer available.

I have no idea how many flies we own. I can't name half of them.

THE KNOTS

I envy those careful fishermen who dote on smooth and efficient knots, tie them with relish and flourish, and speak glibly of the relative knotting qualities of this or that monofilament. I am sloppy, careless, and awkward with knots, but I am trying to do better. Undoubtedly, almost every man, at one time or another, finds he's momentarily forgotten how to tie his necktie. I do, several times a year.

Although I have lost innumerable fish when my hasty knots came untied, my most sweaty-necked horror came when Ben Williams, a longtime fishing friend, appeared to have broken off a big tarpon when we were many miles from a dock. I had tied the big streamer to the 80-pound shock tippet, and although I tried to get there first, Ted Smallwood beat me to the flyless tippet as Ben reeled it in. There was no denying the curlicued end.

"It came untied," Ted said, in a voice commonly associated with death sentences.

The first requirement of a knot is that it hold, and most of the fly fisherman's are made in monofilament of various sizes. Splices of line to backing can be made in several ways, and although there is some difference in their size and smoothness through the guides, most of them will hold until the leader breaks. So your problem is the mono near the fly.

Whatever the knot tied in monofilament, it must be properly snugged. The practice of applying saliva before pulling it up is a big help. When heavy monofilament is used, it is essential that it be stretched hard before the knot is tied. The common error is to stop the stretching too soon. Unstretched, monofilament has a snakelike habit of crawling out of a knot. When fishing, the knot should be checked regularly to make sure it hasn't begun to open. In heavy fishing, if fish are not leader-shy, the "bitter end" of the leader should not be snipped too short.

The nail knot is commonly used to attach the leader butt to a line, and once it's snugged up, it stays, usually until long after the line finish breaks from continual flexing. I've never had a nail knot give way. There is a quick and easy way of tying it that's shown on page 359, since it's a little hard to describe.

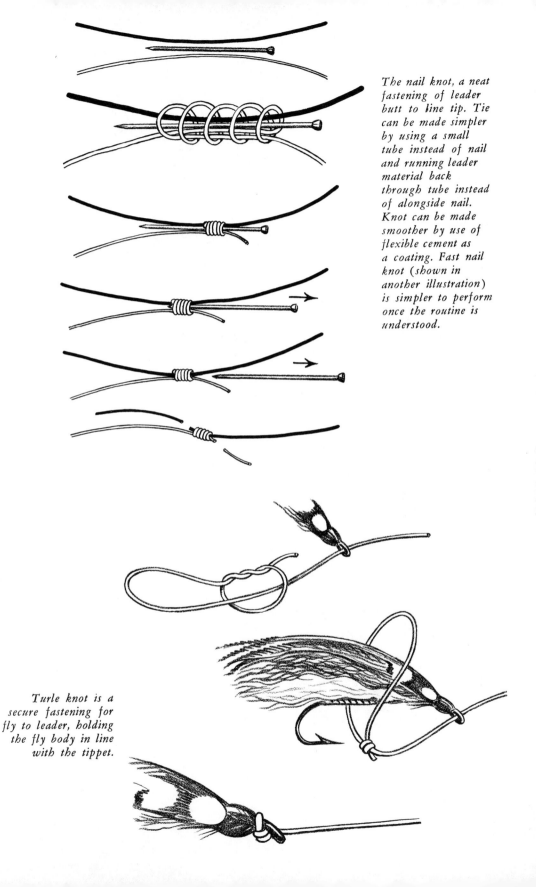

The nail knot, a neat fastening of leader butt to line tip. Tie can be made simpler by using a small tube instead of nail and running leader material back through tube instead of alongside nail. Knot can be made smoother by use of flexible cement as a coating. Fast nail knot (shown in another illustration) is simpler to perform once the routine is understood.

Turle knot is a secure fastening for fly to leader, holding the fly body in line with the tippet.

The clinch knot has high breaking strength but must be snugged up tightly or some monofilament will work out of it. The improved clinch (below) places even more premium on careful tightening, especially with large-caliber monofilament.

The nail loop is a strong fastening for leader to fly and enables fly to swing loosely in the loop. Under heavy stress in playing a fish the knot will tighten down on the hook eye but continues to hold. This tie is especially popular with heavy shock tippets for big-game fishing.

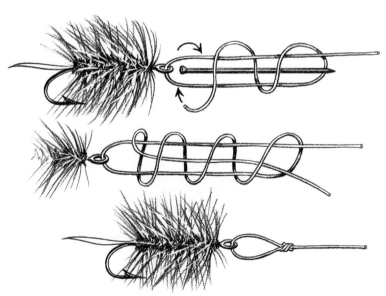

360

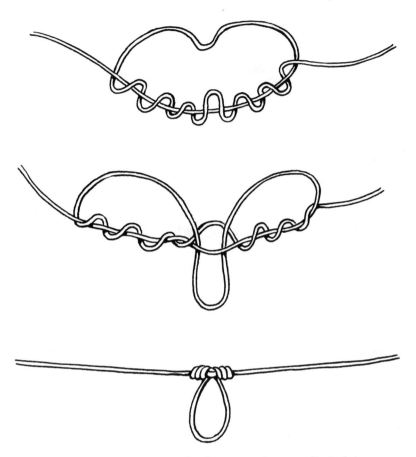

This dropper loop is used when more than one fly is being
fished at once. The second fly can be attached to the tightened
loop by a separate piece of tippet material.

Standard connection for two pieces of leader material of
similar size is the blood knot, making a neat and strong
connection. It requires careful snugging.

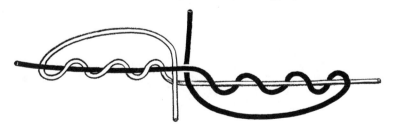

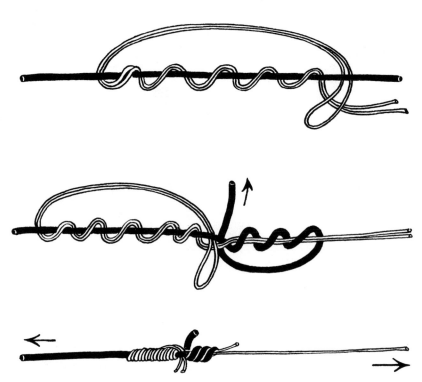

This improved blood knot or *Stu Apte knot* is used for attaching large shock tippets to relatively small leader material and simply involves doubling the small monofilament. It requires smooth pull up and goes much better with an application of saliva. A recent improvement involves wrapping the doubled material back over its turns instead of continuing to make turns in the same direction before tucking back through opening.

The surgeon's knot is a simple splice of leader material although not quite as neat as the blood knot or barrel knot.

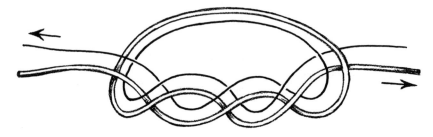

The fast nail knot is simpler to tie than the conventional one but the description is difficult. Remember that the material in the loop will end up as the leader butt which is attached to the line. Therefore, make the loop large enough to give the proper length of leader butt when it is pulled through.

In this knot the nail is simply a stiffner. A right-handed tyer would grasp the line, nail and leader loop with his left hand, then make a series of about five turns with the loop over the ends of the leader, line and nail, working his turns back toward his left hand, using his right. Then, using his right hand, he pulls the end of the leader and the original loop is snugged up on the nail and the line. The nail is then removed with care that the line does not slide out of the loops and the knot is tightened and smoothed with the fingers, after which the line and leader tips are trimmed.

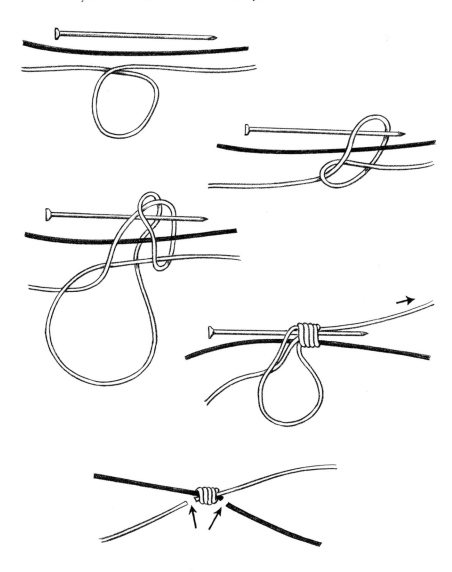

The blood knot, or barrel knot, used for construction of tapered leaders, is another good one. Get it snug and it holds well. I've had more trouble with the heavier sections than with the lighter ones, simply because I've occasionally been too light on my pull-up pressure and the knot works out. That's probably happened a total of six or eight times with me. The surgeon's knot is used by some leader tiers and seems to hold well enough, although it isn't as neat as the barrel.

Fastening a heavy shock tippet to 12- or 10-pound test mono is the toughest connection of all. I will show you the methods of doing it, but they take a little practice. The Stu Apte knot is a barrel knot with the small material doubled. It's easy, but requires a quick, sure pull-up. The latest kink on that one is to wrap the small stuff back over itself as you wind it, rather than working in the same direction as you make your six-or-so turns. This causes the thing to pull up more neatly. You'll probably bungle this one several times.

Attaching the hook eye to the tippet can be done in several ways. Unfortunately, most of those knots which allow the hook eye to swing loosely in a loop are a little short on strength, and are risky with light tippets. A nail-knot procedure can be used well with heavy mono, leaving a loop for the hook to move about in. It adds to the action of large streamers or bugs, and pulls up snug under pressure with no danger of breakage.

Since most of us like heavy butt-sections for our leaders, as an aid to casting, there's bound to be some kinking as the leader comes off the reel. This is no problem with heavy flies, but a nuisance with small ones. A split rubber bottle-stopper is good for pulling those sections through, although a folded piece of inner tube is more often used. Rapid rubbing will warm mono, causing it to lose some of its set and straighten more easily.

Like the rest of the fly-fishing game, knots are a simple matter of attention to detail.

Index

Index